WHAT THE MARKET TEACHES US

What the Market Teaches Us

Limitations of Knowing and Tactics for Doing

CHARLES W. SMITH

OXFORD
UNIVERSITY PRESS

OXFORD
UNIVERSITY PRESS

Great Clarendon Street, Oxford, OX2 6DP,
United Kingdom

Oxford University Press is a department of the University of Oxford.
It furthers the University's objective of excellence in research, scholarship,
and education by publishing worldwide. Oxford is a registered trade mark of
Oxford University Press in the UK and in certain other countries

First Edition published in 2015
Impression: 1

Published in the United States of America by Oxford University Press
198 Madison Avenue, New York, NY 10016, United States of America

British Library Cataloguing in Publication Data
Data available

Library of Congress Control Number: 2014960131

ISBN 978–0–19–874511–2

Printed and bound by
CPI Group (UK) Ltd, Croydon, CR0 4YY

This book is dedicated to
Claire, Jonah, Rebecca, and Joshua
our beloved grandchildren
and
A Sensible World They Deserve

Acknowledgments

Through the many decades that the central themes of this book were evolving literally scores of people from a range of different places provided me with vital support of varying sorts. The numbers are such, and the past sufficiently hazy, that only a comparatively few are formally noted here.

Given the central role that the market plays, not only in this book but in my professional writing over the years, it seems appropriate to begin with my lifelong market alter-ego who not only first introduced me to the market, but continued to be a crucial "prime informer" on the market for a half century: Gerald D. Weintraub. Over the years many hundreds of other market participants, both professional and non-professional, have also assisted me with their own accounts, connections, and insights. In my more recent encounters with derivative transactions, particularly option transaction, I am in debt to Marty Kearny of CBOE for always managing to make time for me and my pestering questions.

The theoretical themes of this book also have significant historical roots. While, as is noted in the Preface, I approached the market with philosophical concerns from the very beginning, the key role of "critical realism" in reframing these philosophic concerns began a full decade later. From its quiet beginning in the early 1970s, critical realism has become a major theoretical force in both philosophy and social science, with hundreds of supporters. While I am indebted to scores of these scholars, I am most indebted to three of the early founders of this movement, Rom Harré, Peter Manicas, and the recently deceased Roy Bhaskar.

With rare exceptions, books require more than data and ideas if they are to become a reality. They need a home or habitat in which they can mature and grow. For most academically grounded books this means that they need a discipline, or often a sub-discipline, in which to thrive, a place where early ideas and drafts can be presented and critiqued. In the case of this book, sociology as a discipline played a central role here, as is noted in the Preface. Its more defined home for the past two decades, however, has been the sub-disciple of "economic sociology" that after more than fifty years of slumber re-emerged in the early 1990s. While this emergence involved numerous people, a key event was the Russell Sage Seminar in Economic Sociology held in 1990 in which I managed to take part. Again many people played a role in this emergence. Four to whom I am especially indebted are Mark Granovetter, who chaired the seminar, Richard Swedberg, who edited the book generated by it, Harrison White, who gave my qualitative research a seal of approval, and

Viviana Zelizer, who managed to get me invited to the seminar. All four of these colleagues have offered me support over the years that has been greatly appreciated given the academically solitary nature of the ethnographic research I rely upon. I am especially indebted here to Viviana Zelizer, who shares my strong, but minority, cultural orientation toward markets and money. In this context, I need to acknowledge one other colleague, Karin Knorr Cetina. With her own interests in the market, cognitive sciences, and ethnography, Karin has been a very special colleague and friend.

Two other talented women also need to be acknowledged. The first to be noted, Abigail C. Saguy, is also a sociologist, but not an economic sociologist. Her areas of specialization are primarily culture and gender studies. Most importantly, given the task at hand, she is an unbelievably earnest and knowledgeable supporter and critic of whatever her father writes. The second woman is similarly an earnest and knowledgeable supporter and critic. I refer here to my wife, Rita C. Smith, who has shared every day of the fifty plus years that this book has been evolving. My final acknowledgment goes to Dr Jonathan C. Smith. Yes, he is my son, but more importantly in this context he has also served as my prime informer on thyroid and parathyroid surgery. Without him I know that I would have lost each and every patient introduced in this text.

A book such as this requires further assistance than that noted above if it is to become a reality. It needs the critical and supportive care of a talented group of editors and publishers. In this regard I am grateful for the assistance of numerous Oxford University Press professionals, Clare Kennedy, Barbara Ball, Kirtiga Balakrishnan, and Stephen York, but most particularly my editor David Musson.

My sincerest thanks to each and everyone.

Contents

Preface

We know less than we think, but can do more.

"Why are you so engrossed by the market?[1] You're not a trader. You aren't even an economist. You're a sociologist and a theoretical one at that." This question has been put to me continually for decades. The root of the matter is that though I have participated in and written about markets for many decades,[2] my primary concern has not been to "know" the market, a futile objective as we shall see, but to extract from it a deeper understanding of various facets of human behavior. More specifically, I have been interested in learning about how people cope with ambiguities and the unexpected. The futile task of predicting the market I leave to others. But why the market?

The answers I give tend to revolve around two replies I obtained from two different stockbrokers in the early 1960s when I first began to study the market. Both had been recommended to me as savvy, knowledgeable, and wise market professionals. The first reply was in response to the question of what attracted him—at that time and even now market professionals tend to be men—to the market: "It is the best game there is! It embodies life. You want to figure out what life is all about, figure out the market." The other was in response to a more pointed question querying how professionals "made sense" of the market. His answer had an interesting twist: "Look, any professional broker can give you a very convincing story of why the market did what it did yesterday, but not one of them can tell you what it is going to do tomorrow." Taken together these responses spoke directly to how people tried, but generally failed, to make sense out of ambiguous and uncertain situations which was then, and has remained, a

[1] Throughout this book, the term "market" is regularly used to refer primarily to financial markets, or even more pointedly to equity and their derivatives markets. At other times the term is used to include pretty much all price-setting markets. In those places where the intended meaning might be unclear I have tried to be more specific, though in most cases such specificity is not really necessary. An appendix, "Understanding Markets from a Sociological Perspective," has been included to provide a fuller overview of markets than those that are focused upon in what follows. In both presentations, as indicated in the title of this appendix, a predominantly sociological perspective is used.

[2] Smith 1981, 1989, 1993, 1999, 2005, 2007, 2011, 2012.

key interest of mine. Clearly the market wasn't then, and isn't now, the only site capable of offering insights into how people attempt to cope with such situations.[3] Few, however, are as abundant when it comes to the variety of ways in which these situations are managed. The market has an additional advantage. It was, and still is, comparatively more accessible to field study and qualitative research, particularly participant-observation and ethnographic research, for which I had a strong methodological preference, than most similarly vibrant natural arenas.[4] Whatever the reasons I was hooked.

Over the past half century, the more engaged I have become, both as an academic researcher[5] and as an active trader,[6] the more I have come to appreciate how price-setting markets, particularly financial markets, not only reveal the various multifaceted ways we attempt to cope with puzzling and challenging situations, but also where, how, and why we are likely to succeed in some situations and fail in others. The way financial markets have evolved, mutated, and grown over this period has served to enhance both of these processes by generating new puzzles and attempts at new solutions which, like earlier solutions, tend to work in some ways and fail in others. At the same time these markets have acquired a visibility and social importance significantly greater than they had when I began to study them. The chapters that follow are aimed at seeking out the teachings of these markets by exploring the various types of ambiguities and unexpected events that pervade them and the different practices that are employed in coping with them.

This book is clearly not the first to explore the market or price-setting markets in general or even these issues. Markets are the prime concern of the

[3] Two other sites, kayaking and surgery, in fact, will be drawn upon in Part III when the coping strategy of "acting sensibly" will be explored.

[4] In the early 1960s, Brandeis University's Sociology Department, where I was a graduate student, emphasized ethnographic/participant-observation training in the earlier Chicago tradition. The "stock market" became my "prime" research site (Merton 1987). My continuing long-term reliance upon these research methodologies has served not only to shape the ways markets are presented, but also the related literatures most cited. The existing literature dealing with financial markets and markets in general is overwhelming. Even the more limited sociological literature on markets has in recent years become immense (see Appendix A). The more ethnographically grounded literature, however, remains, comparatively small, with only a minority of it dealing in a significant manner with the central theoretical concerns of this book. As a consequence, the supporting citations in this text tend to be of earlier writings of the author. A fuller discussion of this methodological issue, which explores the symbiotic relationship between the methodology used and markets, is presented in Appendix B: "The Interplay of Ethnography and Markets."

[5] I came to sociology quite late in my academic career that in my undergraduate years and early graduate studies focused upon philosophy and psychology. It was only later that I encountered sociology and, as a field project, the stock market. The stock market then led to other market settings that have collectively occupied me for the past five decades.

[6] My first stock market trades occurred in the early 1960s and were pretty much limited to equity transactions, followed later by bond trades and in the 1980s, commodities. Since the late 1980s, options have assumed a dominant role. I became deeply involved in non-financial auctions around the same time derivatives entered my life, though my participation in such markets tended to be limited to rugs and isolated collectibles.

very weighty and multifaceted academic discipline of economics. Markets also constitute a very large segment of human day-to-day activities. The search for order and meaning, knowing and trying to make sense out of what we know, meanwhile, has been a primary concern of the human species for many millenniums. The existing literature, both academic and non-academic, that speaks to these issues is unending. It entails different mixes of theoretical cogitation, experimental studies, collection and analysis of various sets of data, and comparative field research. Where this book differs from the great majority of this literature is in its primary focus upon the actual practices of the market and the suggestions and implications they present for the ways we cope with uncertainties rather than any given paradigm or theory of how this is done.[7]

To ignore all of the paradigms, theories, and writings that bear on this subject would, however, be not only arrogant and disrespectful, but also wrongheaded and silly. The problem, particularly given that this book is intended for a broad audience, is determining how best to utilize these writings. The path selected is to let the market speak for itself as much as possible by presenting examples, often in the form of vignettes, of both its uncertainties and its related coping practices, coupled with the various outcomes. The ability of vignettes to embody the cognitive, behavioral, and emotive components built into different situations is of particular value when dealing with the types of complex, multilevel happenings that are common in the market. Here one need only picture someone trying to decide whether to sell or buy some particular stocks in a market that has been erratically and significantly moving up and down for a day or so while supposed market experts have been issuing a stream of conflicting explanations and predictions. Such vignettes, of course, are bound to be subject to my own framing that has itself been shaped and framed by the specific theoretical writings that most influenced me. How readers are likely to understand this presentation will in turn be shaped by their own past experiences, both theoretical and concrete. Such vignettes, I would suggest, nevertheless, provide the market, or any grounded situation, with a voice more of its own. An eclectic existing literature will be utilized when it might help to clarify matters.

[7] While the sociological literature actually grounded in the everyday practices of these markets constitutes a comparatively small part of the total sociological literature dealing with these markets, such studies do exist. Most are noted in one place or another in the text that follows and in Appendix A, though their work, in keeping with the guidelines noted above, is not subject to detailed examination. I feel obliged here, however, to acknowledge minimally five who have spent many years and hours looking at these markets from within one sector or another. They are all I might add authors or co-authors of chapters in Part II, "Financial Markets in Action," of *The Oxford Handbook of The Sociology of Finance* (2012): Karin Knorr Cetina, Donald McKenzie, Alex Preda, David Stark, and Caitlin Zaloom. One or more of their works are cited in the Selected Bibliography.

The prime objective of the eclectic mix of the references noted below is not so much to explicate the vignettes and practices presented, but to indicate general territories and set boundaries. American classical pragmatism, prospect theory associated with the works of Kahneman and Tversky, practice theory associated most often with Bourdieu and Giddens but linked to a range of different social scientists, rational choice theory, and organizational theory will all be used. The works of Emile Durkheim, George Herbert Mead, and transcendental/critical realism associated with Rom Harré and Roy Bhaskar will also be utilized, as they have individually and collectively served to shape the central arguments of this book. More detailed information on where and how this literature will be used will be indicated when brief overviews of the various chapters are presented below. With few exceptions, all those mentioned in the text are listed in the Selected Bibliography section at the end of the book with one or more of their writings cited for those who would like a first-hand experience of their thoughts.

From what has been said it should be clear that while this book is concerned with exploring what markets, primarily financial and auction markets, might teach us, it is not intended to be a "how to" book for dealing with the market, though it does make various suggestions as how market situations might better be approached. It is concerned, rather, with examining and understanding the various types of puzzles and responses that markets offer and what we can learn from them. More specifically it deals with conflicting accounts, unexpected happenings, and contingencies that pervade the market and the various coping responses that they elicit. A key contention of the book is that the complexities and contingencies of the market have undergone significant changes in recent years that have altered not only the traditionally dominant "making sense" coping practices of explanatory accounts when dealing with contradictory information, but also "acting sensibly" coping practices that rely primarily upon taking appropriate actions in response to unexpected happenings. While similar changes have been occurring in other social sectors, markets, particularly financial markets, are featured in this discussion because, as noted earlier, they not only provide an exceptionally rich inventory of these situations and the coping practices used to handle them, but are also comparatively accessible. Two other sites, kayaking[8] and surgery,[9] however, will

[8] As with the market, the comments on kayaking are derived primarily from many years and many miles of "participant observation/ethnographic research," augmented by secondary resources and hundreds of hours of instruction from various gifted instructors in numerous places including white water, ocean surf, choppy seas, rivers, sounds, and open waters. Though I am clearly an experienced kayaker, I am definitely not an expert in any sense. I have kayaked enough, both by myself and with others to know that it is an activity that requires any serious practitioner to act sensibly, if they hope to continue to paddle.

[9] In contrast to the market and kayaking, the surgery material presented is grounded primarily on the experiences of a "prime informer" backed up by secondary resources.

also be included when exploring the "acting sensibly" coping skills in an attempt to broaden and enrich the presentation. A central message in what follows, based on what the market is telling us, is that such acting sensibly coping skills are likely to require much greater attention in the future.

The emphasis given to acting sensibly is not intended, however, to undermine the importance of making sense, which itself takes various forms and continues to function as our dominant coping strategy in most situations. This book is itself, for example, more an attempt to make sense than an instance of acting sensibly, which explains in large measure why the more detailed discussion of acting sensibly has been postponed to Part III. In order to properly grasp acting sensibly, it is useful if not necessary to appreciate types of puzzles we confront and the more usual ways we attempt to cope with them as well as where and why they succeed and where and why they fail. Parts I and II attempt to do this. This approach also provides a sounder foundation for Part IV that explores the emergence of comparatively recent hybrid coping practices that draws upon factors from both making sense and acting sensibly practices as well as countermeasures that might help us better to deal with these new hybrids. These hybrid coping practices, which utilize what is commonly called "big data" and various types of statistical/probabilistic/algorithmic explanatory models have emerged in large measure to deal with the introduction of various new financial instruments and the correlated increased volume and volatility of modern global markets.

While uncertainties present themselves in a variety of different forms, they commonly present themselves either as ambiguities embedded in some narrative or other mental medium, or contingencies embedded in some sort of activity, happening, or other type of physical flow. Put slightly differently, we confront them primarily either in acts of "knowing" and/or "doing." Most of our coping skills are similarly intended to solve particular puzzles of either "knowing" or "doing," though there are often overlaps. Greater attention has historically been given to unraveling the enigmas of knowledge for the fairly simple reason that, being embedded in knowledge, they have tended to demand explanation of some sort or other. The mysteries of doing in comparison are often overlooked for an equally simple, if quite different, reason; namely, that they commonly don't "fit" into familiar knowledge categories. A classic example of this is the parable of Alexander the Great's response to the puzzle of unraveling the "Gordian Knot." Where others had previously attempted to disentangle the knot by determining its structure, Alexander simply split it in half with his sword. One might say that he "thought outside of the box," but it is just as likely that he simply "responded/acted" to what he experienced to be an adversarial challenge.

"Doing" puzzles and their associated "coping" component have tended to be overlooked in comparison to "knowing" puzzles; this book seeks to redress this primarily in Part III. The reason for emphasizing such doing puzzles is not, as noted above, that they are inherently more important, but rather because they have tended to be overlooked and dismissed. There is the added fact that our limitations in dealing with such puzzles have become more costly as the number and importance of such doing puzzles have increased. In exploring "doing" puzzles, however, "knowing" puzzles cannot be ignored. Puzzle solving, even when primarily behavioral, as in untangling a knotted string rather than merely splitting it, has a significant knowing component. As such, in order to get a firm grip on coping it is necessary to maintain a balanced approach utilizing both "knowing" and "doing" components. Another factor that requires attention as it has shaped and continues to shape the way these uncertainties are experienced and the coping practices employed is that they have evolved and changed over time and continue to do so. But we are getting ahead of ourselves. A more detailed chapter-by-chapter account of the discussions to follow and how they are related is in order.

The book is divided into four parts: Part I, "Uncertainties in Knowing and Doing," explores the two major types of uncertainty—ambiguities and contingencies—that permeate what we know and what we do. Price-setting markets, especially financial markets, entail a higher percentage of both types, but especially in the case of doing, than most structured social arenas; Part II, "Traditional Coping Practices: Denying and Binding, Insulating and Propelling," examines the historically dominant forms of coping—accounts and routines—that normally prevail; Part III, "Acting Sensibly: Eluding Hazards and Grasping Opportunities," focuses upon "acting sensibly," primarily in terms of the behavioral practices utilized in responding to unexpected, contingent happenings; and Part IV, "Teachings for Tomorrow," examines the recent emergence of "hybrid" coping strategies employing statistical, probabilistic, algorithmic accounts, modern technological instruments, and what is commonly designated as "big data." This section then suggests ways, including more hands-on practices, which we might beneficially utilize to cope with these developments. All of these chapters will rely quite heavily upon market and contrasting vignettes in an effort to privilege the voice of the market as alluded to earlier. Below is a brief, but fuller section-by-section and chapter-by-chapter account of the subjects addressed, including selected references, and related teachings offered by the market. While intended as a general overview it is also offered as a guide for those readers with particular interests or who are desiring to jump around.

Part I, "Uncertainties in Knowing and Doing," is composed of two chapters. Chapter 1, "Knowledge is Fickle," lays the foundation for much that follows by highlighting some of the various ways in which "knowledge" fails to meet the various standards of rationality and factual accuracy that are commonly expected. More specifically it will explore how, despite a general consensus regarding the rules for thinking rationally, we seem to consistently fail to do so. This paradox has been a subject of interest from the early beginning of

Western philosophy. The primary explanations offered have tended to revolve around various inconsistencies in the ways we use language. These inconsistencies have, in turn, fostered various attempts to generate logically consistent symbolic accounts by specifying various decision-making rules. Rational choice theory, particularly as defined within modern economics, is perhaps the most prominent of such systems, though philosophy from the time of Aristotle's logic has given rise to a range of other systems. Other philosophers, however, have argued that language is inherently incommensurable with the types of rationality these systems embrace. Ludwig Wittgenstein's (1953) concept of "Language Games," which grounds the meaning of language within its particular context, is probably the best-known formulation of this position. The market embraces a mix of these perspectives as reflected in the innumerable detailed, analytically rigorous reports it generates and the equally numerous "double-talk" explanations and predictions it fosters.

While these historic debates regarding the inherent rationality/non-rationality of linguistic and mathematical scripts continue, other factors bearing on decision making have more recently been introduced, particularly in terms of economic decision making and behavior. I refer here to the "irrational" behavioral tendencies that shape decision making that have been explored by behavioral economics and cognitive psychology, particularly in the form of prospect theory, noted earlier. The concerns of this camp revolve not around language per se, but rather around the way we process alternatives and behave. In some important ways the critiques offered by this camp echo Wittgenstein's contention noted above that how we think and act needs to be seen within the context within which it occurs. A fuller discussion of this will need to wait until we are engaged in Chapter 1. In making a case that knowledge limitations are grounded in the ways we experience/access the world in which we live, however, an even more radical stance could be taken; namely, that such limitations echo the muddled nature of reality. As such our cognitive fickleness may have its own worth insofar as it mirrors and fits the uncertainties that characterize the world we live in. This claim serves as a segue to Chapter 2.

Chapter 2, "Stuff Happens," continuing to draw heavily on market examples, switches the focus from knowing and ambiguities to happenings and contingencies. This switch also entails focusing more upon undefined future events than to past patterned events. The central theme of this chapter is that concrete reality is composed of a myriad of interrelated open systems, which are individually and collectively subject to change due to unrecognized underlying causal forces. It is this configuration that gives "reality" its intrinsically contingent character. This is not an original thesis: it can be traced back to the pre-Socratic philosopher Heraclitus, who summed up the changing nature of the world in his observation, "You can never step twice into the same stream." More recently this unfolding character of the world has been embraced in a somewhat different form by what is commonly referred to as transcendental/critical realism, and associated with Roy Bhaskar (1975, 1979), Harré and Madden (1975), Harré and Secord (1973), and Peter Manicas (1987, 2006) among others.[10] What we experience is a product of a multitude of different factors, many of which are minimally difficult to directly perceive. An important corollary of this theoretical perspective is that the future is not determined by the patterns of the past, at least not by behavioral/empirical patterns that can be known, but by underlying causal forces. This perspective is similar to modern chaos theory insofar as both schools embrace causality and remain highly skeptical of our ability to predict future outcomes.[11] Whereas chaos theory generally attributes our inability to predict the future to our inability to grasp the causal forces in play, critical realism attributes this failure to the ontological nature of these causal forces that has them operating at different levels within open systems. This latter perspective is also generally seen to be inherent in Darwinian evolution. While this chapter seeks to provide an overview of these various philosophic accounts, its primary objective is to provide a series of concrete "grab bars" such as the maxim "stuff happens,"[12] and vignettes that can help us hold onto this crucial, but elusive conception of the structure of this reality. Markets, particularly financial markets, again provide us with one of the, if not the, richest veins of such contingent events and behavioral crosscurrents that generate them.

Taken together, Chapters 1 and 2 are intended to make the case that ambiguities and contingencies are not only pervasive and important, but are also deserving of greater attention. This is particularly true of contingencies. A prime reason why "the market" and other price-setting markets are supporting witnesses of both of these positions is that such markets have been deliberately structured to foster conflicting evaluations and interpretations. This is often overlooked due to our tendency to succumb to our desire for consensus. Why this is so, how we do it, and how this plays out, particularly in price-setting markets, are the primary subjects of Part II, "Traditional Coping Practices: Denying and Binding, Insulating and Propelling." Like Part I, Part II

[10] See also Porpora (2007). The essential insight of this perspective rests on distinguishing between the underlying causal forces that shape worldly and behavioral outcomes and the actual patterns of these outcomes. It is linked also to more traditional transcendental realism. This theme is also central to Giddens (1984). The emphasis given to concrete situations and experiences echoes many aspects of pragmatism, particularly that of John Dewey (1925/1929) and George Herbert Mead (1934).

[11] A key difference among proponents of different versions of this perspective is whether our failure to be able to predict is a theoretical given or not. Some argue that if we had full knowledge of the causal forces in play prediction would be possible; others argue that such full knowledge is theoretically unobtainable. Most chaos theory proponents fall into the first group; most critical realists fall into the second. The literature on this is such that a web-search is probably the best way to go.

[12] That another "s" word, which is commonly used rather than "stuff," will be part of this discussion.

is composed of two chapters: Chapter 3: "Making Sense: Denying and Binding," and Chapter 4: "Routines and Performances: Insulating and Propelling." These chapters examine the two most common means for coping with ambiguities and contingencies: Explanatory accounts and behavioral routines. As is the case with the topics of the first two chapters, these topics have also been the subject of numerous different investigations in a wide range of different disciplines. While references will be made to a good number of these works, emphasis will again be given to various market practices in presenting both explanatory accounts and routines. The theoretical framings that will be utilized in dealing with these procedures, however, will be primarily sociological. My reason for doing this is that these sociological framings address more directly a number of the key "why" and "how" facets of both activities. I refer here primarily to the works of Emile Durkheim and George Herbert Mead mentioned earlier.

In highlighting the social and collective character of governing accounts and narratives, Chapter 3 echoes what is perhaps the key insight of sociology; namely, that knowledge, like language, is an inherently social evolutionary creation. An important corollary of this is that its primary function is not to accurately mirror "reality," whatever that might be, but rather to enable social interactions to occur, with different types of narratives and accounts capable of enabling different types of interactions. While Durkheim is commonly credited with articulating the theoretical foundation for this perspective numerous others have contributed to it in different ways. For the purpose at hand of presenting a general overview of how governing narratives function as coping mechanisms, however, Chapter 3 by and large circumvents tackling this more extensive theoretical literature. The one major exception to this is George Herbert Mead's work that applies not only to Chapter 3, but also to Chapter 4.

The median carryover into Chapter 4 is directly linked to the more central role played by behavior in routines, which are the focus of concern of Chapter 4. Routines as such fall under the general umbrella of what is commonly referred to as practice theory, which is tied to various more modern social theorists including Anthony Giddens and Pierre Bourdieu. While this literature is referenced, particularly Giddens, primary attention will be given, as in the earlier chapters, to the market itself and the various routines it fosters. A central objective of this chapter is to indicate what routines manage to do and what they do not do along similar lines used in the previous chapter to describe accounts. While both of these assessments tend to emphasize the limitations of each in actually dealing with the ambiguities and contingencies confronted, each chapter seeks first and foremost to clarify the extent and degree to which these procedures are inherently attractive and often successful in circumventing the ambiguities and contingencies confronted. It is not an exaggeration, in fact, to recognize them as central to our historical survival as a species. In making this case, both chapters underscore the collective, social, and cultural components that make human society possible and describe and epitomize the human condition. Without these practices, whatever their weaknesses and limitations, there would be no markets. Put slightly differently, these practices make it quite clear that markets are not essentially individual or purely economic activities, but rather deeply social activities.

In Part III, "Acting Sensibly: Eluding Hazards and Grasping Opportunities," the book takes a critical turn. Without in any way rejecting the importance and centrality of the two coping mechanisms examined in Chapters 3 and 4, Part III switches our attention to a generally less utilized, but clearly more engaging form of coping, labeled "acting sensibly." While acting sensibly plays an important role in a range of different activities where "stuff happens" regularly, a case can be made that it is perhaps most central in markets. In a very real sense, Part III presents the book's essential theme. It has been positioned where it has been to benefit from the framings of Parts I and II. As in the earlier chapters, market examples are used extensively, but other simpler examples are drawn from two other settings in which acting sensibly plays a key role: sea kayaking and surgery.[13] Following a brief introduction, it contains six chapters. The first of these, Chapter 5, "The Elements of Acting Sensibly: An Overview," presents the five major steps/stages that constitute acting sensibly, each of which revolves around a different task: 1) identifying and juggling objectives; 2) recognizing and monitoring markers; 3) generating and utilizing rules of thumb; 4) adjusting and correcting one's course; and 5) monitoring and utilizing escape routes. In addition to presenting these steps/stages, this chapter also describes in greater detail some of the more significant changes that have occurred in financial markets over the past few decades, primarily in response to the growth of derivatives.

The following five chapters that constitute Part III focus in greater detail on one of the five steps/stages introduced in Chapter 5, as their titles indicate:

[13] While markets, particularly financial markets, are both extremely rich sites for exploring how we deal with uncertainties of varying sorts and a more prominent sector of society, they nevertheless present certain difficulties when it comes to illustrating the puzzles and uncertainties and the related coping processes that they generate. These difficulties are tied to the increasing complexities and intricacies of many new financial instruments presently being traded and new computerized trading practices used. While rich with examples and highly accessible, many aspects of these modern markets are likely to be unfamiliar to anyone not actively engaged in them. The decision to include a few kayaking and surgery vignettes is intended to counterbalance this situation, not because these two settings are more familiar than the market, but because they rely upon more familiar factors and parameters than some of the many esoteric market practices that will be examined, primarily in Part III. While quite different in ways from both financial markets and each other, both of these sites, like financial markets, are not only subject to uncertainties of ambiguity, but to an even greater extent uncertainties of contingency, i.e., unexpected happenings, which force them to utilize a fuller range of coping mechanisms than most other venues.

Chapter 6: "Identifying and Juggling Objectives," Chapter 7: "Recognizing Markers," Chapter 8: "Utilizing Rules of Thumb," Chapter 9: "Adjusting and Correcting One's Course," and Chapter 10: "Monitoring and Utilizing Escape Routes." Each chapter also draws upon the different settings noted above, with primary emphasis upon financial markets, whose teachings are privileged. While acting sensibly continues to play a secondary role to making sense in the lives of most people, a strong case can be made for the stance that it is presently the most crucial coping practice in shaping the world in which we live and hence deserves significantly more attention than it presently is receiving.

In focusing upon "acting sensibly" the discussion, as suggested earlier, moves into fairly virgin territory. This creates its own difficulties when it comes to providing familiar references and guidelines. This is not to say that relevant writings do not exist. Part III draws quite heavily, for example, on the works of G. H. Mead and critical realism. It also approaches, without actually converging with, a range of work commonly associated with practice theory, prospect theory, and organizational theory. As in the earlier chapters, but more so here however, the presentation depends primarily on what the market, and the two new sites of kayaking and surgery tell us through vignettes. References to prospect theory, practice theory, and organizational theory are presented more to emphasize differences with acting sensibly than as examples of acting sensibly. The relationship with Mead, critical realism, and Darwinian evolution is quite different insofar as acting sensibly can be seen as an extension of all three inasmuch as they lay the foundation for such practices without pursuing them.

Part IV, "Teachings for Tomorrow," takes another turn. In its first chapter, "New Teachings of the New Market," what might be called the "new market" of the twenty-first century, with its range of novel contingencies and novel coping strategies, is described. Included in this presentation is a yet fuller account of the new breed of market makers[14] I label in Chapter 3 "market croupiers," derivatives, ETFs, and ETNs (exchange traded funds and notes), and algorithmic trading practices introduced earlier. These new contingencies and their related coping strategies are themselves products of new types of emerging financial markets linked to and shaped by increased globalization and vast digitalization innovations, particularly in the areas of computerization and communication. This includes "high-frequency trading" and the greater reliance upon "big data." While these markets have given rise to a whole new set of puzzles and uncertainties, they have also given rise to a rich

[14] A "market maker" is someone who is expected to provide liquidity in a market by acting as an intermediary between those wanting to buy and those wanting to sell, by both buying and selling when matching buyers or sellers are not present. Such market makers are commonly referred to as "dealers."

collection of new teachings. These new teachings have a range of interesting impacts upon the more traditional teachings related to both making sense and acting sensibly that transcend markets per se. The bottom line here is that while the reliance upon statistical, algorithmic accounts utilized in coping with some specific types of new trading situations has flourished, the market's overall coping capacities have been severely limited in other ways.

The book's final chapter, Chapter 12, "Learning to Act Sensibly by Engaging and Doing," explores some of the implicit suggestions that markets seem to be presenting as to how we may better prepare ourselves and the next generation to acquire the skills and attitudes required to counter the types of contingencies we are likely to confront, particularly when it comes to acting sensibly. Particular emphasis is placed upon "hands-on" experiential learning as embodied in various types of apprenticeships inherent in markets and other highly demanding acting sensibly contexts. While human civilization is built upon shared, consensual orders, meanings, and making sense, the market teaches us that we need to acknowledge and recognize the inherent and emerging contingencies of our highly changeable world and our need to be able to act sensibly. These "teachings" taken together, highlight not only the rich and multifaceted nature of what the market has to offer, but also how demanding a mentor it is, a fact that pretty much every market professional learns sooner or later. The book proper concludes with a brief Postscript.

Two appendixes are also included: Appendix A: "Understanding Markets from a Sociological Perspective," and Appendix B: "The Interplay of Ethnography and Markets."

Appendix A is intended to provide a richer historical and academic account of the various ties between markets and the discipline of sociology that have helped shape this book. In various ways these ties functioned as the scaffolding used to put this book together, but were removed in order to focus upon the central themes of the book. Appendix B, which focuses upon the particular methodological mix employed in writing this book, including the interplay between the methodology and the subject matter being explored, relates more to the grounds upon which the book rests. In a very real sense these two appendixes speak directly to the making sense–acting sensibly pair explored through the book, with Appendix A delving more deeply into the theoretical framings I have used in an attempt to make sense, and Appendix B examining the investigative practices used to do so in a sensible way.

Part I

Uncertainties in Knowing and Doing

As noted in the Preface, Part I sets the scene for the discussion that follows by exploring the roots of ambiguities and other epistemological uncertainties in Chapter 1, and contingencies and ontologically grounded disorders in Chapter 2. The market will serve as our primary research site for exploring both types of uncertainties as it presents us with an unusually rich mix of both these types.

Taken together, Chapters 1 and 2 are intended to make the case that ambiguities and contingencies are not only pervasive and important, but are also deserving of greater attention. This is particularly true of contingencies. A prime reason why "the Market" and other price-setting markets are supporting witnesses of both of these positions is that such markets have been deliberately structured to foster conflicting evaluations and interpretations. This is often overlooked due to our tendency to succumb to our desire for consensus.

1

Knowledge is Fickle

Seek simplicity and distrust it.
Alfred North Whitehead

I am not sure when I first realized that "knowledge"[1] could be a slippery, fickle[2] commodity, but whatever early inklings I might have had were dramatically magnified by being exposed to the stock market. The stockbroker's response noted at the beginning of the Preface—"Look, any professional broker can give you a very convincing story of why the market did what it did yesterday, but not one of them can tell you what it is going to do tomorrow"—clearly played a central role in this process.

At the time I was exploring how market participants, primarily market professionals, generated accounts of how the market worked that "made sense" of the market. At that time, based on some earlier work I had done, I was particularly interested in how much weight they gave to economic factors, technical and chartist indicators, stories and gossip, market action, or some other type of information.[3] Since I was expecting some sort of review of the various pervading "market philosophies" of how the market worked, with greater emphasis on this stockbroker's own particular stance, I was somewhat surprised by his response; it rang a familiar bell, however, as I already knew that Wall Street had numerous conflicting maxims for pretty much any situation:

Avoid the crowd, but also: Don't fight the tape.
Buy on new highs, but also: Sell on good news.

[1] The term "knowledge" is in quotes to underscore that the term here and in what follows is meant to refer to accounts of one sort or another that claim or are assumed to cognitively grasp or explain something or other. No claim is made that such knowledge is "true" on either "logical" or "factual" grounds.

[2] The term "fickle" has been selected as best capturing knowledge's chameleon-like quality of presenting itself in different ways in different situations. Why this should be the case is a question that this chapter will hopefully explicate in greater detail.

[3] This study continued for over a decade and was published in 1981 (Smith 1981).

Diversify your portfolio, but also: Buy only the best performing stocks.
Take your profits, but also: Hold your strong stocks for the long term; and then,
Never panic, but also: When in doubt, get out.

The market, of course, is not the only place where we confront conflicting advice. We find the same conflicts in the scores of aphorisms that are commonly accepted as embodying the distilled essences of whatever we might call "wisdom." On the one hand we have:

1. Haste makes waste.
2. If at first you don't succeed, try, try again.
3. Absence makes the heart grow fonder.
4. Two heads are better than one.
5. You're never too old to learn.
6. A word to the wise is sufficient.
7. It's better to be safe than sorry.
8. Don't look a gift horse in the mouth.
9. Many hands make light work.
10. Don't judge a book by its cover.
11. Don't bite off more than you can chew.
12. The squeaking wheel gets the grease.

But then on the other hand we have:

1. He who hesitates is lost.
2. Don't beat your head against a stone wall.
3. Out of sight, out of mind.
4. Paddle your own canoe.
5. You can't teach an old dog new tricks.
6. Talk is cheap.
7. Nothing ventured, nothing gained.
8. Beware of Greeks bearing gifts.
9. Too many cooks spoil the broth.
10. Clothes make the man.
11. Hitch your wagon to a star.
12. Silence is golden.

What these contradictory truisms reveal is that much we commonly accept as established knowledge and wisdom is pregnant with inconsistencies. Or to be more generous, given that knowledge and wisdom are highly contextual, minimally fickle insofar as different situations and time make for different truths. As disconcerting as this may be, especially when it has been taught for centuries that "inconsistencies" are indications of fundamental errors of some sort, this fickleness of knowledge, rather than merely highlighting some cases of faulty knowledge, may actually be revealing other constructive facets of knowledge. More specifically, it would suggest that "knowledge," even when logically and factually inaccurate, provides us with acceptable, which generally means consensual, answers of one sort or another. While such a stance clearly conflicts with the widely supported view, especially in the rational-prone worlds of economics and markets, that knowledge should be both logically and factually correct, it is not a unique or original thesis. As noted in the Preface, it comes linked to a variety of explanatory factors, the three major ones being inconsistent language, cognitive biases, and an incommensurate fit between mind and matter. The market presents us with numerous examples of all three. Each requires a fuller discussion, however, to be properly appreciated.

While language, including it should be noted mathematical language, contributes to the fickleness of knowledge in various ways, the grounds in all cases is the simple fact that the primary objective of language is not to mirror the world, either as it is or how it is experienced. Language is meant to foster communication between different people and, as such, a level of cognitive order. These are the basic functions that have governed the manner in which language has evolved. This evolutionary process, however, has, in the case of language as in all other known cases, given rise to a number of incongruities such as those presented above. A prime example of such language paradoxes that goes back to the pre-Socratic philosophers is the simple statement, "I am a liar." If the statement is accepted as true then the speaker's claim must be false. If the speaker is not a liar but truthful, than the statement should be true, and hence the speaker cannot be truthful. While most self-contradictory statements can normally be "straightened out" if various rules are followed, such statements as a whole are inherent in language due to the capacity and tendency of language to be self-referencing.

While philosophers and others who have wrestled with these issues have managed to identify the core practices that give rise to these language inconsistencies, and in so doing establish rules capable of countering them in many controlled circumstances, the dominant view commonly attributed to Wittgenstein is that the meaning of any language is framed and shaped by the social context in which it occurs. As a consequence, similar, even identical, language can have quite different meaning in different situations. The way in which the meanings of language overlap and differ in distinct contexts is embedded in what Wittgenstein refers to as "language games," by which he meant to show that the meaning of language is a product of the way it is used and understood in everyday practices. Wittgenstein's stance here does not exclude formulating more logical and rational, deductive, decision-making models, but any such model would need to stipulate the necessary governing logical and rational guidelines.

Descartes' renowned statement, "I think, therefore I am," doesn't meet these standards, given the ambiguities of pretty much every word uttered. Game theory and rational choice theory associated with economics, sociology, and mathematics that emerged during the last half of the past century probably come closest to meeting the standards for such logical, rational, decision-making models. It is important to recognize, however, that all of these theories refer to decision-making models, not actual decision-making processes, where "double talk," in one degree or another, remains the standard. More specifically these models have not been drawn from actual practices, but rather created theoretically, and tested and reworked in various laboratory settings. Moreover, while game theory and rational choice theory have been created with economic behavior and markets as their most fitting venues, the market itself has continued to be probably richer in double talk than any other sector of society including politics, with almost any market happening generating a half dozen or more interpretive descriptions and explanations. Another way of describing this situation over the past half century would be to say that while various market-oriented academics, primarily economists, have embraced market rationality in the form of various academic models, the market itself has continued to confirm Wittgenstein's language-game view of how meanings and decisions are made. Over the past few decades, however, new twists have been added to this mix.

The new twist that has been added to this issue of the fickleness of knowledge, particularly in the market, entails an interesting mix of elements from the two camps just described. In essence, it entails locating the decision-making practices of game theory and rational choice theory within more specified concrete interactive behavioral situations of everyday life. In keeping with experimental laboratory practices favored by game theorists and rational choice theorists, this mix also utilizes experimentally controlled laboratory situations rather than natural everyday situations. By immersing various decision-making practices in different structured situations this approach is able to explore some of the different ways in which theoretically similar situations are responded to differently due to different situational factors.

The prime focus of concern here is not the rationality of the particular scripts in play but the "rationality" of the way these scripts are processed, or more to the point, the extent to which the script is ignored. While game theory, rational choice theory, and language games differ in various ways, they are similar in focusing upon the particular relevant scripts that are in play. Little to no attention is given to the way these scripts are processed. Put slightly differently, they focus on the meanings inherent in these scripts, with little to no attention to the way in which humans cognitively, emotionally, and behaviorally process these meanings. This is clearly more the case with game theorists and rational choice theorists than with Wittgenstein and his followers, but even this latter group tends to privilege the scripts per se. In academic terms this new approach brings cognitive psychology into the decision-making process. Not surprisingly, it reveals that different situations commonly override the theoretical "rational script" due to the psychological proclivities that they generate.

Given that the discipline of economics and economic markets are commonly seen to be today's citadel of rationality and rational behavior, one might have assumed that there would have been serious resistance to yet another attack on the rationality of the market. As it turned out, however, this innovative cognitive/psychological way of framing market behavior actually became the foundation for a whole new economic sub-discipline commonly referred to as behavioral economics. The writings and research of Amos Tversky and Daniel Kahneman, commonly referred to as prospect theory, in conjunction with the work of other behaviorally oriented economists, particularly Richard Thaler, are generally seen as providing the foundation of this sub-discipline.[4] The foibles documented by Kahneman, Tversky, Thaler, and others reveal a range of different "biases" in the way we think, such as privileging recent experiences, agreeing with the majority, and focusing on the familiar. In addition it shows that we employ different types of reasoning in different situations, particularly when there are different degrees of risk involved, both in acquiring wealth and in losing it.[5] Overall, this literature documents that market behavior is likely to differ in fundamental ways from what game theory and rational choice theory would favor. Again there is nothing really surprising here, especially for anyone who has spent much time in the market. For most, however, this does not create any great alarm as, this research has also shown, most people believe that they are considerably smarter than other people. In the market, for example, while most people are comfortable relating stories about how other people fail to understand what is happening in the market, they seldom include themselves. This is the underlying point of the trader's message to me noted earlier about the disconnect between the plausible explanations offered about the past and the failure to accurately predict the future.

This judgment pervades financial markets, being embedded in the thinking of both non-professional and professional investors, market analysts and

[4] The label of "prospect theory" given to the theoretical account generated by Tversky and Kahneman comes from their 1979 article of the same name. It presents a powerful critique of the limitations of classical utility theory in explaining decision making under risk. Kahneman received a Nobel Prize for this work; Tversky was ineligible as he had died. For a selective list of their joint and individual publications, see Tversky and Kahneman (1986, 1991), Kahneman and Tversky (1979, 1982, 2000), Kahneman, Slovic, and Tversky (1982), and Kahneman (2011). Prospect theory will be addressed in a number of discussions in the following chapters. For Thaler, see (1991a, and 1991b).

[5] Most of these factors are discussed in the printed version of Kahneman's Nobel Prize address (2003).

columnists. What makes all of this even more confusing is that pretty much everyone in one way or another knows this to be the case, though everyone continues to present their own views as sound. It is so well known that a large percentage of those involved in the market, be they professional investors, analysts, columnists, or lay investors, like to characterize themselves as contrarians, which means that they justify their own views and assumptions by claiming them to be opposite to those generally accepted. So many market participants claim to be contrarians that it is sometimes difficult to know what is and isn't the "accepted" position, especially since there are normally a handful of different views and assumptions, each with its contrarian counter position. The one thing that they have in common is that they all simultaneously embrace particular views based on the claim that most views are groundless.

However critical one might be of such cognitive limitations and irrationalities, there are grounds to suggest such thinking has various evolutionary advantages; as such, it would be presumptuous to dismiss it as without any value. Common ways of thinking, even when biased and "irrational," can be shown to foster rapid decision making, even if such decisions often prove not to be the best choice in the long run. In the market, being able to act quickly is often a significant advantage, especially since it is likely that others will be reacting as irrationally as you are apt to act. In fact, given the irrationality of others, acting rationally can sometimes prove to be very costly. A stampeding herd may lack rationality, but it seldom is sensible to get in its way, as anyone familiar with financial markets can attest. "You don't fight the tape!" continues to be a wise admonition. There is also the dynamics of the self-fulfilling prophecy that can serve to counter for some time the inherent irrationality of a particular stance. A well-developed account, even with its numerous built-in biases, can be useful in other ways, which is an issue to which we will return later. For the present, however, it is the limitations of these accounts that are of concern.[6]

Whatever particular advantages biased accounts might generate, they are clearly not rational according to accepted principles of rational thinking. Furthermore, though such ways of thinking may be useful in particular situations where rapid decisions are required, they tend to be counterproductive in the long run. Equally troubling is the fact that from a theoretical perspective, both cognitively and behaviorally, such actions deviate

[6] One other "benefit" of our being cognitively limited worth acknowledging was noted by Konrad Lorenz (1963). He points out that if early humans possessed the level of instrumental knowledge we prize, we would have likely self-destroyed ourselves by either killing each other directly or destroying our ecological niche and habitat. Nazaretyan (2003, 2005) expands upon this thesis in a most interesting way. Given the damage we have done to ourselves and our habitat in recent years linked to our ability to release nuclear power, alter the weather, and manufacture biological agents, Lorenz's fears may still be relevant.

dramatically from generally accepted rational accounts of how the world works and how we should act. Such "rationality" is highly praised and valued rhetorically in financial markets, where rationality is in many respects a "holy grail."

In pursuit of this holy grail, and in an attempt to counter the various types of limitations described above, particularly the cognitively biased limitations identified by Kahneman, Tversky, and behavioral economists, a growing number of market professionals in recent years have attempted to impose rational constraints upon their market behavior by subjecting it to computerized algorithmic programs of one sort or another. Rather than relying upon their own momentary market judgments, these traders have created elaborate and sophisticated mathematical models with which they program equally sophisticated computers to trade for them. The governing idea here is that, while we can know what is the rational thing to do in most situations, we cannot program ourselves to be able to act this way in response to the tremendous amount of constantly changing information within the time limits demanded by markets, but we can program computers to do so. These developments have impacted financial markets in numerous ways. The most significant of these has been the exponential growth in computer-generated trading that has lead to a massive growth in overall volume, accompanied by greater and more rapid fluctuations in prices.

While it is generally known that such computerized algorithmic trading practices are being utilized by hedge funds and other sophisticated traders using proprietary programs, the full extent to which similar, if less sophisticated, trading programs permeate the market has by and large been overlooked. There has been an equal if not greater growth in such trading among what might be called semi-professional traders, commonly referred to as day-traders, whose present estimated number is at least in the millions. Nearly all of these traders rely exclusively or heavily upon some sort of computerized algorithmic trading program. Scores of lectures, seminars, and expositions are scheduled around the country in numerous cities, including Las Vegas, New York, Los Angeles, Chicago, Boston, and New Orleans, by numerous companies that offer a wide range of trading platforms, algorithmic programs, and online accessibility to many markets. Many of these expositions run for days and are attended by thousands of individuals.

The general consensus is that few of these individuals actually make any significant money from their trading, but it has contributed significantly to the increase in overall volume in pretty much every active financial market in operation. Where ten million share days was a busy day on the New York Stock Exchange in the nineteen seventies, multi-billion share days on the combined equity markets is presently quite common. And this figure does not include the many millions of future and option transactions occurring on other exchanges or the numerous transactions that do not occur on a monitored exchange but rather in what are called "black pools." While the great majority of these trades generate comparatively small gains and losses, the exchanges executing their trades make a good deal of money. The consensus seems to be that the more financial instruments there are to trade, the more transactions, and the more transactions, the greater the profit for the exchanges and the professionals traders, who make the markets for the day traders and pretty much everyone else.

While we shall have an opportunity to examine various facets of these developments in more detail later, the relevant issue here is simply what might be called the assumption of rationality, more particularly market rationality, which such programs presume. Fortunately, or unfortunately depending upon your perspective, regardless of how sophisticated such algorithmic programs and computers might be, there are sound reasons to believe that the holy grail of market rationality cannot be attained. Any attempt to circumvent Tversky, Kahneman, Thaler, and company by relying upon algorithmic tools of one sort or another, confronts an equally impenetrable barrier; namely, Gödel's incompleteness theorems, which reveal that the quandary in generating and utilizing "rational" accounts lies not merely in our own cognitive limitations, but also in various mathematical limitations inherent in the accounts that in many ways echo the language "double talk" problem discussed earlier.

A full account of Gödel's theorems is beyond the scope of this discussion. In brief, however, they prove mathematically that any axiomatic system of even modest complexity cannot be both complete and consistent.[7] Put more colloquially, this means that it is impossible for any closed theoretical system to generate a consistent, complete deductive account of itself. While these theorems formally address only mathematical systems, it is generally accepted that they indicate that all relatively complex axiomatic systems are similarly limited. Our reasoning capacities are limited not only by language issues and particular cognitive habits linked to our own evolution, but to limitations that are inherent in any non-trivial deductive reasoning system. As such, even the most advanced computers running the most sophisticated programs can generate what from a broader perspective would seem to be quite irrational results. One does not need to be versed in Gödel's theorems to realize that some of the most sophisticated programs noted above have played significant roles in generating some of the most erratic and irrational price movements to occur in financial markets. The price movements to which I refer are the sudden and short-lived major price moves commonly described as "flash

[7] Gödel published his proof in Germany in 1931. It has since been reproduced in numerous different publications. A recent English translation has lately been available through Google. Fuller discussions can also be found on various websites. Non-mathematicians are probably best advised to seek out secondary sources, which are also numerous.

crashes."[8] The irrational, one might add ironic, nature of the connection between these market movements and the computer-based trading practices that have played such a significant role in their occurrences is that from a purely theoretical stance, the types of algorithmic programs in play should have had just the opposite effect. The grounds for this rest with the way liquidity and price changes are presumed to be related. Put quite simply, the greater the liquidity, that is the greater the number of buy and sell orders in play, the smaller the price movements between sales should be, because there should always be numerous close bid or ask quotes around any given transaction. Unfortunately, the huge number of bid and ask quotes that algorithmic programs can generate cannot adequately be monitored cognitively, at least not by humans as we know them. As a result, the job of monitoring these numerous transactions, with all of their associated bids and ask quotes, needed to be built into the trading program. Even the most sophisticated program has limitations. Unfortunately, the only option that seems to exist when such a program is pushed beyond its limits is to have it in effect shut down. Different programs, however, mean different conditions for a shutdown. If this occurs, as appears to have happened in each flash crash situation, some programs shut down and others do not, and the necessary liquidity evaporates, producing explosive price movements. The resulting damage suffered by many is a direct result of an assumption of rationality that was not and is not to be.

The fickleness of knowledge, however, transcends the limitations due to language issues, cognitive biases, and mathematical theorems. There are times when accepted knowledge seems to conflict directly with what is, or minimally what we directly experience. That is, there often seems to be a disconnect between what we accept as "valid" as it conforms to what we accept as correct reasoning, and what we accept as "factual" based on our own experience. Such disconnects have a very lengthy history going back to the pre-Socratic philosophers, particularly Zeno of Elena, who was born around 490 BC and was a disciple and junior colleague of Parmenides. A number of the most familiar "disconnects" are known as Zeno's Paradoxes, which revolve around different hypothetical situations. The most familiar is a hypothetical race between two contestants, commonly a hare and a tortoise, where the slower tortoise who can only run 1 yard in a second is given a 90-yard head start in front of the hare who runs 10 yards in a second. The question is when will the hare catch the tortoise. The second paradox is simply to hold a book or other object and

[8] One might quibble that such price movements are not irrational, but correctly mirror the bids and offers that are being presented. This approach, however, is circular and fails to confront the simple fact that the prices generated deviate from all accepted valuation processes, including pure market valuations, insofar as such market valuations carry the restriction of by "knowledgeable participants."

ask whether it will fall to the floor if one lets go of it. The third paradox revolves around an arrow or some other object apparently in flight.

The paradoxical component in all situations deals with the way we conceptualize movement and space. In the race situation the paradox is created by claiming that the hare will never catch the tortoise, even though it seems obvious that it will in exactly 10 seconds. The claim that it will not catch the tortoise is based on the argument that before the hare can catch the tortoise it must first reach the place where the tortoise started. During that time the tortoise would have moved further ahead. This will always be the case, which means that the hare can never catch the tortoise.

The paradox with the falling object is based on a similar but slightly different framing. The argument is made that before any object could fall to the floor, it would have to go halfway to the floor. Since there is always a halfway point between two points, it can be argued that the object can never reach its final goal, since there is always another halfway point to reach first. If one chose to frame it somewhat differently, the object could never begin to move, since there would always be a halfway point between where it was and where it wanted to move to, no matter how close that point was. This second formulation can be seen to lead into the arrow in flight paradox, which is somewhat more abstract in form. The argument here is that motion of any object is impossible, as it requires being in two different places at the same time, since to be in motion means to be here and there simultaneously.

The underlying difficulty in all three of these paradoxes relates to the way continuity is cognitively represented: How does something go from here to there? The way we normally do this is by accepting a framing that entails an infinite number of infinitely small points. These infinitely small points allow an object to occupy each and every point between the start-point and the end-point. The catch, of course, as Zeno's Paradoxes reveal, is that if you actually try to move along a path constituted by infinitely small points, you won't get very far. In fact, you won't get anywhere, since there will always be an infinite number of points between any two points, no matter how close they are to each other. This is all admittedly both very abstract and rather difficult to grasp, which explains why most people find Zeno's Paradoxes somewhat unpleasant. What might be called the "deceptive" component of these paradoxes, however, lends itself to other settings, including some associated with financial markets. Of these, two types have done quite well: Ponzi/chain-letter schemes and what might be labeled doubling-up strategies. What links these two processes to Zeno's Paradoxes, is that they both also exploit our cognitive limitation to grasp infinity.

Leaving out the various emotional factors that normally play a role in both of these processes, their main attraction is that they offer what appears to be a sure way to make money. The central idea is that a simple initial investment through a process of repeatable investment will eventually/in-the-end produce a profit. In the "doubling up" strategy the idea is to keep increasing one's investment/bet in a manner to cover all earlier losses until one wins, which is bound to happen eventually. In the Ponzi/chain-letter scheme the idea is to solicit funds with payment from promised future funds that will themselves be acquired by similar promised future funds in a manner that will in reasonable time fully cover the original investment. In most market Ponzi scenarios only the initial or early operators are aware that they are engaging in a Ponzi scheme; most later "investors" assume that their investment has actually been put to work somewhere, even if not necessarily in the most honorable place. The payoffs to the initial investors, however, normally play a significant role in drawing them in.

In contrast, what might be called the Ponzi element is generally made public in chain-letter schemes. While there are many variations to these letters, in all cases participants are asked to send funds to earlier participants in expectation of receiving funds from later participants. These letters clearly spell out how everyone will come out ahead providing everyone does what is required, which generally means paying off the earlier players and sending out a sufficient number of letters to new recruits. And they would, just like the gambler who continues to double his bet, also eventually come out ahead. Unfortunately, there are always limits to the number of times one can double up a bet and the number of people to whom a chain letter can be sent. Theoretically, without any such limits, they should work. Unfortunately, the world doesn't function theoretically, which is perhaps one of the major limitations inherent in purely theoretical strategies.

While such schemes, like Zeno's Paradoxes, continue to puzzle many, they generally do not have much of a lasting effect. After pondering Zeno's Paradoxes, most people simply respond by noting that like the book does fall to the ground and the faster contestant does catch and pass the slower one so there must be something wrong with Zeno's argument. Similarly those receiving chain letters or too-good-to-be-true investment opportunities tend to deposit them in a wastebasket. In doing so, however, they underscore the fact that we are normally more comfortable simply ignoring our cognitive limitations than acknowledging them.

As with Wittgenstein's language games, Tversky's, Kahneman's, and Thaler's cognitive biases, and Gödel's theorems, Zeno's Paradoxes and Ponzi schemes do not keep many people awake at night. Most people accept what they believe to be sound, if not axiomatically provable. There is a good deal of utility in this as will be shown later, but this utility does not eliminate, eradicate, absolve, or explain away the multifaceted fickleness of knowledge. More importantly, as a consequence of ignoring them, we fail to confront an equally, if not more, disturbing possibility suggested earlier to the effect that the fickleness of knowledge reflects a fickleness in the world itself. That the world, not just financial markets, is pregnant with indeterminacies capable of generating various types of fickleness is clearly not a novel notion. It is central not only to quantum mechanics and Darwinian evolution, but to various other scientific perspectives. The quote commonly attributed to Mark Twain that "everyone talks about the weather, but nobody does anything about it," echoes this truth, which nicely mirrors the comments of the market trader made earlier about predicting the market.

While the idea that reality itself is inherently unpredictable does not eliminate or amend the various knowledge limitations presented above, it does put matters in a somewhat different light. The contradictions, surprises, and uncertainties that we continually confront are not necessarily due to our cognitive limitations. The market clearly supports this view. While constantly engaged in wrestling with its rationality, seeking it while simultaneously acknowledging the futility of its efforts, the market, in the form of its various participants and audiences, recognizes that there is more entailed in unexpected happenings of the market then conceptual limitations. There are clearly contributing factors in the dynamics of the market itself. A trader once commented to me regarding a trade that went sour, "I think I handled that one as good as I could have, but it just wasn't to be. The market is like that sometimes." Or, as most traders are likely to say at one time or another, "Hey, the market has a mind of its own." Both of these statements recognize that not only are many uncertainties in large measure products of the market itself, but also that it is important to learn how to respond to them.

The idea that reality is inherently random and hence unpredictable, like fickle knowledge, is a theme that goes back to the pre-Socratic philosophers. It is not merely that things are always changing as reflected in Heraclitus' statement quoted above that you cannot step twice in the same river, but that the forces generating these changes are themselves inherently unknowable. The question as to whether this is due to disorder in the flow of events or merely our inability to grasp this order is subject to debate. Most chaos theorists tend to embrace a world subject to universal determinism, but a determinism subject to numerous undetectable minor causal forces that make it impossible to predict most outcomes. Others, including Darwin and most critical realists, hypothesize a world inherently disordered due to the way in which different systems erratically disrupt each other in confronting each other's agency.

While this latter stance appears to be supported also by quantum theory, there continues to be a pervasive and powerful resistance to this view of reality, as reflected perhaps most clearly in the continuing rejection of Darwinian evolution by a majority of practically all populations. It is a stance, however, broadly embraced by the market. Even in the market, however, differences of opinion as to the source of any given confronted disorder are common. The primary reason for this is that such confrontations occur in the midst of minded actions embedded in concrete situations and happenings in which, not only knowledge and reality, but emotions and other factors play a part.

In such situations it is often difficult to determine the source of the muddle encountered. I discovered this in one of my earlier market dealings, which reminded me of an even earlier existential awakening I experienced as a freshman undergraduate. While this undergraduate experience had nothing to do with the market, it addressed this issue more clearly than did my later market experience. In fact, I am not sure I would have been able to appreciate that my later market experience even addressed this issue if I had not had this earlier experience. I will, consequently, start with it.

The undergraduate experience I had occurred in an advanced physics course I was assigned to as a potential physics major in my freshman year. The course was structured as a "doing physics" experience rather than the more normal, primarily passive, learning/acquiring accepted knowledge process. A key component was an innovative physics laboratory that differed significantly in the ways laboratory assignments were structured. The routine was quite simple. Upon entering what was designated as our laboratory space, we were given a brief written assignment that generally asked us to prove or do something. While the space was quite large and full with all sorts of equipment, no equipment was normally selected for our use. We were free to ask questions of the laboratory assistant and to request different types of equipment and materials. While we were able to get pretty much any equipment or materials we requested, it was considerably more difficult to get answers to our questions beyond bits of clarification. We were, in short, pretty much expected to work things out on our own. The message was pretty clear: "You guys think that you want to be physicists, so start acting as such."

One of the first lab assignments we were given was to confirm Newton's second law of motion, generally called the law of gravitation, which was presented to us in its then common form of being 32 feet per second per second acceleration of free-falling objects. In short, our assignment was to work out some way to document that free-falling objects do in fact accelerate at this rate. We quickly discovered that the laboratory had a supply of 20-foot high contraptions fitted with wire guidelines, weights, paper rolls, and electric spark machinery. The goal was to use these materials to build an appropriate free-falling mechanism that could record the trajectories of the falling weights by means of timed electric shots from the falling weights to the stable backboard through the paper sheets. Our task would be to do so in a manner that would generate a sufficiently accurate 32 feet per second per second acceleration record to confirm Newton's second law.

After many hours over a period of days of pampering and refining our instruments, dropping our weights numerous time, greasing wires, and measuring innumerable burn spots, we all produced pretty much the same results: series of burn spots that approximated the 32 feet per second per second acceleration that we expected, but with variations that were considerably larger than those we expected and were required to meet. No matter how hard we attempted to fine-tune our equipment, the variations exceeded what was acceptable; and time after time, we were sent back to get "better" results. The real "kicker" and associated frustration came, however, when we were finally informed that there was nothing wrong with our results. Newton's laws, like all scientific laws, cannot be expected to reveal themselves experientially in as pure a form as we might expect. Better equipment would improve our results, but there would always be some disparities in our findings. In essence what we were told was that accepted theoretical rules such as Newton's second law of motion do not present themselves in concrete events in pure form. Put slightly differently, underlying causal forces shape concrete reality, but given the plurality of such forces at work in any given situation, no particular force is mirrored in its pure form.

My early trading experience was somewhat different, but it entailed similar dynamics. It revolved around a series of trades. The first of these was a purchase of some shares of RCA. There were a number of factors supporting this move, including its recent bullish market action in which it had showed itself to be the best performing stock, its fundamental economic credentials as the lead player in the growth of color TV, and the fact that it had recently weathered a number of critical reviews, and in doing so appeared to have established a formidable stop-point—a support price where long-term buyers had been willing to buy any stock for sale. Taken together, these factors made it a very attractive buy at the time as they evidenced a set of causal forces generally seen as capable of lifting the price of any given stock. Shortly after this purchase, however, after advancing quite briskly, the stock started to fall. As it gave up approximately half of its recent gain I nervously sold my shares. The next day the stock shot up leaving me quite dejected on the sidelines. I had clearly acted improperly allowing my fear of a loss to cause me to sell unnecessarily, my own exhibition of prospect theory many years before prospect theory was formally introduced.

Selling the stock, however, wasn't in itself a huge mistake. It is never a major error to liquidate a position if one becomes significantly uncomfortable with it. As the saying goes, "When in doubt, get out." It is what I did next that was the mistake. While still off balance watching the RCA climb in price, I jumped on the next stock that caught my eye. In this case it was IBM, which had also been behaving bullishly, but not nearly as strongly as RCA had. More importantly, at the time I was not fully abreast of the company's financial situation or its future growth potential. Even this move was in itself not that terrible. What made it into a dangerous move was that I ended up making a significant profit on it. What, one might ask, was dangerous about making a profit on this trade. It was dangerous because I had acted impulsively in response to superficial performances rather than a set of grounded causal factors starting with the initial decline of RCA followed by the rise of IBM. The decline of RCA in no way negated the factors that I had relied upon in buying it in the first place, whereas the rise in IBM was part of a general up-market lead by RCA. I had, in short, relied upon various apparent patterns rather than appropriate causal factors. The profit I made could easily have reinforced a tendency to rely on such patterns lacking evidence that there were legitimate causal factors in play if I had not been properly chastened by an experienced market mentor. Whereas my physics experience was intended to teach me that even highly controlled causal forces do not present themselves in perfect form, this market experience was intended to teach me that behavioral patterns in and of themselves tell you little if anything about the factors that generated them.

As it was, as my mentor made sure I understood, it did prove costly insofar as shortly after making this purchase the market as a whole had a minor correction, at which time I could have re-established my RCA position. I couldn't because my funds were tied up in the IBM position. Over the next few months RCA significantly outperformed IBM. The central point in this case as in the physic laboratory is the disconnect between causal factors in the world and their particular manifestations.[9] Put slightly differently, how we experience the world does not necessarily inform us correctly of the nature of the underlying causal forces at work. We both miss forces at work and see forces that do not exist. Both processes pervade the market place. In highlighting the disconnect between how we frame events and how events actually unfold, this difference would seem to echo the various paradoxes presented by Zeno discussed earlier. There is a fundamental difference, however, that is commonly overlooked; namely, that Zeno's Paradoxes focus upon our cognitive limitation in the way we frame the reality we confront, whereas these disconnects are directed at the disconnects between the reality we confront and the underlying reality that generates it.

Over the years since my own RCA–IBM experience, I have observed numerous market participants wrestle with this conundrum. I recall listening to an old-fashioned market fundamentalist in the late 1970s explaining to an aggrieved client that, while the true value of a stock is linked to the underlying earnings of the company, the stock price often does not reflect it. Whether this broker's belief that his economic principles were as sound as Newton's second law is a different question to which we will return. Whether sound or not, his

[9] "Causes" tend to be framed and understood in a variety of different ways. Aristotle claimed that there were four different types of causes: material causes that referred to the causal powers inherent in materials; formal or structural causes related to the structures of things; final or teleological causes that were related to the objects or ends of events; and efficient causes that referred to eternal forces that impacted on items and events. Most recent discussions of causal forces deal with what Aristotle referred to as efficient causality, which is how it is used in this text unless another meaning is clearly noted. This holds true for expressions of "causal factors," "causal mechanisms," "causal forces," and "causal powers." While "causal mechanism" tends to be the most commonly used phrase, it assumes a mechanical, structural conception that conveys an overly deterministic stance that "causal powers" and "causal forces" do not. As such, the discussion that follows relies upon these latter two framing.

message to his client was basically the same message that my physics instructor was trying to convey to me. The fact that your empirical results do not conform to certain assumed governing principles/laws does not necessarily invalidate those principles/laws. To dismiss them as governing principles/laws would be like throwing out the baby with the dirty bathwater.

While I remember being sympathetic toward this fundamentalist-oriented broker, I responded less sympathetically when I heard a chartist-oriented broker offer similar, but quite different, counsel to one of his clients. Again the market had not performed properly according to the broker. There was, however, an important difference in how the two brokers responded to their particular situations. For the fundamentalist, the underlying economic dynamics that he valued had not materialized as expected. Nevertheless, he continued to accept his view of the market; it was this particular situation that he hadn't gotten right. The traditional cyclist–chartist doesn't have this option. What "determines" his market are particular market patterns. There are not underlying causal forces at work, except perhaps some sort of transcendental "hand" of the market. For this chartist, getting the market wrong means that the chart/pattern relied upon was wrong in some way. For this chartist the market is not only an ordered world, but one whose order is discoverable. While most market professionals accept that the world is ordered to some degree, and there are clearly differences here, the great majority are more skeptical when it comes to getting a hold on it. And then there are those who remain agnostic regarding just how ordered the market and the world as a whole is. Few, if any, of these individuals would argue that there is no order to what happens, but most would argue that there is considerably less order in the world than most people assume. For these individuals, the fickleness of the market is clearly not due only to limitations in what and how we know: their world is itself fickle.

The market is clearly not the only arena where fickleness is seen to be rooted in both knowledge and the world. Where the market differs from most other everyday arenas is the degree to which it accepts market uncertainties and contingencies as inherent in the world, rather than our inability to properly grasp the way the world is ordered.[10] More important than simply recognizing and accepting the uncertainties and contingencies inherent in the external world is the extent to which the market, or more accurately a subgroup of market participants, seeks to deal with them. There is more at work here than the fickleness of knowledge.[11] To put the matter more colloquially "stuff

[10] Various other arenas could be suggested from wars—true, but not really "everyday arenas"—to sporting events—acknowledged, but more tangential. We shall, in fact, explore two more focused activities—kayaking and surgery—in Part III. Markets, however, are really in a class of their own here.

[11] There is another possible reason why what we thought to be the case did not materialize as expected. The information we relied upon wasn't so much fickle as it was falsified. While this

happens," and much that happens isn't due to limitations and ambiguities in what we know. Often it is grounded in contingencies we confront in the world we inhabit. The market has a good deal to say about such contingencies. It is to these situations we now turn.

clearly may be, and in some situations is, the case, the conviction that information was falsified is more often than not a defense against accepting the fickleness of knowledge. This is commonly the situation in the market.

2

Stuff Happens!

You shall see my back, but my face you shall not see.

Exodus 33:23

Give me lucky generals.

Napoleon

Stuff happens! Be it a tsunami caused by an earthquake thousands of miles away or a storm-surge tidal wave, a peaceful ocean can quite suddenly transform itself and destroy anything that stands in its way. On a lesser scale, an unexpected falling branch may lead to a car accident that turns a score of people's lives upside down, people may win lotteries, teenage girls get pregnant from their first sexual encounter, long-lost jewelry may be found, apparently healthy people get sick, and some very sick people suddenly recover. But there are few places that experience stuff happening more than do financial markets. On a grand scale there is the apparently healthy bullish equity market, totaling literally trillions of dollars with hundred of millions of investors, including a significant percent who are considered highly knowledgeable, which suddenly collapses within minutes, erasing 10 percent of its total value in a matter of days if not hours. On a lesser scale these markets house sudden price changes, unexpected changes in trading volume, and an almost constant flow of stories and information that serves to reframe, often significantly, how the market is perceived.

Pretty much everyone knows of such instances and most have experienced one or more in their lifetime both in and out of the market. Some attribute these events to a divine power, others to fate or simply blind luck. For most people, however, even those who claim to "know" the source of such events, the "whys" of specific events remain a mystery. As difficult as it may be to cognitively and emotionally accept these events, most people find it easier to do so and move on than to pursue and confront the even more mystifying sources of such events. Such avoidance strategies enable people to retain a view of the world as fundamentally ordered even if subject to aberrations here and there. Unfortunately, such avoidance strategies hinder our ability to grasp properly the numerous implications and meanings inherent in the two simple, but quizzical words: "stuff happens."

Why "stuff"? While clearly more vulgar, the more common "s" word in this saying is "shit happens." The primary grounds for this is that the unexpected that "happened" is generally experienced as highly unpleasant. The fact remains, however, that the number of pleasant unexpected happenings tends to equal the number of unpleasant happenings, but the pleasant ones often go unnoted. Our propensity to emphasize unexpected negative happenings more than unexpected positive happenings is consistent with much cognitive psychological research along the lines discussed in the previous chapter; namely, that individuals tend to take credit for the good things and attribute the bad things to external factors. But given that "what" happens is just as likely to be positive as negative, the more neutral term of "stuff" is more appropriate.

But neutral or not why "stuff," given that "stuff" generally refers to leftover bits and pieces of some sort? What does it mean to designate what happened as "stuff"? Whatever else it might mean, the usage of the term "stuff" denies the unexpected happening its own identity; it cordons it off from the normal flow of events. Given that the events to which the word "stuff" refers are generally not trivial, it would seem that it is their "unexpected" lineage that is the grounds for distancing them. "Stuff" conveys the message that while something did occur, its happening was aberrant, and as such marginal. What is significant is that which is normal and constitutes our lives. Tsunamis and tornadoes "happen," but they are not integral to our lives in the same way as the sun, which rises every day at a predictable time in an ordered way. Put slightly differently, it suggests that such events are essentially chance events and as such should not overly concern us.

This does not mean that such events, or chance itself, are of no consequence. Chance has a rich and lengthy history that has given rise to a similarly rich and lengthy literature, too rich and lengthy to be treated adequately here.[1] Fortunately, for the more limited purposes of exploring unexpected events, an exhaustive analysis is not required. In contrast to events framed within ordered accounts, three features of nearly all "unexpected" events are of particular importance: 1) Such events are ontologically real; they occur in the world. They are not merely products of the way we frame things or experience things; 2) Such events, nearly always, are experienced both emotionally and cognitively and more often than not either positively or negatively; and 3) Such events are grounded in a spatial–temporal context; the boundaries of these contexts, however, are indefinite insofar as they are both expandable and contractible. An event described as occurring in New York City on

[1] For three interesting overviews, see Beck (1992), Bernstein (1998), and Reith (1999). Knight's (1921) book is one of the earliest books to deal with economic and market risk.

September 20, 2008, for example, may equally well be described as occurring on the northwest corner of 50th Street and Fifth Avenue at 6:07:24 a.m., September 20, 2008 or in the northeast of the United States of America during the first decade of the twenty-first century.

While each of these facets is distinct, they are also interrelated and overlap. The blurry nature of their boundaries, coupled with their grounding in the real world, feeds into and is fed by their unexpected status; these same factors in combination foster emotional as well as cognitive responses. In combination, these factors endow these events with a multifaceted mystique. Where are they from? What is their meaning? How should we deal with them? Notwithstanding the vast multi-disciplined literature focused on these and other related questions noted above, the unexpected events relevant to this discussion can be explicated in terms of a comparatively simple "stratified, open system model" of reality. Open stratified system models come in varying forms and permeate numerous disciplines in both the natural and social sciences. The particular model employed here draws heavily upon modern critical realism associated with Bhaskar (1975, 1979), Harre and Secord (1973), Harre and Madden (1975), Harre (1981, 2009), and Manicas (1987, 2006), to name some of the theorists whose works have significantly influenced me.[2] It has also been informed by fifty years of personal ethnographic research of a wide variety of auction markets, particularly financial markets (Smith 1981, 1989).[3] It has also been fostered by Darwinian and neo-Darwinian evolutionary theory, quantum physics, particularly the Heisenberg theory of inconsistency, the thoughts of Wittgenstein, pragmatism, developmental psychology, various strains of social theory, and a wide variety of everyday experiences. The lineage of this model, however—where it gets what—is quite secondary to the fact that it embraces a world of layered open systems that generate both emergent and unexpected outcomes.[4]

As indicated in the previous paragraph, open stratified systems pervade the world as we know it. There are good reasons, in fact, to maintain that they constitute the basic structures of physical reality in all of its various forms, including physical, chemical, biological, semantic, and meaning systems. This is not unexpected given that they are products of what colloquially is referred to as the "big bang," which is responsible for their basic structure. The "big bang" served to transform a "one" into a "many"; that is what the "big bang" was all about. From the moment that the many was generated, however, each

[2] The references cited are really just the tip of a very large transcendental/critical realism literature. See (2007) for a focused chapter on causation.

[3] A more detailed discussion of the particular nature of the ethnographic methodology utilized is presented in Appendix B: "The Interplay of Ethnography and Markets."

[4] To draw on an important distinction discussed by Rom Harre (2009), while the "open system" model is used in the discussion that follows primarily as an explanatory tool, it is presented as a model of reality, not merely as heuristic tool.

segment of the many has been engaged in different degrees with active interrelationships with the other segments, both internal and external. As these ties were formed creating a level of physical reality, new entities emerged that over time became linked together to generate an emerging new strata of reality. This process is commonly seen to have begun with what we generally call physics that begot chemistry, that begot biology, that evolved in numerous ways, including generating numerous animal species including humans who have generated whole other strata of mind and meanings, such as languages, religions, science, kinships, groups, organizations, nation states, and so on.[5] What each of these processes reveals in one way or another is a search for a new, more bounded, "oneness" of sorts.

In physics, reality is framed primarily in terms of gravitation, the strong/nuclear force, the weak force, and electromagnetism, which link the many parts together.[6] Chemistry, focusing primarily upon the structure, properties, and interaction of matter tends to frame reality in terms of molecular and chemical bonds and forces.[7] Biology focuses primarily upon the morphology, physiology, anatomy, behavior, origin, and distribution of living matter/organisms as well as their bonding forces, including reproduction and various interactional practices. The social sciences, for their part, tend to focus upon humans, their cognitive skills, individual and collective routines, and different ways of interacting, including forms of exchange.[8] Humans have managed to combine their interactive practices and biological facilities to generate what George Herbert Mead[9] labeled reflective thought, language, and mind, which appear to be subject to the same dynamics as other systems. In all of these cases individual entities of one sort or another are shown to influence and be influenced by other entities and as a consequence are linked to these others through a changing, ongoing, never-ending series of such linkages. At every level some sets of linkages acquire a relative degree of closure that endows the sets with their own identities. They exist as quasi ones. But all such quasi ones remain incomplete and caught up in more encompassing links, and subject to internal

[5] There continue to be debates as to the nature of these cognitive and social entities, including their ontological status. While important and interesting in their own right, I have elected to avoid them as much as possible, as most of these debates are tangential to the concerns of this book.

[6] Most readers interested in a fuller discussion of these forces are probably best advised to search on line where they will find numerous informative websites.

[7] The advice given in the previous note applies here as well.

[8] Exchange in the form of material goods clearly plays a, if not the, central role in economics. Exchange of authority and power is also central in political science. Sociology and anthropology wrestle with their own exchanges that govern family structures, friendships, culture, and organizations of varying sorts. All of them are equally engaged in the exchange of various sorts of information.

[9] Numerous books and articles have been written on Mead. One article that I would strongly recommend that is not know widely is an article by Gillespie (2005).

alterations due to the incompleteness of the linkages that constitute them. This inherent incompleteness generates the inherent dynamism and activity of all entities from sub-atomic particles to the cosmos itself. Nowhere is this more powerfully manifested than in Darwinian and post-Darwinian evolutionary theory and evolution itself.

We may think of ourselves, for example, as distinct entities, but our existence is symbiotically entwined with our environment; we depend constantly on foreign sources, not only for nourishment and oxygen, but also on the foreign organisms that reside within us to process these external resources. The earth itself is dependent upon the sun and moon, to name the two major players, not only to exist as it does in its orbit but also in terms of such things as temperature and atmosphere. Such dependencies do not refute the equally apparent fact that the earth and most individual human beings exist as highly stable, comparatively closed systems that function by and large as unified entities. The key point here is that even the most stable of entities are innately open systems subject to "foreign" forces from both within and from without. Understanding the constitution of these forces, their interplay, and how they affect different entities has been and is one of the major objectives of the physical and social sciences.

Since the "big bang," reality as we know it has figuratively been subject to the pulls and pushes of such forces, giving rise to various clusters that have morphed into ever-growing interrelated assemblages of stratified clusters, with certain clusters, from the smallest to the largest, obtaining levels of mutuality that have endowed them with particular identities; these identities range from sub-atomic particles to galaxies with chemical elements, biological entities, and collectives of varying sorts, including social groups as by-products of the process. However strong the ties and forces constituting such entities, all continue to be constituted by various vital subsystems and subject to external forces that bind them to encompassing systems of varying sorts. This "chain of being" runs from the smallest particle to the universe as a whole and its inherent, unending pursuit for completeness energizes it all.

We not only encounter variations of this account in numerous philosophical, religious and scientific texts, but also personally experience its pulls and pushes in our daily lives. What we often fail to realize, however, is that the forces that hold a particular system together are the same forces that break the system down. Love and attraction hold families together and break them up.[10] The same secretions that enable us to digest what we eat can cause us to expel what we eat. Gravity not only holds the earth in its orbit but also governs the collisions of meteorites upon moons and planets. Ethnic and national loyalties hold groups together and generate conflicts between such groups. The same

[10] For a perceptive sociological framing of this process see Collins, R. (2004, 2008).

economic practices and beliefs that generate economic growth in one context produce bankruptcies and economic collapses in other contexts. These dynamics result from the fact that all entities are open systems to one degree or another because no matter how strong and numerous the forces holding them together, they remain incomplete; as a consequence they are continually engaged in varying degrees with other systems, both within and without, and subject to their forces. An entity such as a gold molecule, a solar system, a coral reef, an ancient tree, a 200-year-old whale, a nation state, or a priesthood that has existed for more than a thousand years may be comparatively stable and apparently immune to such forces, both external and internal; all, however, remain subject to such forces, which can, under certain conditions, transform them in fundamental ways, including demolishing their present essential makeup.

Having said this, it should be noted that most historically stable entities/systems tend to endure for significant lengths of time, specifically because they are comparatively closed systems held together by numerous, strong ties. This does not mean that there are not an equal or greater number of loosely structured systems that are simultaneously emerging and crumbling. There probably are. It is the more stable systems, however, that we recognize and which because we see them exist for us. The transient systems commonly come and go without attracting notice. There is nothing inherently wrong with this tendency to privilege the more stable systems. It is the relatively stable systems that constitute the world that we experience and with which we are understandably concerned. In contrast, that which is in flux is unknowable in any real sense, and as such beyond our abilities to influence, let alone control. It could be argued that there are also deeper forces at play here insofar as the comparatively integrated and stable system could be seen as representing the original one from which the many emerged. The search for order and meaning that encompasses pretty much all human thought would also seem to embody this force.

Given their pervasive presence, it is not unexpected that integrative forces assume many different forms depending upon the particular context. Anthropology, biology, chemistry, linguistics, philosophy, physics, psychology, and sociology abound in a multitude of theories and concepts that seek to codify how these forces work in different situations. From love to logic, assimilation to accommodation, conquest to submission, hierarchy to equality, weak force to strong force, DNA to genes, networks to culture, syntax to semantics, to name just a few, mankind has been engaged in a search for order and meaning for thousands of years. In a very real sense, it could be argued that the cosmos has been engaged in a similar, if more ontological, pursuit, though the emergence of "negative energy" has put this into question. Whatever the relative ultimate strengths of the forces of the one and those of the many, at any given moment we tend to be more sensitive, both consciously and unconsciously, to familiar "ones," be they in the form of identifiable entities, stable systems, or customary practices. Our tendency to ignore "stuff happening" is simply a by-product of this dominant perspective that reality has an essential oneness and order, even if it presents itself differently at different times. It identifies the "unfamiliar" event as an aberration in the expected, while at the same time underscoring the fact that such things do occur.

Somewhat surprisingly this tendency to ignore or tolerate the disorder inherent in "stuff happens" doesn't function well when it is grounded in our own mind and meanings. Exposure to the unexpected twists and turns generated by the pushes and pulls exerted by different systems, subsystems, and encompassing system upon each other when operative in the external world in which we live is one thing; confronting similar disorders in how we mentally comprehend our world is quite another thing. The discomfort that this latter type of disorder tends to generate has both individual/psychological and collective/social roots embedded in our unique mental abilities. From a purely biological perspective our reasoning ability clearly endows us with the capacity to both connect and dissect experiences. Both capabilities have significant value in coping with the world we live in. Ordered accounts, however, from a psychological perspective have the added existential value of calming us by putting us in an ordered and less threatening world.[11] Such ordered accounts also have perhaps even more important social powers. They provide the bases for consensuses that are themselves the bases for social collectives.[12] Whereas "stuff happening" in the external world confronts us as inherently unthreatening contingencies, they are commonly experienced as anxiety-provoking ambiguities in mind and meaning. Each type is dealt with in its own way.

As noted above, the common response to encountering "stuff happening" in the eternal world is to regard the events as idiosyncratic, due metaphorically to such things as running into bumps on the road, taking a wrong turn, or, to use a nautical metaphor, getting caught in crosscurrents of some sort. Whatever the particular form, most explanatory accounts for unexpected events—stuff happening—tend to focus on the flow of the event, the "happening," rather than the "stuff." The "cross-currents" metaphor probably catches this view best as it frames the "unexpected" figuratively in terms of a particular type of flowing water; namely, intermingling flows of currents moving in different directions and often with different force. While this framing ignores the underlying dynamics of open systems and causal forces articulated by

[11] For a fascinating book depicting this process see Festinger et al. (1956).

[12] Numerous sociologists, social psychologists, and philosophers have fostered this view in one form or another—too many to acknowledge all properly. In the discussion of this subject in later chapters, the writings and thoughts of Douglas Porpora, Emile Durkheim, and George Herbert Mead will be privileged for the fairly mundane reason that they have most influenced my own thinking on this subject. A fuller discussion of this issue is better left until later.

critical/transcendental realists, it does serve to emphasize the way things are related, rather than the things themselves; particular events are subsumed in larger accounts that depict their changing relationships and contacts with other entities over a period of time. In doing this the "stuff happens" adage not only underscores the dynamic character of objects/stuff, but also includes the interactive nature of what happens. The Latin root of the terms "contingent" and "contingencies," introduced earlier, grasps this, as it has two previously unrelated entities physically coming together by touching, or better, bumping into each other. This coming together reverberates through both entities as each entity exerts different forces upon the other. We have a chance event insofar as this coming together did not exist, was not perceivable, in either of the two entities before they "touched." Stuff happening, by its very nature, transcends what we are aware of at that moment.

This "transcendence of what we know" links "stuff happening" and "chance" together. In so doing it also sheds light on why markets are commonly seen as games of chance and forms of gambling. Like games of chance, markets are built around contingencies. Not necessarily the contingency of rolling dice in which the dies are deliberately brought into contact with an extraneous table of some sort, but multiple and simultaneous exchanges of goods and currencies subject to the independent actions of a multitude of different people. Like most games of chance, markets emerged as a way of transcending what might be referred to as "accepted" human understanding. Most early games of chance, or more accurately venture of chance, were intended as a means of communicating with transcendental powers of one sort or another. In more recent times they have a simpler function as a means of circumventing existing structures of varying sorts. Markets for their part, as will be explored shortly, were adopted as a means for circumventing established normatively governed ways in which material goods could and were allocated. In both instances we confront the tensions between order and control, freedom and growth.

Albert Einstein was quoted as saying that he didn't think that "God would throw dice with the universe," though, it should be noted, much of his own work indicated that this clearly was a possibility. Most Darwinians, if perhaps not Darwin himself, appear to opt for the dice insofar as they see evolution as transcending determinism as it is generally understood. Market practitioners tend to do likewise. Most will contend that, while markets in the long run reward those with the proper skills and strategies, chance plays a role in every market transaction. Where market players differ from each other is in their views as to just how significant this role is and how it differs in different markets and at different times. There are those who argue that all financial markets are little more than a casino. For even these market practitioners, however, the market is not gambling. Whatever role chance might play and however prevalent the unexpected, markets are subject to their own rules and patterns, and as such manageable. Differences of opinion on how best to depict and explain the dynamics of these capricious markets remain. Moreover, in recent years, these "unexpected, unpredictable, erratic" aspects of financial markets have acquired an even more dominant and central status under the heading of "volatility," which has its own market roots in the now quite famous Black, Merton, and Scholes option-pricing model. We will have an opportunity to discuss and explore both "volatility" and pricing models in greater detail in subsequent chapters. "Volatility" is introduced here, not only to buttress the theme of this chapter that stuff happens, but also to underscore the extent to which financial markets are currently perceived as the embodiment of "stuff happens," with its open systems, contingencies, ambiguities, anxiety, and crosscurrents. Stuff happens everywhere, but few if any arenas acknowledge this fact and force us to confront it to the degree to which the market does, which is an important teaching in its own right.

The fact that markets are permeated with ambiguities and contingencies—fickle knowledge and stuff happenings—doesn't mean that these conditions are endured and accepted passively. Every action generates a reaction, and ambiguities and contingencies are no exception; while markets harbor more than their share of both, they are also home to an abundance of countermeasures. The great majority of these countermeasures can be grouped into two major types: accounts and routines. Though accounts, which include different types of narratives, tend to be utilized most in response to ambiguities, and routines most in response to contingencies, there is also a good deal of overlap with accounts used to minimize contingencies, and routines used to mask ambiguities. There is nothing unusual about any of this as accounts and routines are the coping mechanisms commonly used in response to ambiguities and contingencies wherever they are confronted. Where markets differ from most other settings is in the greater number and complexity of the accounts and routines they generate in response to the similar richness in numbers and complexity of market ambiguities and contingencies described above. It is to these coping practices that we now turn.

Part II

Traditional Coping Practices: Denying and Binding, Insulating and Propelling

While Part I sets the scene for different types of uncertainties, Part II reviews the major traditional coping practices that have and are used for dealing with uncertainties. Chapter 3 focuses upon the practices employed in attempting to manage narratives and accounts that rely upon cognitive solutions of one sort or another. Chapter 4 focuses upon the practices that have been utilized in attempting to deal with concrete uncertainties embedded in the flow of events.

3

Making Sense

Denying and Binding

Life can only be understood backwards, but it must be lived forwards.

Kierkegaard

It is generally accepted that some things make sense and other things don't. There is considerably less agreement, however, when deciding what makes sense and what doesn't, and why some things make sense and other things don't. Despite these differences, certain factors commonly play a role in the way people go about making such judgments. Familiarity is clearly one such thing: people generally tend to accept what they know and what is normal for them as sensible. Such familiarity can be based on past experiences. What is agreeable and enjoyable is also commonly judged sensible, as it normally fits with who we are. A governing account, in the form of a consistent, logical story, explanation or narrative, however, is the most common means of ascertaining whether something is sensible, particularly in situations where its sensible status has been put into question. While we may be inclined to accept familiar and enjoyable events as sensible, such feelings are unlikely to convince those who do not share them. In contrast, well-fashioned accounts can often be used to reframe events previously experienced as non-sensible by others into sensible events. Such accounts do this by fitting together what were previously perceived as disjointed elements into an integrated narrative.

Such accounts and narratives come in a variety of shapes and sizes, from simple declarations such as, "I wanted to round off my holdings to an even thousand shares," made in response to the question, "Why did you buy that hundred shares of Yahoo yesterday?" to a grand narrative characterizing not only Yahoo shares, but the entire industry, the market as a whole, and a wide range of other factors. Whether brief or all-encompassing, such accounts and narratives seek to order and make sense of some questionable event or thing by placing or linking it to a more encompassing narrative order. By linking things together in an ordered and apparently reasonable manner, such accounts are often able to smooth over the disconnects that characterize ambiguities and contingencies. In doing so, what was previously experienced as disordered, broken, incomplete, contradictory, or out of place is reframed to be seen as ordered. This is not an insignificant accomplishment, as indicated earlier. The pursuit of order, completeness, and harmony is an essential and pervasive force in practically all situations and endeavors. It is what religions, philosophies, and sciences are all about. Disorder and confusion in both the physical and mental worlds we inhabit can be very frightening and anxiety provoking. Accounts, which serve to shelter us from such situations, are prized.

Unfortunately, we are commonly subjected to different accounts that present things quite differently, which is likely to generate its own apprehensions. There is the added problem that most, if not all, accounts tend to be inaccurate in a variety of ways; such inaccuracies, in turn, are prone to expose us to other dangers as they lessen our anxieties. As a consequence of these weaknesses, relying on accounts, however useful they might be in protecting us from the worries of ambiguities and contingencies, often results in transporting us from the frying pan into the fire. As implied by the "any professional broker can give you a very convincing story of why the market did what it did yesterday" comment noted at the beginning of the first chapter, financial markets are permeated by such conflicting accounts. This fact alone would make the market a promising site to explore such accounts, but market accounts provide us with additional facets, a number of which were embedded in a response I received many years ago when querying another broker about the basic function of the market. His concise answer was "The market is about defining value."

While in accord with the comments about "making sense of things" or "mirroring life," which is another facet of markets claimed by many, this answer cut more deeply into a number of theoretical issues associated with accounts. While price as monetary value is included, the use of the term "value" usually indicates something beyond price. The broker just noted was referring to the underlying grounds that shape prices. Moreover, by attributing such pricing to the "market," he was also framing it as a collective endeavor of those engaged in the market. As someone who was transitioning from philosophy, which tended to privilege individual cognitive processes in acts of making sense, to sociology, which tended to see such acts as inherently social and embedded in concrete situations, this framing caught my attention. His answer also sensitized me to the implicit distinction he was making between surface prices and the multiple underlying factors that generate such prices at any given moment.

I clearly didn't grasp all of these implications upon hearing his statement: they emerged in the more lengthy discussions that followed. Over the years additional facets emerged in response to other market encounters and various themes drawn from the writing of different theorists. Together they served to shape minimally three teachings that the various market accounts I encountered presented. The first was implicitly noted at the beginning of this chapter. Market accounts are not normally assumed to be factually or logically accurate. Their primary function is to provide an account that is consensually agreed upon. This understanding has an illustrious sociological pedigree normally associated with Emile Durkheim (1933), who argued that the prime function of our conscious conceptions was not to be factually accurate, but rather to foster social solidarity. A second teaching that echoes the insights of George Herbert Mead (1934) is that market meanings are embedded in market interactive practices; another way of phrasing this is that the market is to a large extent a self-defining entity insofar as its actions generate its changing character. A third teaching revolves around themes raised by critical realism presented in the previous chapter regarding the importance of causal forces and the distinction between these forces and behavioral patterns. All three of these insights not only speak to modern markets, but also their emergence over past centuries, a process that Karl Polanyi is commonly credited with best describing.[1]

While we tend today to take modern price-setting markets, including financial markets, pretty much for granted, they are, in fact, comparatively new ways for allocating goods and services. As Polanyi notes, exchanging goods rather than simply allocating them according to established customs is a comparatively recent practice; goods were initially used by those who fashioned them, or given or taken by designated individuals. Exchange of goods grew with the growth of more complex societies that served both to undermine the taken-for-given normative structures governing simpler societies and to expose individuals to different framings.[2] Even then most exchanges normally were carried out by means of direct exchanges of goods through various forms of barter between individuals and/or social groups. The great majority of exchanges between individuals tended to occur between individuals with whom there were blood or other recognized cultural/social ties, and then such exchanges commonly did not entail a tit-for-tat exchange at a given moment; they functioned, rather, as a reciprocal giving system that tied specific, designated individuals together. As such, the exchanges were governed by a commonly shared normative set of cultural meanings and rules similar to the accounts advanced by Durkheim that stipulated who could exchange what with whom.

[1] Polanyi presents his basic argument in his book, *The Great Transformation* (1957: 250–6). It is briefly outlined below, and will be explored in greater depth later. His theoretical understanding of markets also plays a central role in Appendix A: "Understanding Markets from a Sociological Perspective."

[2] The growth of more complex societies is noted not only by Polanyi, but also by Durkheim (1933), who relates the types of rules governing different societies directly to their level of homogeneity and heterogeneity and contact with other social groups.

The emergence of early markets served to transcend these cultural barriers that limited who exchanged what with whom. These markets tended to be grounded in specific "market places" where "non-related" individuals could exchange goods with each other. A preponderance of such early markets also relied primarily on barter, where goods were exchanged for other goods. This also required a fairly well-developed notion of private ownership. While such barter exchanges also allowed for a degree of bargaining of how much of one item should match how much of another item, the exchange value of most goods tended to be established within specific markets according to the shared values of those participating. The power of these markets was not primarily in the flexibility of value that they provided, but rather in the flexibility of individuals with whom one could engage in an exchange.

The emergence of modern price-setting markets, where the monetary value of specific goods is set in the market, represents a further development that only emerged later with the emergence of various classical empires that provided the monetary grounds for such transactions and exchanges between people with different evaluations of goods. The driving force of this transformation was directly linked to "markets defining value." More specifically, price-setting markets emerged due to the breakdown, or more correctly absence, of a consensus among buyers and sellers as to the proper value of the goods being exchanged, this lack of consensus being a direct result of the fact that markets entailed the participation of people not necessarily culturally similar. Such markets, lacking cultural consensus, required that they generate a consensus of their own sufficient to enable the particular transactions to occur; namely, establishing an agreed-upon price. What made this possible was that these markets also provided the types of interactions that consensual definitions require. This link between generating shared meanings through interaction with others is central to George Herbert Mead's (1934) seminal theory on the evolution of mind, self, and society. This brings us back to where we began, "markets defining value" and the importance of shared market narratives capable of generating consensual prices. Markets may be about defining value, as the broker quoted earlier said, but it is their narratives that determine what that value is likely to be. Unfortunately or fortunately, few markets, subject as they are to a multitude of different groupings, are limited to a single narrative; financial markets, which tend to be highly international, are particularly fond of a multitude of narratives. More to the point given the case being made here, the great majority of market professionals believe that these narratives determine market prices rather than the dominant economic view that factors such as "supply and demand" and individual "rational" decision making determine prices; this reveals a more pervasive sociological framing of the market by these professional than is generally recognized.

The extent to which financial markets generate numerous narratives has been experienced not only by anyone who has spent any time in the market, but by anyone who has ever been exposed to a radio or television market report. Pretty much all such reports will include a reference or two not only to the prices of various market indexes, but also to some economic/business factor that played a part in the market's action, some technical information on daily volume, highs and lows, and some market gossip as to who might be buying and who might be selling. Lengthier reports that go into greater detail are likely to quote one or more market analyst and have a word or two dealing with market movements and trends. All of these references are grounded in particular, quite different market narratives of one sort or another. It is the application of these narratives to the market that serves to "make sense" of the market.

Forty years ago, when I first began to explore how people made sense of the stock market, it was these narratives and their proponents that became my focus of attention (Smith 1981). In summarizing my findings then, I described four dominant orientations and their proponents. What distinguished each group was the particular aspect of the market that they focused upon. What I called "market fundamentalists" focused upon the economic fundamentals of companies and the economy as a whole. For them, market value was determined by such things as earnings, dividends, economic growth, interest rates, trade, and cash flow. The bible for most adherents to this perspective was Graham and Dodd's classic *Security Analysis*, first published in 1934, and still cited by Warren Buffett often as his investment bible. Those I then called "market insiders" were more concerned with who was buying and who was selling, particularly those buying and selling in large numbers. Their motto tended to be that it mattered more "who you knew" than "what you knew" since getting the jump on major buys and sells required knowing ahead of time what was to occur.

What I called the "cyclist–chartist," often linked to the "wave theory" associated with Ralph Nelson Elliott (1938/2012), focused primarily upon the past trading/price patterns of financial instruments and the market in general.[3] Many of the most committed of these cyclist–chartists saw these patterns as controlling the market movements of financial instruments. Their charts revealed the hand of the market gods. The last group that I described were the "traders," who, for lack of any better term, I described as focused upon "market action," how particular financial instruments—stocks, bonds, etc.—responded to the overall movement of the market, news, and other market-related occurrences. Gerald Loeb (1957) is often considered to be the godfather of this perspective. Given how loosely the term "trader" is used, they probably should be described as "market-action traders" or "response traders."

[3] Elliot first spelt out his theory in 1938 and followed up with numerous articles and another book in 1946. While his books are seldom used today there are literally scores of books that are built around his earlier writings as even a cursory browsing of the Internet will reveal.

When applied to given individuals, however, the term "trader" still tends to indicate market behavior that is shaped in large measure by market action. I have tried in what follows to stick with this meaning though there are times when it is used in its more general sense as someone simply in the market. When capitalized, however, I am clearly focusing on these "real" traders.

In revisiting and updating my account of the market in 2001, I expanded upon these four types and narratives by including two new types. The first of these, the "efficient market" perspective, was not actually a new type since I had encountered this type in the early 1960s. At that time and for many years later, however, it was very much a minority perspective within the market itself. This was not surprising as it argues that the market on its own is the most efficient pricing tool available. Put slightly differently, it claims that you cannot actually "beat the market" as the market prices at any given moment are the best "informed" prices there are. Its primary home during these years was the economic academia, where it was commonly associated with a book by Malkiel (1973) entitled *A Random Walk Down Wall Street*. By the 1990s, with the expansive bull market in progress, this perspective gained many adherents, as it argued that an investor could benefit most by simply being in the market, subject to a proper allocation of resources.

The second new perspective that I described as governed by "transformational ideas" was also not so much "new" as significantly more visible. More particularly, it claimed that "new ideas," particularly those with a technological component and a technologically new product, were what would control the market of the future. Economic fundamentals, smart money, charts, past market action, and normal market responses could and would all be overridden by innovative, generally technologically original, products that would not so much meet market demands, but would actually create such demands. Think of Apple and Steve Jobs. At the time I described this perspective as "post-modern" to underscore the extent to which it privileges ideas above and beyond pretty much everything else. At that time I also noted that this view had flourished, riding an upward market move for nearly twenty uninterrupted years, and questioned whether it "had the legs" to survive in down markets as well as an up market. After the quite violent ups and downs of the past decade, I would have to say that while new technology continues to have a life of its own in the market, it nearly always requires an economically sound, market-connected home if it is to flourish. Moreover, it usually needs to show that it can perform in the market if it hopes to acquire the market support required to flourish in the market. For now it continues to have supporters, though ironically they now often identify themselves as fundamentalists rather then the reverse.

The "transformational idea" perspective is not the only governing narrative that has undergone modifications over the years: pretty much all of them have undergone modifications of some sort though none have been absorbed in the manner that the transformational idea has. This absorption has been due in large measure because the fundamentalists' narrative has expanded its own economic boundaries to include such ideas as financial assets, especially if they have been copyrighted. While a good number of these ideas pertain to the world of computer hardware and software, others are grounded in medical and pharmacological companies. The fundamentalist narrative has also expanded its boundaries to embrace international markets and finance markets to a greater extent than it once did. Warren Buffett, who once refused to invest in high technology businesses because he said he didn't understand them, in 2011 became a major shareholder of IBM. For whatever it is worth, he exited with a loss in 2014. Nevertheless, in expanding its definition to include technology in this way, the fundamentalist narrative has maintained its central position and profile in practically all financial markets. This has not been the case with the "market insiders," who have been confronted by a number of obstacles.

As indicated above, the proponents of this perspective prize information, particularly privileged information. They not only believe that such information is what moves the market, but they depend upon such information in managing their own investments and trading. Historically the "best" of these professionals managed to secure the information they needed through maintaining a wide network of knowledgeable contacts. New technology and regulations have made this much more difficult if not often impossible. Twenty or thirty years ago, a broker or individual investor willing to put in the effort required could call pretty much any company and engage in a discussion regarding how "things looked" for the next quarter. The information received was not legally "inside" information insofar as pretty much anyone willing to go to the bother could have access to it. Often the information garnered was being prepared for a more general distribution in the near future. In most cases it also needed to be properly interpreted to have much value. There were also a good number of proprietary analyst reports generated that were restricted to large investors that an earnest insider could access.

New Securities and Exchange Commission (SEC) regulations instituted over the past few decades coupled with email and the Internet have changed all of this. Many of the SEC regulations have restricted the way information was often distributed. At the same time the Internet and email have dramatically reduced the time spread needed to disseminate information. In short, without transgressing SEC regulations it has become very difficult to access non-public information, and nearly all public information is almost instantaneously disseminated. What was once market rewarded "not-yet-public" information is presently at least "crony capitalism," if not illegal. This does not mean that this perspective has disappeared. Many market professionals continue to believe that it is applicable to current markets and that it is still in use. The number of major announcements that are immediately preceded by significant moves would lend support to this view. By and large, however, few market professionals will publically admit to actually employing such an approach. But they will add that there are "others" who do.

The accounts and practices of traditional cyclist–chartists and Traders have also been subject to meaningful change, due in large extent to technological changes and the overall growth in market activity. In the case of the chartists this change has been reflected primarily in the types of charting-tools that they rely upon. Historically most chartists employed graphic charts that pictured the price patterns that were believed to control the market. Modern algorithmic programs have made it possible not only to grasp novel movement patterns grounded upon mathematical models, but also to integrate a number of such models into a single program. Such programs have the capacity not only to generate simultaneously numerous graph charts, but also to chart the differences among these numerous charts and emit audible signals in response to numerous programmed differentials. For many if not most chartists these flashing, beeping, digital charts still reflect the hand of the market, but the hand is now in constant movement. For others these charts and programs are seen primarily as means for simultaneously monitoring various facets of the market. This approach is seen to be more technical in nature than cyclist. That is, it is specific market movements that are the focus of concern rather than any overall market patterns that are so central to cyclists. In this respect their perspective embodies the traditional market Trader perspective in that it seeks to grasp the "action" of the market rather than its trajectory. This is reflected in the general practice of referring to the large number of professional and semi-professional market participants who daily trade using such programs as "day-traders."

There is something of an ironic twist in the way in which modern computer technology has served to transform many chartists into quasi-traders. The very programs and technology that have literally highlighted "market action," which has been the primary focus of traditional market Traders, has served as an obstacle for many traditional market Traders. The increased speed, volume, and changes in price of the market, made possible by modern computer technology, makes it more difficult to get a proper "feel" of the market. This same technology has also been part of the emergence of new markets, primarily derivative markets, which has made it more difficult if not impossible to "read" the market accurately. This latter problem is related to the fact that derivative markets have the capacity to hedge, that is counteract/offset, trades made in "primary" markets. As a consequence of these developments many Traders have been forced to limit their trading to more constrained situations where their skills can still be exercised and where being able to judge market direction plays a lesser role. We will have an opportunity to explore this matter in greater detail in Part III.

Proponents of the "efficient market" perspective echo many of the Traders' judgments when it comes to computer-based, high volume, erratic price movement markets of recent years. Rather than complain about these developments, however, they celebrate them as they reinforce their long-held position that there is no way over time to "beat the market." The only sensible investment strategy is to properly allocate your funds among various types of investment according to your resources, risk preferences, and desired return, rebalancing these allocations periodically between every six months and a year. The view that there is no formal strategy that can "beat" the market, however, is not limited to Traders and efficient market proponents. It has in a slightly modified form actually given rise to what might be considered a whole new framing of these markets, which might aptly be called the "croupier" perspective. It concurs with Traders and efficient market proponents that the market cannot be beaten under normal conditions, but they neither withdraw from the market nor simply accept it as it is. They rather seek to profit from such markets by establishing themselves in managerial roles serving as croupiers. Rather than taking positions in the market, they seek to remain neutral, but to profit by extracting small transaction costs from multiple transactions, provided primarily by numerous, relatively recent, technical chartists, aka day-traders, described above.[4]

Taken together the various metamorphoses described above have produced some strange bedfellows. We have cyclist–chartist and efficient market proponents both accepting these new markets, but for completely different reasons: cyclist–chartists because they provide them with a whole new generation of charts, graphs, and trading programs; efficient market proponents because they support their claim that the market can't be mastered. We have old-fashioned economic fundamentalists and post-modern transformational idea proponents morphing together in their search for the "right" fundamentals. And then we have traditional Traders and insiders, who historically marched to very different drummers, both, for quite different reasons, more alienated from the market. Throughout all of these changes, however, we find that each type has managed to hold quite closely to its traditional view of how the market works. What changed were not these views per se, but rather the applicability of these views, with insiders and Traders experiencing the most difficulty. We have also seen, however, a significant flourishing of what might be labeled market agnosticism. There has always been a strong agnostic streak in the perspectives of both Traders and efficient market proponents, though again for very different reasons. Where Traders have historically disparaged market canons of all sorts, they have had faith in their own capacity to exploit market gyrations; most efficient market proponents, in contrast, have claimed

[4] Croupiers will receive considerably more attention in Chapter 11, "New Teachings of the New Market," when in conjunction with programmatic trading and what is commonly called "big data," they will be the main focus of attention in an attempt to explore the contingencies of tomorrow, which we are likely to confront.

to understand the dynamics of the market, but denied their own or anyone else's ability to predict how these dynamics will play out. The road to success for them is simply to stay with the market for the long term. The croupier perspective shares both the efficient market negative view in outguessing the market and the Traders' negative view of canon-based faith in the market. The way to make money in the market for the croupier is not to try to outsmart it or stick with it, but rather to "tax" the other players.

The croupier perspective is considerably more complex, however, than the above would suggest. It entails a quite sophisticated understanding of how modern algorithmic, computerized markets function, both individually and collectively. The proponents of this perspective, in short, are similar to efficient market proponents in possessing a quite sophisticated understanding of how markets function, though they operate more like Traders when it comes to the way they participate in these markets. If there is a single factor that best grasps what this perspective is all about it would be the way it redefines price movements and embraces them as the central factor in market dynamics. For the croupier, price movements are framed in terms of the pricing models noted near the end of Chapter 2 and labeled as "volatility." As "volatility," price fluctuations acquire significantly greater importance as they no longer merely reflect degrees of price movements, but become the basis for measuring and determining "value." This transformation requires an explanation of its own as it impacts on the encompassing governing narrative.

Prior to the mid 1980s, it was unlikely that you would have heard the word "volatility" being used in the market. Even in the late 80s, when "volatility" data was being generated, few market participants paid it much attention. Everyone was interested in understanding how market prices varied, but given that this "volatility" was being measured in terms of a mathematical model generated by academic economists, it was considered peripheral to the market itself. With the growth of option markets in the '80s and '90s, which were themselves more and more subject to various pricing models, the concept of volatility became a more popular "handle" for denoting degrees of price fluctuations. By the beginning of the new millennium in 2000, a few years after the Professors Merton and Scholes were awarded the Nobel Prize for their pricing model work,[5] "volatility" had become the term of choice to denote price fluctuation, not only in derivative markets but in most financial markets. By then, however, it had spread from the academy to the market.[6]

As noted earlier, the fact that market prices varied over time has been recognized and accepted from the very inception of financial markets. "The

[5] Black was not included as he was deceased.

[6] In this process various other pricing models that modified Black, Merton, and Scholes came into play to deal with various issues not dealt with in the basic Black-Merton-Scholes model. These adjustments are discussed in the text to follow.

Market will fluctuate," as J. P. Morgan[7] is attributed to have responded when asked what the market could be expected to do, says it all. Such fluctuations were generally seen to be due to the various risks and rewards associated with owning the particular financial instrument. As such, they were also seen to embody the gambling, risky nature of financial markets in general. This did not prevent more adventurist traders from attempting to profit from these fluctuations through the use of rights/options to buy, "calls," and sell, "puts," financial instruments at specific prices in the future.[8] The pricing model attributed to Black, Merton, and Scholes served to domesticate these price fluctuations by grounding them within the price of the financial instrument. Prices were not so much subject to price changes, but rather carried these changes within themselves. The mathematical formula, upon which this pricing model rests, accomplishes this by expressing the price in terms of various variables, including volatility.

The price of a stock that had maintained the same price for some time would be seen as having little to none of its price assigned to its volatility. The price of a stock whose price varied up and down significantly would, in contrast, have a significant part of its price assigned to these variations.[9] Determining how a given volatility should compute into the pricing of a particular option required including information on the 1) present price of the underlying financial instrument, 2) the strike price—the price at which the underlying instrument could be bought, 3) whether it was a right to buy—a call, 4) a right to sell—a put, 5) the expiration date—when the right to buy or sell ended, and 6) various other factors such as interest rates, dividends, etc. While all of these factors impact on the price of a given option at a given time, the key variable remains volatility. The key claim of the pricing model is that it could mathematically compute accurate option prices for any financial instrument that traded regularly in sufficient volume. From a purely academic perspective, this quite elegant pricing model was seen to be a major accomplishment deserving the praise and awards it received.

For the market, however, the results were even more rewarding. The pricing model provided the means not only to price options in a manner that enabled them to be exchange traded on an enormous scale, it also, crowned with its Nobel Prize, legitimated options as sound financial instruments. Moreover, volatility, as a universally applicable measurement of price variability and hence risk, enabled hedging and arbitraging, not only between particular financial instruments and their own derivatives, but between and among an

[7] This response is also attributed to Bernard Baruch, but the general consensus is that it should be attributed to Morgan.

[8] Such transactions were limited to OTC—over-the-counter markets.

[9] Based on the assumption that stocks were equally likely to go up as down, such variations were calculated in terms of the price variations from the mean price during the given time period.

almost unlimited number of linked instruments and derivatives. And to top this all off, these linkages enabled bundling these various instruments together to form new instruments, all of which could themselves be used to generate new derivatives. For academics, a Nobel Prize entails a good deal of wealth, but in purely financial terms the pricing model earned exponentially more from the garden of financial products it generated when it was planted in the market. As often happens in such migrations, however, the plant underwent some structural alterations.

Among some of the more important, but not transformative, alterations were the following: An adjustment to deal with American options, which can be exercised at any time, in contrast to European options, which cannot be so exercised, and were the focus initially of the pricing model; various adjustments to deal with recognized skews in distribution that are not part of the normal distribution used in the Black-Merton-Scholes model; adjustments to manage future dividends; and adjustments to manage discontinuities in pricing. The most significant transformation, in contrast, required no specific modification to the model at all. What it entailed was "reversing" the relationship between the price of options and their accepted volatility. Rather than accepting a price based on past volatility, which struck most professionals as flawed, the option market, elected to collectively set its own prices that were then used to generate "implied volatilities"—volatilities that matched their prices. Price determines volatility rather than volatility determining price. While historical volatility held the fort in the initial conquests of the pricing model, particularly in its success in legitimizing derivatives as rationally grounded financial instruments, implied volatility is king in the market place. The market judged its own ability to assess future volatility as superior to whatever the historical volatility might have been. In doing so the market managed to generate a whole new world of financial transactions.[10]

The preference of most market professionals for implied volatility is also due to the way in which option markets work. Before the adoption of option-pricing models, options were traded almost exclusively in over-the-counter markets through OTC dealers, due in large measure to the difficulties in pricing them. While the great majority of options are presently exchanged traded, they still are primarily traded through market makers. There are a number of reasons for this: first while many options are traded in large numbers, there are numerous options for any given underlying stock that do not trade regularly, which makes it less probable that there will be a non-dealer to see an offering, let alone accept it; second, a large percentage of option

[10] In doing so, it also managed to generate a vast new library of books intended to describe and explain how these new instruments, particularly options, could best be used. See, for example, Natenberg (1994) and McMillan (2002, 2004), which continue to play a big role in this area.

trades are complex trades entailing the simultaneous purchase and/or sale of different options. Again, finding a non-dealer willing and able to respond to such trades is unlikely; thirdly, non-dealer traders are normally not sufficiently enmeshed in the market to be comfortable deviating from the implied volatility prices being offered by dealers. As a consequence, when a non-dealer is attempting to execute an option trade, the party on the other side of the trade is almost always a dealer who is actively involved in the pricing of the options being traded. What this means is that, most of the time, the present posted bids and asks are those of a dealer and reflect the dealer's implied volatility figure. This enables the dealers to maintain a sufficient bid–ask spread to profit from these transactions while maintaining a neutral position. This is a perfect position for a dedicated croupier, especially as such dealers are normally in the position to hedge whatever position they take by buying or selling linked instruments.[11]

This ability to hedge is related to the emergence of volatility as the central means for keeping track of one's market position in whatever form it might be—options, futures, stocks, ETFs (Exchange Traded Funds), or ETNs (Exchange Traded Notes). The reverse side of this is that a market participant who elects to adopt the neutral stance of a croupier can by and large do this by using options, ETFs, ETNs, other derivatives, and other bundled instruments to maintain a neutral volatility position. If economic fundamentalists perceive markets as governed by economic fundamentals, insiders as governed by information, cyclist/chartist/technicians by patterns and programs, Traders by market action, and efficient market proponents by all of these factors, croupiers perceive markets in terms of volatility and probabilities. In attempting to maintain a neutral position, croupiers adopt a similarly agnostic position as to the direction of the market, as do efficient market proponents and most market-action Traders. In their case, however, this agnosticism is not due to the greater inherent wisdom of the market revered by efficient market proponents or the temperamental nature of the market that concerns Traders, but to their conviction that they can do better financially by extracting differences in bid–ask spreads "making markets" for others. Their ability to extract these differences from the trades of others without committing themselves to any particular market direction is due to their ability as dealers to maintain a profitable bid/ask spread.

While these "taxes" tend to be quite small, the increase in the number of different instruments being traded with the advent of derivatives and various

[11] That these croupiers tend also to rely heavily on hedging their positions has a certain poetic justice to it as the derivative-enabled growth in hedging played a major role in forcing numerous market professionals to become croupiers. Historically many of these professionals maintained an edge in the market by being able to interpret market direction through access to order flow information and in some cases access to order books. The growth in multiple hedged orders, however, makes it next to impossible to interpret such information now.

bundled financial instruments, coupled with the exponential growth in the number of transactions, generates huge sums daily. If it all sounds a little bit like running a casino, it is because as in a casino profits come from costs charged to play, in this case bid/ask spreads. Another similarity is in the ability of the house and dealers to maintain a probabilistic neutral position. In Part III, when we take a closer look at how market-action Traders operate, we will also have an opportunity to take a closer look at some of the ways this is done. We will take a more encompassing look at the implications of this comparatively new orientation in Part IV when we will examine Statistical/Probabilistic Accounts. At that time we will also take a look at another strategy grounded in its own statistical/probabilistic account which received a great deal of attention after the 2008 market crash. I refer here to the "Black Swan" theory of Nassim Taleb (2007). For now, however, we need to return to the question with which we began this exploration of these different governing narratives; namely, the issue of their function. From what we have seen, none of these narratives guarantee or even assist our ability to master these markets, though some do seem to be of use to their proponents. So what is happening here?

In the market, as elsewhere, a prime task of governing narratives is to reduce anxieties and enable collaborative behavior by providing a sensible shared account of what is going on. How they do this really doesn't matter: what matters is a relatively coherent framing and story that enables putting what initially might have been experienced as disparate, if not conflicting, pieces together into a reasonable whole of sorts. Their task is to "make sense" of what has happened. The proponents of the six perspectives described above—economic fundamentalists, insider/information proponents, cyclist–chartist–technical proponents, and market-action/Trader proponents, efficient market proponents, and croupiers—can, as my informer noted many years ago, all provide you with reasonable accounts as to why the market did what it did. While none of them are able to predict what the market will do tomorrow, the last three are unlikely to even attempt to do so, but all are able to convey a sense of order to the market. While this ability is not likely to produce market gains, it is very useful in assuring anxious investors. Given that most market professionals make their living through their clients, or more specifically the clients' money they manage, rather than through their own investments, such calming narratives endow them with a "knowing" persona that can help maintain these customers as customers.

Such shared accounts generally also enable collaborative behavior insofar as they present the world in a similar if not identical way to a multitude of people. This is particularly true in situations like markets that lend themselves to a multitude of interpretations. A shared view not only fosters social solidarity, but also enables cooperation among those sharing it. To the extent to which such accounts are endowed with normative powers, they have the added capacity to mold behaviors in conformity with what they claim to be behaviorally inherent. This process is commonly described as being governed by a "self-fulfilling prophecy." This dynamic is a central theme that runs through most, if not all, sociological and social-psychological theorizing. It is generally seen to be a central force in the emergence of human culture and human societies as it provides the symbolic tools required for communication and cooperation. In the market, such shared perspectives foster both the collective pricing of financial instruments and the actual exchange of such instruments. Every transaction requires a buyer and a seller, both of whom must agree on a single price. Shared perspectives greatly enhance the possibility of this occurring.[12]

Such accounts, particularly what might be called mature and experienced accounts—accounts that have evolved over time involving numerous, diverse populations—commonly offer another advantage. They normally come with built-in safety nets, which serve to prevent damages from becoming disasters. These safety devices work differently in different accounts, but in essence what they do is set boundaries intended to limit losses by selling at times and avoiding overreacting at other times. This is a particularly valuable factor in financial markets where financial losses are to be expected but can be weathered, but where it is very difficult to recover if one is bankrupted. In one form or another nearly all mature accounts have built into them warning and stop signs that are intended to restrain action when things go wrong, or more to the point when the account has failed. Such warning and stop signs commonly entail absorbing significant loses. While such loses are never pleasant to endure, attempting to correct things by switching account loyalties can often lead to worse outcomes. Abandoning ship, whatever form the ship might have, is advisedly recommended in only the direst of situations. On the other hand, even sturdy vessels, including the unsinkable *Titanic*, sink. The significant point here is to recognize that mature accounts tend to include a variety of safety devices lacking in most impromptu accounts, which have enabled them to survive through thick and thin.

This does not mean that all mature accounts will protect one from suffering major losses, but only that they generally prove safer than jumping about from one approach to another when things get rough. Such jumping about exposes one to what might be considered the greatest danger that market participants face—namely, getting caught up in some form of mass/crowd/mob behavior, be it suddenly liquidating an entire portfolio or blindly buying financial instruments that are exploding upwards in price. Individuals are most prone

[12] Though a number of different theorists have recognized and discussed the social value and nature of shared accounts, Emile Durkheim's formulation has played a particularly important and formative part in sociology. This issue will be explored in greater detail in Chapter 11. It is a crucial theme that not only runs through this book, but also implicitly critiques a missing facet of the prospect theory account of how market values are generated; namely, in ongoing interactions of participants, both actual and hypothetical.

to such behavior when they feel at a loss to understand what is happening, but simultaneously believe that others somehow know something that they don't. Individuals, in turn, are most prone to feel this way when they have no account or framing mechanism of their own that they can use in these situations. Minus a governing narrative of one's own, a highly visible crowd that appears to know what it is doing can be a very seductive force. Whatever their weaknesses might be, most mature governing narratives provide one of the strongest defenses against such crowd behavior.[13]

There is one thing, however, that even the most sophisticated accounts seldom do: they do not accurately depict the reality that they proclaim to. This is really not that startling given that, as implied above, this is not what they are about. Their function is primarily social by fostering social solidarity, enabling individuals to support and benefit each other. Insofar as such accounts do depict reality, it is due to the ability of this shared reality to enhance social ties. It is this ability to strengthen social solidarity rather than representational accuracy that governs their own ability to survive. This is clearly the case when it comes to dealing with ambiguities and contingencies, which by their very nature directly threaten the "making sense" claims and overall coherency of such accounts upon which their collective acceptance depends. Not surprisingly, the resolutions provided by such accounts generally entail avoidance and denial.

This avoidance and denial comes in a variety of forms. Particular events can be rebuffed as not having occurred, and particular claims can be rejected as not having been made. Arguments can be made that the particular event in question was taken out of a broader context within which the perceived inconsistencies would not exist. Analogous arguments can be made that not enough time has been given to judge the final outcomes. In the market place such responses are most commonly offered in response to apparent "faulty" outcomes associated with economic fundamentalist accounts and cyclist–chartist–technical accounts: "That earning report was flawed; it ignored a major tax implication"; "The program is fine, but you need to give it more time"; "You misunderstood the relationship between the way the delta would operate in that strategy"; "A one time extra dividend cannot be treated as a normal dividend"; and so on.

Efficient market proponents, Traders, and croupiers don't need to offer excuses when disquieting things occur since they acknowledge the unknowable character of the market from the beginning. In the case of the efficient market proponents this does not mean that they believe the market to be inherently chaotic: it is quite the opposite. Of all the types depicted above, the efficient market proponents are most committed to the rationality of the

[13] For a fuller discussion of this process, see Smith (1981), pp. 133–43.

market. It just can't be predicted or second-guessed. There is a reason behind everything: we just often aren't in a position to know what is going on at any given moment. The croupier's response is somewhat less trusting in the rationality of the market, but equally dubious about our capacity to understand what is going on. Market-action Traders tend to fall somewhere in between. They tend to be the most negative when it comes to governing structures of any sort, but prone to accept the idea that the market is subject to various patterns. Unfortunately these patterns are nearly always difficult to identify. As market agnostics who by and large avoid prognostications, proponents of these three perspectives are free from having to defend themselves from accounts that go sour. Their agnosticism has its downside as well, especially when it comes to attracting others to accept your guidance. All three of these approaches might work, but there is little if anything in their view of the market that is likely to convince others. All that proponents of these perspectives can offer in defense of their positions is market success. More importantly, if things do not work out well, there is unlikely to be any story with which to placate a client.

In functioning as they do, market narratives function pretty much the same way most successful governing narratives work. They foster social solidarity, they decrease anxiety, and they provide some cautionary safety nets by providing us with a relatively coherent account that manages to hide most ambiguities and circumvent most contingencies. They are among our best defenses against what Giddens (1984) referred to as ontological insecurity. Religious theologies, political ideologies, basically all "isms," nearly all secular "canons," and a majority of academic theories function similarly for most people most of the time. The "factual" and "logical" veracity tends in most cases to be of limited significance. What counts is that the governing narratives have the ability to generate trust and enable adherents to ignore the ambiguities and contingencies of life they confront.

This does not mean, however, that all such narratives are structured in the same way when it comes to these issues. A majority of modern narratives, including market narratives, rely primarily upon causal paradigms of one sort or another in which various causal forces are assumed to have shaped events. In the market this is the case with both fundamentalist and insider narratives. For the fundamentalists various economic factors are seen to be the primary determinants of prices in the long run; for insiders it is who is buying and who is selling that is of primary causal importance. The problem in both of these cases is that there are seldom, if ever, sufficient controls in place to determine whether what is assumed is factually accurate, let alone sufficient to bring about the outcome attributed to them.

Efficient market proponents also tend to rely upon causal forces, but they not only embrace a plurality of such forces, but also maintain that it is impossible to decipher their various impacts more accurately than does the market itself. Croupiers tend to hold a similar view, though they believe that by monitoring a wide range of data, it is possible to judge how accurately the market at any given moment has integrated these multiple causal factors. This leaves us with traditional Traders and traditional chartists. Traditional chartists stand out here because, as noted earlier, they tend to privilege the market's own order over external factors that might be shaping the market. To understand and master the market, one should not focus on external causal factors, but on the patterns that the market itself has and is generating. To put the matter somewhat differently, these chartists accept their chart-grounded narratives as the driving force shaping the market. The market is an ordered world; what one needs to do is to discover this order in how the market performs. The narrative itself is what counts.

The traditional Trader takes a very different stance. Most such Traders share the efficient market view that the market is subject to numerous causal forces, too many to be properly grasped. What can be grasped, however, is the impact that they have on the market. The objective these Traders set for themselves is to be able to read the market itself, which in turn echoes the way in which different forces are shaping it at any given moment, and then to attempt to project where all of this is most likely to go. Another way of describing this is to say that they seek to go with the flow. Going with the flow has other advantages when it comes to dealing with ambiguities and contingencies in that it keeps one moving. For the Trader, this entails constantly responding to the flow in an attempt to identify and follow a desirable course. While most market participants do not have the skills the experienced Traders have to do this, there are other more defensive benefits that such actions are capable of providing to most people. We are talking here about the advantages that routines and habits commonly provide in ambiguous and disordered situations. Here again the market is a helpful tutor.

4

Routines and Performances

Insulating and Propelling

Beware of your habits. The better they are the more surely they will be your undoing.

Holbrook Jackson

Routines, both helpful and harmful, not only play a crucial part in our lives, but also tend to become a part of us. There is a classic story about four young rabbis sitting beside a stream engaged in a theological discussion about God. After many hours of learned discussion and debate, they came to a unanimous conclusion: God did not exist. Just at that moment, one of them points to the sun declining in the sky and in an anxious voice said, "Look, it is late. We need to hurry or we will be late for afternoon prayers." Instantaneously, without a word, all four rush toward their study hall to attend their afternoon prayers. The point of this story is clear. You can believe what you want, but most of what you do, right or wrong, is grounded in routines and habits.[1]

Over the years a great deal has been written in different scholarly disciplines about routines and habits, their power, structure, basis, and cause. While different disciplines take different positions on different aspects of these practices, there is wide agreement that we are highly subject to them. This is understandable given that routines are generally available and familiar given that we have used them previously; having previously used them also makes them normally energy efficient. Like governing accounts and narrative they also serve as a means for ordering what we do. This similarity to accounts is

[1] The term "habit" is included here since it is often used to denote routines. In the discussion that follows, however, an attempt is made to avoid it since, though the term is sometimes used to describe behavioral patterns subject to some sort of meaningful script, it is more likely to be used in instances of "conditioned" behavior. The behavior of the four young rabbis above is clearly a result of the former. Jumping at the sight of a dog is more likely to be a conditioned response related to an earlier experience. Since in the discussion that follows we are interested in behavior that has been shaped by some form of meaningful account, it is used sparingly.

not surprising since in most cases routines are shaped by an account of some sort. Where they differ is that in routines and performances the accounts are behaviorally, rather than mentally, played out. Theological contemplation and debate entails thinking something through; religious prayer normally requires some form of ritualized behavior that is built into our bodies. Though the four young rabbis reached an intellectual consensus, their bodies directed them to behave according to their past routines. The central point of this story is that shared routines commonly trump shared theoretical conclusions. In doing so, however, routines do not counter the dynamics of familiarity or the bonding powers of shared perspectives; they, rather, embrace these same dynamics but in a more physical, grounded way. The relative importance of each is determined, not so much by differences in how familiar or how strong the consensus is of each, but rather how dominating concrete activities are. Here again we find markets to be rich arenas to explore given the central role played by behavioral transactions: markets entail a good deal of doing, not just of ruminating, reflecting, and concluding.

With their ability to reassure by ordering what we do and bonding individuals to each other akin to the way governing accounts and narratives do, routines also function as a means of coping with the unforeseen, unanticipated, and incongruous. As indicated in the title of this chapter, they do so, however, in different ways than do narratives and accounts. They do not try to reframe situations in a manner that "makes better sense," but rather to insulate us from them by putting us on some form of automatic drive. That this "automatic drive" component succeeds is linked to the form in which the unforeseen, unanticipated, and incongruous confront us in these routine-generating situations. Whereas governing narratives are fashioned to provide a coherent account and to make sense and or explain away ambiguities, inconsistencies, and contradictions, routines enable us to traverse contingencies, disorder, and chaotic situations. They manage to do this by keeping us moving in a particular direction to avoid being caught up in the crosscurrents of contingencies encountered.[2]

As with governing narratives, the market provides us with a collection of such routines, including purchasing routines in which a standard amount of money is invested at specified intervals; allocating routines to select financial instruments to be owned in terms of risk versus rewards for age, changing rates of return, and financial needs; balancing routines to maintain preset ratios for different types of financial instruments; loss-limiting routines; and profit-taking routines. The key component in all of these routines is that they entail

[2] In kayaking, an activity that we will shortly be exploring in some detail, the standard rule when encountering choppy water and crosscurrents is to "keep on paddling." The act of paddling does not eliminate the various forces emanating from the choppy water, but it does serve to maintain a balance by cutting through it.

actions of one sort or another. As such, they actually engage in the flow of events, whereas narratives are limited to offering different accounts. The actions dictated by routines, however, are not crafted in specific ways to respond to what is happening, but rather actions that constitute a familiar course of action previously used. A more detailed examination as how the five market routines noted above work, including a fuller elaboration of the relevant market contingencies/crosscurrents that they are intended to insulate us from, will hopefully illustrate this. We will have the opportunity to examine actions fashioned specifically as crafted responses to specific events in Part III. For now, however, we are concerned with simple routines used to transcend encountered discord. To understand how this works we need to identify the major currents likely to be encountered. Fortunately in financial markets they tend to be pretty much the same in dealing with all five of the routines noted above.

To describe the market as being subject to crosscurrents assumes that it entails a flow of some sort. In financial markets this flow is constituted by the flows of money and other monetarily defined financial instruments generated by market transactions among buyers and sellers. This flow, like any river, tends to maintain a dominant direction. Whereas, in the case of rivers, this flow is downhill under the control of gravity, the flow of financial markets tends to be "uphill" in response to the normally expanding and growing economies generated by growing populations. It is this trend toward growth that supports and justifies investing monetary resources into these markets, as shares of today's economy should be worth more in the future. The flow of these markets, however, like the flow of any given river varies over time and in different locations. This presents any potential investors with the problem of deciding when, where, and how much to invest at any given moment.

Proponents of pretty much all of the accounts described in Chapter 3 would be willing to offer their advice on pretty much all of these subjects. Given the quite different suggestions these proponents are apt to offer, it is not unexpected that potential investors commonly find themselves looking for simpler and hopefully more universal solutions. Various routines often prove to be the answers. When it comes to deciding when to invest, for example, a widely followed and recommended strategy is to make investments of similar, predetermined size at regular predetermined intervals. Rather than trying to time one's investment according to any particular market account, for example, one would invest a quarter of one's proposed annual investment funds at the beginning of every third month. Other, structurally similar, purchase routines might recommend monthly purchases or bi-annual purchases; they might also recommend different amounts at different times. The governing principle in all such routines, however, is to avoid being rattled by or attempting to outsmart market movements up or down. It is a routine, in short, that insulates one from the day-to-day turmoil of the market that can serve to undermine a long-term investment strategy.

Where to invest presents a somewhat similar problem for most investors. Here the issue isn't when to invest, but where to invest. Again, proponents of pretty much any of the accounts described in the Chapter 3 will have their views on this subject. More to the point, these views are likely to vary over time depending on a whole range of factors that play a role in each of these different accounts. As with timing, there exist a number of simpler and more universally shared routines for dealing with this issue. These are what we have referred to above as allocation routines. These routines tend to be shaped more in terms of the particulars of the investor than the market per se. The central variables here tend to revolve around the degree of risk and the level of return on capital that is being sought. These issues in turn are generally tied to the age of the investor and their financial resources. In the end, whatever the specific factors, allocation routines address the percentage of any given investment that should be placed in equities/stocks or fixed income/bonds, as well as the particular risk ration of each category.

The alternatives here have grown significantly over the past few decades and continue to grow daily in response to the introduction of numerous new investment instruments discussed earlier. This growth has itself become a significant factor in underscoring the value, if not need, for such routines. Financial markets, over the past few decades, have been flooded by mutual and exchange-traded funds that purport to combine different financial instruments into single financial products that meet every particular financial profile. And if this is not enough, there are numerous other funds that function as funds of other funds in an attempt to expand and refine individual choices more. In and of themselves, however, no particular mix of investments can function as a sound lifetime mix. As noted above, the assumed proper mix of investments varies by age and financial situation. As such, whatever one's particular allocation mix, one must recalculate this mix on a fairly regular basis. Obviously, this need not be done monthly or even every year, but it clearly would deserve attention every decade or so when younger and more often as one neared retirement age.

In recent years, a number of funds have sought to incorporate this function within themselves by reallocating funds as individuals age. That is, they not only claim to offer a full menu of appropriate allocations for different people, but also built-in designs that adjust these allocations as the needs and situations of these different people are expected to change. For most people, however, reallocating their investment mix as they age is a routine that requires individual attention. The guidelines remain pretty much the same whatever one's age or financial situation; the data and results, however, can change considerably. Again, as with purchasing routines, allocation/reallocation routines are not meant to be governed by "rocket science." They are intended to keep things as simple as possible. For most people this often reduces itself into what percentage of a portfolio should be in equity or equity-like investments and what percentage in fixed-income/bond investments. Whatever any particular mix and whenever it may have been purchased, the value of any given portfolio as well as its individual components is likely to change over time. This brings us to the third routine: the balancing routine.

Balancing routines differ from both purchasing routines and allocation routines in at least one important way. Where both purchasing and allocation routines are primarily focused upon the characteristics and needs of the individual investor, balancing routines are focused primarily on the individual's portfolio. More specifically they are concerned with altering the constitution of the portfolio in response to the way it has changed since it was initially instituted. As might be expected, here again, if not more so, the proponents of the different accounts discussed in Chapter 3 would have their own views on how such changes should be managed. Some might argue that exceptionally strong/upward movement by a particular instrument would indicate that one should increase one's holding of that particular investment, whereas another might strongly recommend taking one's profits. Similarly, some might recommend selling investments that have done poorly, while others might recommend that you continue to hold them. All most likely would have suggestions for adding particular items and removing others. Though a slightly more complex routine than either purchasing or allocation, the balancing routine is also not structured as "rocket science." Balancing, or perhaps more accurately rebalancing, entails simply buying and selling in a manner that will reproduce the ratios that the portfolio was intended to have. If equities have fallen below their designated percentage and fixed income has consequently increased, quite regardless of the overall action of the portfolio, you need to sell fixed income and buy equity or at least buy additional equity to return to the intended ratio.

Though clearly focused on particular portfolios, the primary objective of balancing routines, like purchasing routines and allocation routines, is to enable one to maintain a particular course regardless of whatever changes and turbulences might be occurring in the market itself. They are not so much means for managing the market, as they are means for managing oneself. The final two routines presented above, loss-limiting routines and profit-taking routines, have a similar objective though they are even more focused on the market itself than the just discussed balancing routines. While differing from the previous three routines insofar as they entail actually responding to specific profit and loss situations rather than the calendar and portfolio profiles, their primary function is to insulate one from the turmoil and pressures of the market, not really engage with it. Loss-limiting routines are, as their name would indicate, meant to limit losses. The purpose of limiting these losses relates less to one's overall profit/loss market results, however, than it does to one's ability to maintain one's market presence.

If one is in the market one will have both losses and gains. In keeping with the intent of the routines already discussed, if one has allocated one's resources reasonably and maintained reasonable purchasing and balancing routines, one will have more profits than losses over the long run provided the basic premise that the economy will grow holds true. The key notions here are that the economy will grow over the long term, and that you will be part of it for the long term. This requires that you not get wiped out. This requires that you limit the loss that you will incur in any given investment. With a few exceptions this generally means no more than a 10 to 15 percent short-term loss. The partner routine of profit-taking is intended as a balance to the loss-limiting routine. Just as one can expect that one will confront unexpected large losses, so one can expect to confront unexpected short-term profits. In tandem these two routines also serve to insulate one from particular short-term moves in particular investments. These routines are not intended to be applied to general market moves, which would require one to abdicate one's entire position. Market moves are meant to be dealt with by means of the first three routines that entail investing through good times and bad, adjusting portfolio allocations to one's own situation, and rebalancing one's portfolio on a regular basis. Loss-limiting routines and profit-taking routines are intended only for idiosyncratic moves of particular investments and like each other are intended to insulate one.

Though these routines' primary function is to insulate investors from what might be called "market chop," they have a number of secondary benefits much as do governing narratives; to a large extent they are also similar to those of governing narratives. To begin with, routines, like habitual behavior of all sorts, are energy efficient. One doesn't need to waste time or energy deciding what to do and how to do it. Routines also serve to lessen anxiety, especially anxieties due to disorder and the unexpected, including ambiguities and even more so contingencies. They allow us to get on with things. In doing so they not only insulate in varying degrees from the confusion we confront, but also serve to generate their own forms of behavioral order. They enable us to get ourselves into some sort of rhythm even if we find ourselves in what might otherwise be experienced as a chaotic situation. Routines function very much like behaviorally grounded self-fulfilling prophecies, which is understandable insofar as to a large extent this is what they are. Their power to generate order and a sense of normality, moreover, can often be increased significantly when others engage in complementary or similar routines. Regular first-of-the-month purchasing routines when pursued by numerous investors can give markets timely upward support. Balancing routines provide simultaneous buffers on what might be considered over-exuberant moves both up and down, which tend to give markets a disorderly look. Perhaps most importantly, the simple fact that a significant number of other people are engaged in similar routines generates its own stabilizing powers.

There are times, of course, when such routines can have quite different results, especially when collectively pursued. This is often the case with "limiting-loss" and "taking-profit" routines. The collective selling of a particular instrument at a particular time due to a large decline can generate a much more severe decline. This is often the case when a particular stock or other financial instrument drops below a level that it has not been below for some time. Such points are often defined as "stop" points: points below which the stock should be sold. Even in these cases there is a sense in which routines bring a sense of order to the market insofar as they serve to validate such stop points as stop points. Investors who adhere to their limiting-loss routines in these situations may not be pleased with being forced to take a loss, but they are likely to be gratified that they did when they see the stock continue to drop significantly. If the so-called "stop" point manages to hold slightly below its previous level and the stock then rallies back, our investors will obviously not be quite so pleased.[3] On the other hand, they will be able to continue.

Fairly similar dynamics apply to taking-profits routines, though the end results tend to be more agreeable. Situations in which taking-profit routines are called for also entail prices obtaining unfamiliar levels; in these cases, however, the level is higher than recent past prices. These levels are often defined as "tops" or new "highs." Unlike limiting-loss routines, which increase the downward pressure on the given stock, taking-profit routines act to counteract the movement of the stock in question by creating selling pressures on a stock that is rising. As a consequence, the stocks often retreat somewhat after attaining "new highs," which can make those employing taking-profit routines feel rather clever. On the other hand there are also times when stocks gain upward momentum once they have broken through such "tops." Most long-term investors learn to live with whatever disappointments such movements may cause.

Taken together, these various routines, while clearly not always maximizing return on capital in all, or even most, situations, do provide a moderating support to the ups and downs of the market. As one broker once said to me some years ago using a horseback-riding metaphor, it allows them to hold their seat and not get easily bucked off. Sticking with this metaphor, these routines also provide some support in keeping their proponents from being led down wrong trails and paths. The process at work here is similar to the way in which accounts protect their proponents from getting caught up in what was earlier referred to as mass or crowd behavior. The protection here, however, does not inhere in accounts that set normative limits and proscribed behaviors as to what we should do, but in the routines and habitual practices that we have been trained to enact in various situations. It is analogous to the way in which experienced sea kayakers and canoeists are trained to keep paddling when they encounter turbulent water: there is no time or energy to

[3] While both alternatives occur, fear of loss tends to favor the continuation of such declines before another "stop" point is generated.

figure out what is going on. In hindsight one might decide that one would have done better by paddling in a somewhat different direction, but the key thing is to avoid hesitating and being engulfed by the turbulence.

The high degree to which routines mirror governing accounts in the manner in which they enable us to cope with uncertainties, be they ambiguities or contingencies, is not surprising. Routines are in effect behaviors which have had particular governing accounts implanted. Where governing narratives and accounts structure most human behavior they generally need to be interpreted and applied to do so. The final product of these processes is what we commonly refer to as normative behavior, which constitutes the great bulk of what we accept to be human behavior. While intimately linked, we continue to recognize the various components as distinct factors. The rules, meanings, objectives, and actions are seen as related, but not part of a single practice. In the case of routines, integrated practices dominate, subsuming the various components that constitute them.

There is another factor at work in both of these situations, however, that cannot be ignored—namely, the context or environment in which these coping strategies operate. Context and environment are particularly important in determining the outcome of routines as they are embedded in their particular contexts to a significantly greater degree than are governing accounts. Governing accounts are generally related to the external disorder happenings that they proclaim to make sense of, but they are seldom, if ever, directly called forth by these happenings. Routines, in contrast, are normally initiated by specific chaotic happenings that they are meant to offset or counteract. Experienced kayakers don't need to decide whether to paddle harder when caught up in some turbulence: they do so automatically. This difference reflects the fundamental distinction between the behaviorally embedded commands of routines and the required application of governing accounts previously discussed. Thought and action are both shaped and formed in response to the surrounding world in which they emerge. They are both also driven in large measure by a need to complete something that is experienced as incomplete. In both cases, the chaotic and disordered is the foe, represented in thought primarily by ambiguity and the paradoxical and in action by the unexpected and contingent. The degree to which they are intertwined, however, varies considerably between the way governing narratives function and the way routines function.

Alternative accounts of the nature of thought and action and how they function are obviously available. The view being presented here, which is the underlying perspective of this whole discussion, has its roots in American pragmatism and evolutionary cognitive theory.[4] It is also deeply informed by

[4] There is a good deal of overlap between these two perspectives, due in large measure to the central role that evolutionary theory plays in both. A central theme in both pragmatism—

various sociological ideas bearing on knowledge from Durkheim to Giddens.[5] Taken together, these theoretical framings weave thoughts and actions together as collective evolutionary products. As such, minds seek closure and completeness much as does all existence, and fails as does all else. The same drive for closure and completeness is ironically also at the root of contingencies, the unforeseen coming together of the previously unconnected, which gives rise to the unexpected and disorderly happenings that routines and accounts seek to neutralize. This does not in any way offset the worth of governing narratives and routines, quite the opposite. Both, in their own way and own sphere, are the major tools we have for dealing with the ambiguities and contingencies, paradoxes and chaos that we regularly confront. Moreover, in many, if not most situations, they tend to work quite well for significant periods of time. Neither, however, acknowledges the extent and degree to which our world is permeated by both ambiguities and contingencies, nor the degree to which the world is constituted by a hierarchy of open systems.

More importantly, while each in its own way—denial in the case of governing narratives and insulation in the case of routines—often manages to protect us from of the negative consequences of confronting these threats, they do not provide us with the means to actually cope with them. In order to do this, a radically different approach is required: an approach that requires that we actually engage the contingencies and ambiguities we confront, rather then merely shield ourselves from them. To be able to engage them, we need to renounce both governing narratives and routines to the best of our ability. It requires that we abandon any claim for an ordered and complete integrated whole and focus our attention on the underlying dynamics and mechanisms of a messy many to which we must respond. We need to learn how to act sensibly, which generally requires that we relinquish our fixation with making sense and focus more upon what is actually happening. To a large extent this represents an extension of the movement from thought to action implicit in the transition from governing narratives to routines.

But what of "performances," which were prominently cited in the title of this chapter? The dilemma posed by performances, which explains why they have so far been ignored, is that "there are performances and then there are

particularly Dewey (1925/1929) and Mead (1934)—and evolutionary cognitive theory is that thinking is grounded and shaped in our being and actions. Again there is a very large literature in both fields. The two books just cited identify two books that I have valued highly. For Dewey, I would also suggest McDermott (1973, 1981).

[5] This inclusive referencing of Giddens' work is both deliberate and proper, as his work, intertwined as it is with the writings of Durkheim and Mead and critical realism, wrestles with the way thought, structures, and actions interrelate and as such has made a foundational contribution to this book.

performances," or to put it more directly, performances can and do take quite a different form in the extent and ways in which they mix thought and actions. The great majority of everyday practices labeled as performances are, in fact, routines of one sort or another. They are scripted behaviors in which script and behavior have become one. There are other performances, however, in which the script functions more as a governing account that dictates the behavior, but where the behavior lacks the spontaneity or emotive powers of most routines. There are other performances that differ in another way and serve as a perfect segue to acting sensibly practices that Part III of the book addresses. These performances are scripted similarly to routines, but they are scripted in a manner that requires the actors to also respond simultaneously to the flow of events encountered. Put slightly differently, these performances require a significant improvisational component. They embody what is commonly referred to as the "dramaturgical" paradigm that speaks to Shakespeare's famous line that "All the world's a stage, And all the men and women merely players; They have their exits and their entrances," but can in slightly different form be traced back to Socrates and forward to the writing of Erving Goffman (1959) and scores of others.

Performances entail not only scripts and actors: they also require stages and settings. They utilize not only entrances and exits, as noted by Shakespeare, but also beginnings and endings. All of these components in different ways serve to provide not only cognitive, emotional, and value orders of varying sorts, but spatial and temporal boundaries as well as behavioral guidelines. From religious rituals to sporting events, from musicals to dramas, from live theater to television and radio, from family dinners to high-school dances, and all the other instances of performances that we experience, they serve as central coping mechanisms for us. They are so pervasive that we tend often not to see them or the role that they play in smoothing our way over the bumps and gaps that we regularly transverse, often unknowingly. Before we can appreciate how these performances manage to counteract these bumps and gaps, we need to recognize the various forms in which they present themselves and the particular types of bumps and gaps they address.

In light of earlier discussions regarding stuff happens, open systems, crosscurrents, and contingencies, it should come as no surprise that the bumps and gaps that performances address, are generated primarily by the disconnections we encounter. These disconnections come in varying forms, including disconnections of place and time, disconnections of needs and resources, disconnections of giving and taking, and disconnections of individuals. Here again financial markets provide us with a rich trove of examples, including examples of how particular performances and settings are used to deal with them. That markets, financial and otherwise, should provide rich sites should come as no surprise, given that this is what markets are all about. They exist to enable individuals who would otherwise have few if no grounds to engage in transactions to do so.[6] Depending on what is exchanged, the different parties involved, and a range of other factors, different markets go about their business differently. In all major markets, however, it is necessary to establish guidelines bearing on place, time, commodities, and participants.

Where most early markets dealt in familiar agricultural goods and were restricted to participants who needed to be physically present at the market, but were otherwise physically dispersed, time and place tended to be most important. This led to the specification of both market places and market days. Prices and quantities were generally left to the participants to negotiate. In situations in which individual commodities were less familiar and more diverse, leading to less agreement regarding price and more discord regarding allocation, such markets often spawned spinoff auctions of one sort or another. While the participants in such markets tended to be local, strangers, particularly travelling merchants with less available goods, were normally welcome.

Financial markets have historically presented a somewhat different profile. While both place and time have played their part in the evolution of these markets, neither was subject to constraints linked to the commodities being exchanged as in agriculturally based markets. Both place and time were, rather, subject to constraints linked to the needs and availabilities of the participants. Even more constraining than the needs of the participants, however, were pressures directly linked to the commodities themselves. Financial markets by definition deal with financial commodities, or as they are often referred to financial instruments: currencies, bonds and other debt obligations, equities, and various rare minerals such as gold and silver. What all of these commodities have in common, which designates them as financial commodities, is that they are seen to embody specific financial value; put simply, their primary facet is their specific prices.

What these prices should be at any given moment, however, is nearly always uncertain. Determining these prices at any given moment is the job of the market. In short, where prices are used to guide the allocation of most commodities and goods, in financial markets the allocation process embedded in the transactions themselves generates the prices (Smith 2007, 2011). Given

[6] This thesis is commonly attributed to Polanyi's (1957: 250–6) analysis of his three major types of allocation systems—reciprocity, redistribution and (market) exchange. While all three systems are subject to ideational/normative constraints, markets function significantly more as open systems than do the other two systems in enabling exchanges between otherwise unrelated individuals and negotiated prices. Such markets are consequently able to manage crosscultural transactions (Smith 1989: 3–5, 24–35). To be able to support the necessary negotiations required to establish the conditions governing a particular transaction, however, there need to exist structures of some sort. The structures that have been and are commonly used correspond to those that support performances of varying types that enable interaction between participants. Markets are consequently able to function under conditions of initial ambiguity and disagreement regarding such things as price, quantities, who's buying and who's selling.

that the factors that relate to this pricing process vary from instrument to instrument, distinct markets with separate locations/places have tended to emerge for distinct instruments. Since these various instruments, despite their differences, all deal primarily in one form or another with monetary value, these markets, whatever their particular location, also tend to have an ubiquitous presence, which resists both spatial and temporal boundaries.

Historically, these various pressures gave rise to what might be considered various compromises. Most financial markets elected to mirror the normal workweek, enabling them to be active while most businesses were active, but to close when they closed. In addition to separating into distinct markets according to distinct financial instruments as noted above, financial markets also morphed into what could be called stratified markets, in which a central market restricted to members engaged in primary transactions for clients, and other major players entered into their own transactions using the prices generated in the central market as guidelines. The scripts and stagings for all of these different processes were subject to modifications in response to both internal and external pressures, including government regulations. This, in turn, gave rise, to numerous iconic performances from the New York Stock Exchange's opening bell, its numerous trading posts, runners, and miles of ticker tape to the Mercantile Exchange gold pits. The bottom line in all of these performances was and remains the same as it always was: by means of a sound script, the proper setting, and established routines to ensure that the show goes on, whatever the bumps and gaps.

Financial markets and their various shows have changed significantly over the past few decades in response to a large extent to the technical, digital revolution that has impacted upon everything (Knorr Cetina and Bruegger 2002). Cyberspace has in many ways replaced physical space, with most transactions occurring over the Internet. Trading is no longer focused on a particular walled space: through cyberspace it has gone global. Temporal boundaries have also been bridged. Most markets continue to have official opening and closing times, but as one market closes, a sister market tends to open on the other side of the world, and as if that was not enough, after-hours trading goes on continually. To further complicate matters, new financial instruments, as noted earlier, continue to emerge, with each new instrument introducing a possible new wrinkle in the way in which existing instruments are likely to be exchanged and priced. As markets proliferate and grow, more people are drawn in. At the same time, and in response to this growing population, the market is downloaded and drawn into more and more homes. The show not only continues, it permeates.

However robust or even viral in their ability to expand and replicate themselves, financial markets universally fail to resolve the ambiguities and contingencies that they harbor. If anything, their growth has served to infuse their own vibrant ambiguities and contingencies into other sectors of society.

While proclaiming the ordering abilities of their own governing accounts and recommended routines, market spokespersons and gurus have not brought any sort of serenity to populations as a whole. The great majority of people not only grasp intuitively the extent to which financial markets are highly subject to ambiguities and contingencies, but also the extent to which these ambiguities and contingencies seep into other sectors of society. In doing so, they contribute to a general unease and apprehension that feeds into a need for simple answers and fundamentalist accounts and associated behavior. Unfortunately, such accounts and routines are no more likely to eradicate the ambiguities and contingencies we confront in these other sectors than the accounts and routines of the market are able to eradicate them in the market. They may well serve to help us deny their existence and even to insulate us from them in particular circumstances, but they will not assist us in actually responding to them in a beneficial manner. In order to do this we need to explore another coping strategy; we need, as we have noted, to grasp what it means to act sensibly.

Part III

Acting Sensibly: Eluding Hazards and Grasping Opportunities

Though "acting sensibly" is presented in the discussion that follows as the preferred strategy for dealing with contingencies in most situations, it is clearly not being presented as a means for resolving these contingencies, let alone ambiguities that by definition require some form of cognitive fix. As discussed in Chapter 1 and Chapter 2, contingencies are inherent in the world in which we live. They are not going to go away or be eradicated, no matter how sensibly we might behave. Moreover, as indicated in Chapters 3 and 4, making sense narratives and insulating routines and performances, more often than not enable us to weather ambiguities and contingencies more efficiently than engaging them directly, which acting sensibly commonly requires.

There are times, however, when accounts and routines are likely to be inadequate; in these situations some form of acting sensibly is likely to be the best option we have. In these instances, acting sensibly may not only enable us to limit damages in a manner in which neither governing accounts nor routines can, but also enable us to take advantage of unexpected opportunities. By acting sensibly one does not attempt to resolve ambiguities or eradicate contingencies; the objective is, rather, to avoid or minimize the costs and damages that they might cause, and benefit from them when we can.

When we act sensibly, behavior is privileged over thought, though the modifying adverb "sensibly" clearly serves to retain the presence of thought. As such, acting sensibly is similar in some ways to routines and performances discussed in Chapter 4. Where it differs is in understanding and utilizing mind, not in the form of an account, program, or script, but rather as a faculty for comparing and judging.[1] Hopefully, this will become clearer as we proceed. For

[1] This difference echoes in many ways the distinction between the different types of cognitive systems proposed by Kahneman (2011), Kahneman and Tversky (2000, 1982, 1979), and Kahneman, Slovac, and Tversky 1982. It differs significantly insofar as acting sensibly entails a series of actions. This will be elaborated upon in the discussion that follows.

now, however, a simple comparison of two quite different meanings given to the notion of "navigating" might be helpful. In both cases, "navigating" is understood to be a means for correctly determining how to best move across some space, more often than not water, by determining how best to go from one point, generally where you are, to another point, generally where you want to go. Pre-compass, this was done not only by locating oneself in terms of designated objects—celestial objects, currents, winds, islands, and rocks—but also by "reading" winds and current changes to judge when one's directions needed to be altered. Post-compass and the proliferation of maps, travel routes and directional changes were plotted on maps and then "followed" as best one could with the help of various guidance instruments on the water or over land or in the air.

Acting in accordance with a governing account or narrative and routines and performances entail this second form of navigation. Acting sensibly relies almost exclusively upon the first form. It relies upon responding knowingly to the events encountered, rather than any form of predetermined course. On its surface this might appear to be a relatively straightforward and quite simple strategy. Given the many different situations and complexities that cross-currents and other contingencies are apt to generate, acting sensibly can become a very demanding and complex strategy very quickly as it normally entails a number of distinct sub-actions. Chapter 5 gives a brief overview of the most salient of these sub-actions; Chapters 6 through 10 seek to give a fuller account of each.

One additional feature that separates acting sensibly from both making sense and routines and performances is worth noting as it speaks to a basic article of faith that is operative in all of these situations. Governing narratives and accounts, and the drive to make sense of the world that they embody, and routines and performances are fundamentally affirmations and commitments to the power and primacy of existential order. They do not merely seek order; they accept such order as an inherent factor of reality. This holds true, not only for markets, but for the canons that pertain to pretty much all human spheres, be they religious, political, economic, or ethical; it similarly holds true for routines, be they personal, institutional, or organizational, and performances, be they theatrical, musical, dance, or otherwise. Even rule-governed sporting events, despite the pervasive presence of conflicts and the unexpected are structured and subject to spatial, temporal, and normative constraints that serve to hold the various parts together in a manner that produces a single, integrated event.

Acting sensibly, in contrast, is basically agnostic about any sort of future or possible universal order; more importantly, it clearly rejects the notion that such an order presently exists to be followed or even discovered. Acting sensibly relies more on various forms of "improvisation," which were deliberately ignored in the earlier discussion of performances. It accepts and acknowledges both ambiguities and contingencies as inherent in the world. In many cases, including most markets, it often prizes them as possible sources of significant rewards. Such attitudes are normally tempered by the recognition that they also are potentially dangerous and can be the source of great harm. The objective is to maximize the positive and limit the negative by acting sensibly. As with accounts and routines, the market, primarily as embodied in the practices of Traders, provides a rich inventory of situations and examples that speak to these issues. The underlying dynamics depend upon the fact that, while these Traders are agnostic when it comes to predicting what the market will do, they generally accept, as noted earlier, that the market is subject to causal forces that shape it. Moreover, they have historically believed, based on their past experiences in dealing with these forces, that they could commonly spot, evaluate, and respond to them when they came into play.[2] It enabled them in other words to "act sensibly," and we now turn to the details of this.

[2] Efficient market proponents clearly reject this premise. Croupiers take what might be called an intermediate position on this matter. They tend to be highly dubious when it comes to grasping the causal forces in play, but they are positive when it comes to utilizing past market actions. This will be explored in Chapter 11 after we have dealt with acting sensibly.

5

The Essentials of Acting Sensibly

An Overview

Acting sensibly, as noted previously, is inherently less ambitious in what it seeks to accomplish than either "making sense" or "routines." It has no pretentions of resolving or eliminating either ambiguities or contingencies; rather, it seeks to avoid or sometimes correct mistakes, which tend themselves often to be errors of omission rather than errors of commission. Insofar as personal responsibility comes into play at all, the great majority of these failures are tied to failures of attention more than any other factor. The primary source of most of these failures is normally seen to reside in the contingencies encountered. In the context of recent work in cognitive psychology, acting sensibly entails an interesting mix of what Kahneman and Tversky labeled "Cognitive System 1": intuition and perception.[3] It differs from both of these cognitive systems, however, in a number of important interrelated respects.

First, it is primarily a behavioral process not a mental process: what is central is what is done, not what is thought, though clearly thoughts are attached to these actions. Secondly, acting sensibly occurs over a period of time, which tends to be determined by the event(s) with which it is engaged; it transcends individual behavioral, cognitive, and perceptual responses. Thirdly, it is not so much intuitive or even emotive, though it tends to entail significant elements of both, as it is somatic: it tends to employ the body. It is not so much a form of passive knowing as it is an assimilating–adapting–probing activity. In these respects it echoes Mead's (1934) understanding of mind as being located, not only in our brains, but throughout the entire nervous system of our bodies. All of these factors, as well as other characteristics it shares with various comparatively non-rational, intuitive, emotive thought/action models, will be depicted in greater detail in the chapters that follow, in which the five basic components that constitute acting sensibly will be examined in market

[3] See Kahneman (2011, pp. 19–30) for a clear presentation of each system.

and other contexts. For now, however, it seems more appropriate to simply provide each component with a label and a brief description. That will be followed in this chapter by an attempt to delve in more detail into the mindset and sensibilities that these components entail and reflect. Hopefully, this will facilitate seeing how these various strategic steps are applied in particular situations.

1. Identifying and prioritizing objectives—the key point here is to recognize that in acting sensibly there is no single objective. The constantly changing conditions that generally apply require one to hold simultaneously a number of different objectives, which need to be continually reprioritized.
2. Monitoring manifest and potential markers—in acting sensibly, the major difficulty is not simply that there are numerous markers that must be monitored, but that these markers come and go. The crucial task here is not to become fixated on any given set of markers at any given time since new markers of importance are apt to appear suddenly while others are likely to disappear.
3. Identifying and juggling rules of thumb[4]—the need to identify and juggle a range of "rules of thumb" underscores the fact that in acting sensibly one needs continually to make modest adjustments, with the emphasis on "modest." Grand strategies seldom if ever work. It is necessary to match appropriate practical minimalist actions to particular situations. This commonly requires focusing upon various pertinent, but limited, underlying factors, rather than upon the total situation including underlying causal forces that will be explored in more depth later.[5]

[4] The expression "rule of thumb" has been assigned numerous different origins and definitions, including a recently proposed origin that it specified the size of the stick that could be used to "correct" or "punish" a wife in eighteenth-century English law. There is considerably more evidence that it has numerous other origins built around the use of a thumb as a measurement guide. What most of these different accounts have in common and which constitutes the general meaning of this expression is that it is a simple, easily applied decision-making procedure applicable in a wide range of circumstances to govern specific actions. It is in this general sense that the term is used in this text, though in the discussion to follow a number of more detailed facets will be expounded. As such it has much in common with the central Wikipedia definition:

> A rule of thumb is a principle with broad application that is not intended to be strictly accurate or reliable for every situation. It is an easily learned and easily applied procedure for approximately calculating or recalling some value, or for making some determination. Compare this to heuristic, a similar concept used in mathematical discourse, psychology and computer science, particularly in algorithm design. Rule of thumb also used to be used by navigators; the safe distance to pass off any point of land was the width of one's thumb, regardless of the scale of the chart being used.

A key point here is that though it might entail some sort of measuring, such rules are intended to govern some action.

[5] In examining causal forces we will also be returning to the perspective of critical realism introduced in Chapter 2.

4. Adjusting and correcting one's course—the need to adjust one's course is linked to identifying and juggling rules of thumb. The emphasis here, however, is upon recognizing the ways and extent to which previous actions or lack of actions need to be addressed to successfully attain one's present objective(s).
5. Maintaining an escape route—the principle of maintaining an escape route completes the circle back to identifying and prioritizing objectives, since fleeing the situation is clearly an alternative objective. The underlying assumption here is that, when all else is said and done, survival remains the objective of last resort. What might constitute a viable escape route at one moment, however, may not constitute a viable escape route later. As such, monitoring and maintaining a viable escape route commonly also entails identifying and locating new escape routes as conditions change, much as is the case in identifying and monitoring markers. Most importantly, however, electing to utilize an escape route represents a clean break from adjusting and correcting one's course. It requires that one "abandon ship."

All five of these components involve/entail a response of one sort or another. In the case of the first two, the responses have a dominant perceptual character. This is most clearly the case in monitoring markers, which tends to rely heavily upon visual signs, though all forms of sense inputs are relevant. Insofar as identifying and prioritizing objectives tends to be visually framed, their perceptual character is similarly central, though most objectives are usually experienced as more than a visual goal; certain "affordances"—future possible situations inherent in the present situation—are commonly also attached.[6] Identifying and jugging rules of thumb, in contrast, tends to call forth both more manual and cognitive imagery as they normally are framed in terms of particular physically manipulative actions we might take. In acting sensibly, such actions, however, are seen as particular responses to given situations. Adjusting and correcting one's course is similar to identifying and jugging rules of thumb insofar as it also entails both physical and cognitive responses, but it differs insofar as the focus shifts away from any skills that the actor might have to a "reading" of the alternative possibilities that the environment may have to offer. In this way, adjusting and correcting one's course also entails a large visual component. Maintaining an escape route, insofar as it is a particular mixture of objectives and course choices generated by quite special markers and an apparent useless toolbox, embodies all of the imageries of the other four components, plus its own quite distinct fear factor.

Taken together, these components give acting sensibly a very different feel than that associated with making sense and routines. The mind is engaged, as it is in making sense and routines, but it is subject to a constant stream of new

[6] For more on "affordances" and "ecological psychology" see James Gibson (1979) and Heft (2001).

factors that demand to be included. Predetermined framings and procedures linked to governing narratives and routines that function to divert attention away from what is being directly experienced both externally and internally are hindrances. History is full of such situations, the sinking of the *Titanic* being one of the most notable insofar as it entailed blatant failures on all five counts. Sticking to a predetermined course, ignoring clear danger markers, and failure to follow established appropriate rules of thumb contributed to a quite unnecessary disaster. Financial crashes, most sea-kayak fatalities, and botched surgeries generally entail similar failures. They also contribute to missing many promising opportunities such as unexpected profits, prized paddling experiences, and surgical shortcuts. In nearly all of these cases, the root failure is to disregard the inherently contingent character of the situation and to approach it as if it were a fully ordered, predictable, and understandable situation. What makes such attitudes so distressing is that to a significant degree the contingent nature of all of these situations is implicitly known and often intended.

Market Traders know that every day they can expect something to occur that will appear "off" in some way and unexpected. Moreover they depend upon such situations to provide them with an opportunity to outperform less skilled market participants. They are not alone, however, in this respect. Experienced sailors' skills, be their vessel the *Titanic* or a one-person kayak, are needed to traverse waters known to be subject to various contingencies. Surgeons cut into patients in pursuit of active bodily abnormalities. A surgeon who cuts into a body seeking to remove a cancerous growth can expect to encounter mixed clusters of blood vessels, nerves, muscles, and fat, which may have little resemblance, not only to the way they are depicted in anatomy books, but also in the way they appeared to be depicted in recently taken medical images, be they X-ray, CT and MRI scans, or ultrasound imagings.

The contingent nature of these situations, moreover, is not accidental. In the great majority of these cases, encountering such uncertainties is at the heart of what they are about. In many, if not the great majority, of these encounters the tasks and the rewards are linked to parrying the uncertainties with minimum cost. In other cases, however, the encountered surprise is seen to be a found treasure that pays for the costs of uncertainties not successfully parried. For a kayaker it may be an unexpected current, and for the surgeon an unexpected secondary growth. When it comes to contingencies and crosscurrents, however, financial markets are probably the richest sites there are, both figuratively and literally. This is not surprising given that, unlike most other situations that confront these conditions, markets were and are deliberately structured to foster contingencies and crosscurrents. This point was noted earlier in the reference made to Polanyi's three forms of economic allocation described in his book *Trade and Markets in the Early Empires* (1957). A few additional comments are in order here as they relate to the way the three settings used in the next few chapters, kayaking, surgery, and markets, differ. A fuller presentation of Polanyi's different forms of allocating goods is also in order, but first a few comments on the three settings that are used in the following chapters.

As presented in Chapter 2, "Stuff Happens," and following discussions, contingencies have been defined as grounded in what we normally call physical reality, in contrast to ambiguities that have been grounded in meaning systems of one sort or another. This holds true for the contingencies of markets as they are generated by crosscurrents in the flow of transactions that constitute markets. While these transactions are subject to pricing and other definitional framings that emerge from a range of different meaning systems, they are directly and indirectly also related to items embedded in happenings in concrete reality. One can admittedly argue that this is also true of ambiguities insofar as even the most abstract meaning system is subject to concrete happenings in some way or other. There is a qualitative difference, however, in the pervasive and continual impact of such happenings upon most price-setting markets and whatever impact they are likely to have on family routines, classroom routines, religious practices, and other primarily normatively governed activities. On the other hand, the contingencies of markets are clearly more subject to normative and interpretive constraints than is the weather, which is the prime source of contingencies impacting upon kayakers, or the normal and abnormal functioning of the body undergoing surgery. It is specifically this "middle" position that endows markets with their quite special capacity to sensitize us to the limitations of accounts and routines in coping with the unexpected and disordered. It also, however, presents markets with the opportunity to utilize other coping practices—one might want to say obliges them to utilize other coping practices, particularly those utilized by those confronting contingencies that are by and large detached from normative and interpretive constraints, such as those confronted in kayaking and surgery. Back to Polanyi and his account as to how this "middle" position evolved.

Polanyi's historical and anthropological account of the evolution of economic systems, grounds early economies within what might be called traditional societies and cultures. As such, Polanyi argues that economic practices were governed similarly to the way in which the rest of these societies were governed, the earliest being cultural designations and practices of normatively established reciprocity, followed by imperial powers and imposed redistribution practices grounded primarily on taxation and booty. Emerging markets, in contrast, depended upon the voluntary exchange of goods between willing individuals where the cultural and political status of individuals was of secondary importance to their needs and resources. Among a range of different factors that must also accompany this transition, such as acceptance of the notion of private property, the needs and resources of the individuals involved must differ if there are to be exchanges. If such exchanges are to entail more than charitable gift giving, the haves giving their surplus to the have-nots, the needs and surpluses of the participants need to differ. This would require that they have access to different sources of goods that they are willing to bring to the market. Without a flow of goods for sale, there is no market. The market is likely to be defined by the types of goods that flow through it, but the life of the market will depend primarily upon the features and vitality of the various flows that it embodies.

The significance and importance of what is being exchanged and the rhythm of the exchanges tend to differ depending upon whether one is a buyer or a seller. In most retail markets, most buyers are periodical participants and primarily interested in obtaining particular goods; the sellers in these markets tend to be permanent participants and more focused on the flow and rhythm of exchanges. Where buyers are primarily concerned with selecting goods, sellers need to focus on price, inventories, and movement of products. In practically all modern retail markets, prices are set by the sellers. These markets are commonly referred to as "fixed-price" transactions (Cassady 1967, Smith 1989).

In wholesale markets, buyers tend to share the concerns of the sellers in the retail markets, which makes sense since they tend to be the same people. Both buyers and sellers are regular participants in these markets, and both prices and good mixes are commonly negotiated, which serves to emphasize the flow and rhythm of the market. Cassady (1967) labeled these markets as "private treaty" markets. Flea market, automobile or house transactions, insofar as they entail negotiating both price and exactly what the exchange will entail are similarly classified as private treaty markets. All such markets in differing degrees tend to highlight the flow and rhythm of the transaction. Similar flows and rhythms characterize all auctions, which include most financial auctions, the exceptions being various private treaty financial exchanges limited to a few participants.

The flow and tempo of auction markets, however, particularly financial markets, tend to be even more intense, due to the multiple bids and offers that constitute most auction markets. Even here there are differences between different types of auctions.

While many "one-of-a-kind" auctions—auctions of particular, often iconic items such as a famous painting, a rare antique, a prized racehorse, or a first edition—often proceed in a highly ordered, often subdued manner, most collectible and commodity auctions, the latter covering financial markets, tend to be turbulent affairs with bid and sometimes ask offers coming in from numerous participants simultaneously (Smith 1989). Moreover, existing prices are continually replaced with new prices, sometimes higher and sometimes lower. As a consequence, all that there is to grasp hold of in such markets is often the market's flow and rhythm. Navigating such markets is very much similar to navigating a vessel in a stormy ocean. In both cases one is confronted by contingencies of varying types. It is this prevalence of contingencies that accentuates the importance of acting sensibly in these situations in contrast to attempting to make sense or to adhere to a given routine. It is also why markets provide a rich site for examining the intricacies of acting sensibly strategies.

There are a number of other benefits which these markets provide that most experimental settings, be they behavioral economic experiments or cognitive psychology experiments, lack.[7] First, markets are inherently longitudinal: they are seldom momentary events, but rather continue over periods of time. As such, they provide sites for observing how given responses generate new consequences that demand new responses. Second, real markets, in contrast to market models of one sort or another, are inherently social entities with particular histories and cultures, and pervaded with a range of social networks that experimental settings and theoretical models lack. Thirdly, most markets provide us with knowing confederates in the form of market professionals, who are not only knowledgeable in the ways of the market, but also, when properly approached, eager to share their understanding, since for them understanding the market is central to what they do. This is itself tied to the fact that nearly everyone is continually seeking to "refine" their own understanding, given the tenuous nature of such "understandings."[8] Profiting from these markets is clearly a prime objective of all market professionals engaged in these markets, but the game component, including how well one plays the game quite distinct from winning, also plays a central role. All of these factors, when coupled with their comparative transparency and accessibility, make these markets not merely testing sites for various behavioral and cognitive theoretical hypotheses, but a rich source for generating significant general behavioral and cognitive teachings.

There is one additional facet to acting sensibly that financial markets reveal. Though acting sensibly entails the most direct exposure to contingencies, it is not inherently a defensive strategy. Some acting sensibly practitioners, including the great majority of market Traders and many kayakers, and even some surgeons,[9] are often eager to engage the contingencies of their worlds in

[7] Prospect theory and the great body of behavioral economics research rely primarily on such experimental studies. Given that these approaches focus primarily upon how participants experience and respond in particular situations, such experimental settings enable researchers to get a better reading on how different participants respond to different situations. It significantly hinders one's ability to get a good reading as to how such actions unfold over time and interactively.

[8] This facet of markets is explored in some detail in Appendix B.

[9] I hesitated for some time to suggest that even some surgeons actually get a lift out of such situations, but there is good evidence that this is the case as Joan Cassell's book *Expected Miracles* (1991) reveals.

contrast to the proponents of making sense and routines who are more prone to circumvent them in one way or another. This is clearly not true of all: some prefer to use their acting sensibly skills defensively. Others, including most surgeons, tend to follow a more neutral path. All of them, however, need to be attentive, sensitive, and responsive to the contingencies they encounter if they are to be successful. They need to have a feel, not only for the crosscurrents that they encounter, but also for their own reactions and responses, both cognitive and emotive. When it comes to the familiar flight–fight response, they are significantly biased toward fight over flight, though as we will see, flight is never dismissed. They similarly tend to be more oppositional than conforming, but again they will often go with the flow. It is all part of acting sensibly.

As useful as markets are in providing examples of coping strategies, particularly examples of acting sensibly, they are not the only sites. Pretty much any activity that commonly entails confronting and dealing with contingencies and the unexpected will have its own share of instances and examples. Some of these activities have an added benefit of presenting simpler and more familiar examples than do financial markets, though their familiarity is generally based more on dramatic—movies and television—exposures than actual exposures. In an effort to enhance the following chapters, which focus on acting sensibly, examples drawn from the two non-market sites introduced in the Preface—sea kayaking and surgery—will be used to augment the market examples. When it comes to market examples, equity option markets will be featured due to the multifaceted situations they are apt to generate. While the origins and nature of the contingencies and unexpected happens of these different sites vary, all three confront a greater number of contingencies and unexpected happenings that cannot be ignored or easily circumvented than most other sites do. An additional reason for including these other two sites is that they present us with significantly different types of contingencies than does the market that speak to the different ways in which the flow of events and accounts impact on each other.

As indicated earlier, the fundamental difference between ambiguities and contingencies is that ambiguities are epistemologically grounded—they exist within meaning systems/accounts of one sort or another—and contingencies are ontologically grounded—they are grounded in a physical reality. There are, however, normally overlaps of sort. The contingencies of kayaking, for example, are grounded primarily in geothermal crosscurrents of one sort or other that generate sudden weather and nautical conditions commonly referred to as "storms." Clearly this is a predominantly natural, physical setting. While the great majority of kayak outings do not encounter such storms, active kayakers can expect to get caught in one or two over time. When they do, making sense of what is happening will be limited to acknowledging that what they are experiencing is indeed a "storm," and identifying a limited number of particularities about it: where the wind is coming from, the "chop" of the waves, etc. They need to focus on what is happening and minimize any attempt to try and make sense of it in terms of the underlying forces in play.

The situation for surgeons is both similar and different. The world that surgeons confront—the human body—is also a natural, physical/chemical/biological setting. Unlike kayakers, however, they can nearly always expect to encounter "disorders" of one sort or another: they are operating because something is not functioning as it should. The "disorder" that they expect to find, however, while commonly a consequence of some sort of contingency, is not itself an unexpected happening. Moreover, in most cases, what the surgeon finds will by and large "make sense." The "unexpected happening" that the surgeon might encounter would be due to the "expected" disorder presenting itself in an unexpected way. In these situations, the surgeon will likely be forced to forgo the making-sense framing she has expected to use and focus on what is happening in a similar way to our kayakers' response to the oncoming storm. Even then, the surgeon is likely to call upon a compilation of knowledge bearing on the dynamics of the particular situation, including whatever surgical actions she herself has taken. Where kayakers and surgeons mirror each other is in their ability to prioritize what is happening when the unexpected, whatever its source, occurs.

Successful Traders require this ability also. The situations that they confront, however, differ in a number of ways from those of kayakers and surgeons. The contingencies that market Traders confront are by and large manmade, if not humanly controlled. They are manmade insofar as price-setting markets are manmade. This contingency–market relationship is not accidental. Markets were created to foster transactional crosscurrents. Where traditional allocation systems of goods and services were governed by cultural and organizational narratives, markets, as noted by Polanyi, provided the means whereby goods and service could be exchanged among otherwise unrelated individuals. Such markets created transactional currents of goods and services constrained primarily by the decisions of the individual buyers and sellers participating in these markets. Though such individual decisions tend to be subject to collective/cultural rules of varying sorts, such decisions were not, and are not, subject to any sort of established governing narrative.

The guiding principle, insofar as one existed, was to allow the market to allocate goods and services according to the market's own determinations, that is the decisions of the individual buyers and sellers, which in many respects functioned similarly to Darwinian natural selection except there was nothing "natural" about it. Unlike the other major social configurations created by humans, such as kinship systems, and religious and political institutions, particular actions of markets are only semi-governed by normative narratives and specified routines. There are shared rules and shared definitions, but within these constraints individuals have a great deal of freedom as to what they can do. In and of itself this would be more of a quantitative difference than a major qualitative difference, but these individual "free" actions are linked together to create a flow of transactions which flow back upon each other, creating yet new currents and crosscurrents. It is not surprising, consequently, that markets were, and still are, commonly considered to be undisciplined and uncivil, and as such not an integral mainstay of society, but rather appendages dedicated to managing corollary activities entailing various material goods. It is similarly not surprising that these markets supported a form of individualism that the more collectively oriented institutions, which are seen to constitute the unifying core of traditional societies, commonly condemn. This comparative autonomy from governing normative narratives and routines also explains the more creative and active manner in which "acting sensibly," in contrast to "making sense" and "routines," copes with uncertainties, to the specifics of which we shall shortly turn. Before doing so, however, a few additional observations regarding apparent similarities between acting sensibly and the other approaches, pragmatism, practice theory, prospect theory, and organizational theory noted earlier, are in order to avoid following some familiar but misleading pathways.

All four of these orientations are similar to acting sensibly in embedding knowledge within situated action. Knowledge in all of these cases is linked to doing. More often than not it is also meant to assist us in dealing with a problem of some sort. The specifics of how this is done and the types of problems the orientations encounter vary. Pragmatism as presented in the works of Pierce, Dewey, James, and Mead tends to be an encompassing account of the origin and nature of how we think and act in general. Where it differs from most earlier philosophical accounts is in seeing knowledge as problem oriented and inherently social, having evolved within the natural, physical world. While the various versions of pragmatism differ regarding particular issues, they share these central themes. What is commonly referred to as practice theory, generally the writings of Giddens and Bourdieu, embraces these pragmatist themes, though seldom references any of their writings, the one major exception being Giddens' attention to Mead. Given the ever-widening split between different academic disciplines, in this case between philosophy and sociology, this is perhaps not surprising. There is the added fact that practice theory tends to focus more on the interplay between the agency of actors and social/cultural structures of varying sorts. In this respect practice theorists tend to be more sensitive to Karl Marx's pronouncement: "Men make their own history, but they do not make it as they please; they do not make it under self-selected circumstances, but under circumstances existing already, given and transmitted from the past."[10]

[10] From *The Eighteenth Brumaire of Louis Bonaparte* (Karl Marx 1852). Multiple publications.

Similar themes also run through what is commonly referred to as organizational theory, particularly the writings of Karl Weick (1979, 1993, 1995), Weick and Sandelands (1990), and Weick and Sutcliffe (2007) under the heading of sensemaking. The social/collective nature of meanings is emphasized, as is the need to respond appropriately to a range of unexpected concrete events that can be expected to be encountered. Prospect theory, as noted earlier, similarly seeks to ground decision making in specific concrete situations. It differs from the other approaches, however, in a number of different ways. First, it privileges individual rather than collective decision making; this is consistent with the experimental methodology it utilizes that explores how different individuals respond to particular situations. It also doesn't explore how individuals respond to unexpected situations, but rather what might be called mixed choices. As such, it is structured more than the other perspectives along the lines of economic modeling, which clearly was a choice made by Kahneman and Tversky. Like the other approaches, however, prospect theory also mirrors "acting sensibly" in privileging how people respond to unexpected and/or puzzling situations rather than generating or utilizing an explanatory account or following a pre-set routine. Though similar in these various ways, all of these approaches differ in an important way. While privileging the concrete, commonly muddled, situations that are encountered, these situations, with few exceptions, are defined and presented in terms of the behavioral patterns experienced, rather than in terms of the underlying causal forces encountered. Behavioral data trumps meaningful experience. One is guided to understand the given situation in terms of similar behavior rather than to identify whatever underlying forces are in play. The issue here is that quite similar behavioral patterns can be generated by quite different causal forces, and similar causal forces can generate quite different behavioral outcomes, depending upon a range of other factors in play. This critique is not meant to ignore the value that such approaches can and often do have. We will, in fact, return to this process in Part IV when we take a closer look at what might be called big data or evidence-based accounts. Nevertheless, they differ in this respect from acting sensibly to which we now turn.

6

Identifying and Juggling Objectives

When you come to a fork in the road, take it.
Attributed to Yogi Berra

Numerous sayings attributed to Yogi Berra, including the one above, are always good for a smile, if not a hearty laugh. More often than not, as in this case, they also contain wisdom, even when you need to dig for it a little. In this case, the wisdom lies in recognizing that when a choice is required, it should be made. The ambiguous nature of the choice in this saying also carries with it an additional dose of wisdom, even if it was not intentionally included. Most of the choices we confront often appear without warning and without any clear direction signs. Moreover, whatever path is selected, it is likely to lead to another fork in the road. Among the multiple forks and paths that we are sure to encounter, some are apt to lead to riches of one sort or another, some to opportunities, some to barren lands, some to circles, and some to dangers. More than a few are likely to lead to, or minimally pass through, various combinations of these states of affairs. In deciding which path(s) to follow, consideration for the resources at our disposal will normally play a significant role. The key factor, however, will more likely than not be what our objective is: where we want to go; what we want to accomplish. Unfortunately, depending on a wide range of factors, our objectives and goals are likely to change, as the following examples would suggest.

A SEA KAYAK OUTING

On a sunny, slightly windy autumn morning, three experienced sea kayakers set out to make a 12-mile open water crossing to an island off the New England coast. Four years earlier, they had made this same crossing with a larger group under the leadership of three professional guides.[1] It had been

[1] Unlike surgery and financial markets, kayaking is not for most a profession. There are a few individuals who make their living from kayaking, but most of them also run a kayak business of

earlier in late summer, but the weather had been approximately the same. If anything it was less sunny. The weather forecasts, they checked three different ones, all projected a reasonably calm day, with sun and modest winds off the ocean onto land. Their kayaks were all well fitted as were the kayakers, who had two GPSs, three cell phones, compasses, extra paddles, safety gear, backup clothing, water and food, nautical maps, and sundry other things. They launched their kayaks at a little past 8:00 a.m. They had plotted a course to a point on the island, which they figured would take them under four hours to reach paddling at a modest rate, with one brief stop at a unmanned lighthouse for a break and snack approximately two-thirds of the way across. They planned to head back no later than 1:00 p.m., which would give them over a two-hour cushion before the sun set as they were still on daylight saving.

For the first hour and a half, all goes according to plan. (Kayakers, like surgeons, also plan. They even practice various routines, like rolling and rescues.) A little after 9:00 a.m., however, the wind suddenly picks up as it begins to blow more northerly. The waves, which were running between 1 and 1.5 feet, are running from 2 to 3 feet, with whitecaps here and there. The sun continues to shine brightly, but clouds are forming in the south and east; some appear to be fairly dark. While the water is rougher than it was, paddling is relatively easy and the increased wind is actually increasing the speed of the kayaks. The conditions, however, have definitely changed, with a wind shift, rougher waters, and a potential incoming storm. The immediate question is somewhat removed from whether they should continue to the island, which was their original objective. The question they face right now is whether they should continue to the lighthouse, turn back, or raft-up and attempt to get a weather update. They also need to determine how each of them feels about what is happening and what they should do.

As just described, the three paddlers clearly need to rethink what their present objectives should be. Each choice brings with it different advantages and different disadvantages. The safest choice might seem to be to turn around, but they are minimally two hours from shore, given that the wind has strongly turned against them. The lighthouse would seem an easier destination, but with a storm brewing, the wind and a real possibility of rain, it is possible that they might miss it. Even if they get there, they could be stranded as it is unmanned and their cell phones may not be operable that far out. It probably would make sense to try to get a more recent weather forecast from where they are—their cell phones should probably still be in range of towers on the coast, but given the location of the clouds and how quickly conditions have changed, it might be naïve to give too much weight to whatever they hear. If they do manage to get through, it may also make sense

one sort or another. The relatively few other kayakers who are paid to kayak are kayak instructors who do so mainly as a part-time additional job.

to stay put for a while in case they decide that they need to call for some coastguard assistance.

Given that the storm is still pretty far away, they might also consider taking advantage of the increased wind at their backs and aim directly for the island. With the wind with them and paddling a little harder, they could probably reach the island in significantly less time than they could make it back to the shore. What should they do? I'll leave it to the reader to decide what they would do. The important point here is not what they might decide, but rather that they need to come to some conclusion, and that conclusion if it is to be sensible needs to be in response to where they are and what is happening. No known and established routine or pre-planned navigation course will resolve their present predicament. What complicates their situation further is that whatever they decide, they will need to continue to evaluate what other options exist at any given moment in light of the conditions at that time. That each is simultaneously at physical risk doesn't make any of this any easier. I know what I would do, but that will have to wait until we confront some of the other components that constitute acting sensibly. But first we need to visit our other two sites.

WHERE'S THE TUMOR?

Tumors come in a variety of shapes and forms and can be found pretty much throughout the human body. Different tumors generally require a range of different treatments. Diagnosing the nature of a particular tumor and deciding how best to treat it is a complex task requiring highly trained medical skills and a range of sophisticated medical tools. Before any decision about operating can be made, a significant amount of making sense is required, associated with a significant number of medical routines. Once the decision to operate has been made, however, acting sensibly assumes dominance. There is one type of tumor that presents a range of uncertainties that relate closely to the task of acting sensibly; namely, a parathyroid adenoma, which is a benign tumor of glandular origin. While there are certain exceptions, in most such cases, especially if the patients are symptomatic for hyperparathyroidism, the recommended treatment is the surgical removal of the affected gland.[2]

[2] Parathyroid adenomas are clearly not my specialty as I'm not a surgeon or medical doctor. I did grow up in a medical household, however, with both parents physicians, and held various hospital odd jobs. The surgical material presented in this text, however, is drawn primarily from one informer who is an experienced surgeon who has specialized in parathyroid and thyroid operations for as long as I have been kayaking. While surgery is explored in this book primarily in terms of a broader interest in contingencies, much of what is claimed here echoes what Atul Gawande (2002) refers to as "complications" in his book *Complications: A Surgeon's Notes on an*

It is here that things begin to get more uncertain. The roots of this uncertainty relate to the fact that there are four distinct parathyroid glands, all of which are located on the posterior of the thyroid gland, two on each side, with one higher than the other. The two higher glands are referred to as the superior glands and two lower as the inferior glands. The diagnosed medical problem of hyperparathyroidism can be due to any one of these four glands, which is the most common situation, to all four of the glands, or to a combination of two or three glands. While pre-surgical imagery, especially a Sestambi scan, can often identify how many and which glands are most likely to be the cause of the disease, the glands at times do not present themselves during surgery as expected. The situation is further complicated by the fact that it is not always easy to find and identify all four glands, given their relatively small size when healthy. An added problem is that the surgeon cannot completely remove all four glands without putting the patient at serious risk.[3] Even if all four glands are contributing to the disease, at least half of one gland needs to be kept.

When all of these factors are put together, a situation is created that requires the surgeon to actively review what he or she can and should be doing. Sometimes the first gland found in what is normally a four-gland exploration will reveal itself to be an apparently diseased gland, which when removed is determined to be diseased. If the follow-up blood test indicates a PTH level within the normal range and a decrease of at least 50 percent, the surgeon can assume that the problem has been resolved and bring the surgery to a close. If the first gland found does not seem to be diseased, or if the PTH level does not fall within the accepted range and has not decreased by at least 50 percent, the surgeon will need to continue the exploration with or without removing the first gland. This exploration normally needs to be extended until the PTH level meets the accepted levels or until three and a half glands have been removed. A particularly difficult situation exists when early indications are that all four glands are contributing to the hyperparathyroidism based on two glands already removed, but where the other glands prove extremely difficult to locate.

Such a surgery can be taxing on both the surgeon and the patient, raising questions as to how long it can or should be prolonged. This, in turn, raises questions as to how aggressive the exploration for the missing gland should be. When the pros and cons generated by these different questions are measured,

Imperfect Science. While many complications are probably linked to mistakes of one sort or another, the thrust of the argument here is that a good number are also linked to contingencies. The degree to which surgeons confront situations pervaded by uncertainties is also revealed in the Cassell book (1991) cited above.

[3] This type of risk like the risks that kayakers confront, differs significantly from the more cerebral risks commonly associated with economic behavior. For a sociologically grounded exploration of such physical risk taking, see Lyng and Snow (1986), Lyng (1990, 1993, 1998).

the surgeon needs to decide which of the various objective options is best chosen. The operation may have begun with a single general objective—to remove the diseased gland(s). What actually occurs once the operation begins, however, often requires the surgeon to identify and prioritize a number of quite distinct objectives. Well-trained surgeons usually begin an operation with a rough picture in their minds, based on scans and other diagnostic tools, as to what they are likely to find once they begin. What they expect to find, however, is never meant to serve as blinkers that prohibit them from seeing what they actually confront, and the different risks that might be present for both the patient and the surgeon.[4]

MANAGING EQUITY OPTIONS

The notion of risk is a perfect segue into our third situation. The risk that is in play here tends to be financial rather than life threatening, but it exists here in a highly developed and sophisticated form. We are about to take a closer look at what goes into trading equity options. The decision to focus on derivatives rather than stocks and bonds or currencies grows out of the qualitatively greater volatility of derivative markets than the markets of the financial instruments to which they are linked. Derivatives are in a very real sense about volatility, volatility in turn is what modern financial markets are all about, and financial markets function today as the central engine of globalization and the world in which we live.

The decision to focus on equity options rather than SWAPs, mortgage-related derivatives, and various non-exchange-traded derivatives, which have received significant media attention in regard to the 2008 financial crash and the various economic troubles that followed is based on a number of factors: First, equity option transactions are primarily exchange based which makes them significantly more visible than non-exchange transactions.[5] Second, the volume and variety of transactions in these markets underscores the growing complexity of financial markets and the consequential contingencies of these markets that play a central part in acting sensibly. Third, as the financial

[4] Unlike the kayakers, the surgeon is unlikely to face personal physical danger, but the same cannot be said for the patient. And while seldom in physical danger, surgeons continually confront serious professional and economic risks.

[5] This visibility is rapidly becoming more opaque as a greater percentage of both equity stocks and their derivatives are being traded in what are called "black pools," which are non-exchange-based trading networks sponsored and used by large hedge funds and banks to enable them to buy and sell in high volume without getting scalped by high-frequency traders (Durbin 2010). While potentially a major issue and game changer, it cannot be seriously addressed here for lack of sufficient quantitative and qualitative information.

derivatives used in generating the Black and Scholes pricing model, which remains the theoretical foundation for all financial derivatives, they provide the best measures for comparing the way these derivatives were initially assumed to be traded and how they are actually traded. While this comparison will be spelt out over the next few chapters, it is worth noting that from a modest to negligible existence in 1975, when the Black, Merton, and Scholes model was formally adopted by the Chicago Board Options Exchange (CBOE), to 2011, worldwide equity option exchange markets' transactions increased to 170 trillion dollars, with approximately a quarter of these transactions occurring in the United States.

So what drives this sort of massive buying and selling of these options? What are the people involved trying to accomplish? The most obvious answer would be what it always is in financial markets, to make money. While in some sense true, this answer misses on both counts. It really isn't what equity option markets are about nor other financial markets either. Financial markets, particularly equity option markets, exist not to make money, but rather to manage and safeguard money that people already have. While making money is all well and good, even for those who have a fair amount to begin with, protecting what one has, limiting one's losses, and offsetting one's position are for those who have money generally more important.[6] That there exists a real need to protect this money is directly related to the prevalence of contingencies common to most financial markets noted earlier.[7]

Being aware and appreciating that identifying and prioritizing objectives in financial markets pertains more to the specific situations and positions that one already holds than to hypothetical new situations and positions is central to grasping what acting sensibly is all about. In surgery, it is being in the middle of an operation. For the kayaker, it is being in a boat in some body of water. For the financial Trader, it means being in the market, which entails having various financial positions. The task of identifying and prioritizing

[6] The differences between the way in which people value wealth that they possess versus the way they value wealth that is not theirs is a critical distinction inherent in prospect theory (Kahneman and Tversky 1979) that counters classical economic utility theory. Whereas Kahneman and Tversky emphasize the impact this distinction has on individual decision making, they basically ignore its role in managing pricing negotiation strategies in auction settings (Smith 1989).

[7] There are, of course, other reasons to put funds into such markets, such as the excitement of being part of the market, meeting people, self-image, etc (Smith 1981, 1999). First and foremost, however, you need to have some funds. Even then, and ignoring the other reasons that might have played a role in directing funds into equity markets, the objective of "making" money is seldom found in simple or pure form: individual objectives tend rather to mirror the overall feel and flow of the market. In highly volatile markets, especially bullish/up markets, objectives are likely to take the form of significantly increasing the monetary value of one's portfolio/holdings. Less bullish conditions, however, might quickly force participants to lower their expectations: to make a little money; to not lose any money; not to lose too much money; and then not to be wiped out.

objectives, in short, is not about getting in or out of the market, but rather managing the positions one presently holds. The difference between having money in the market rather than in your mattress, a saving account, or long-term government bonds is that, as in the surgery and kayaking, your situation requires that you have the skills to navigate the crosscurrents and highly fluid character of these situations. These skills are for the most part acting sensibly skills.

Financial markets, particularly equity option markets, differ in a number of different ways from the two situations discussed earlier. One of the most critical ways is in the greater number and varieties of alternative objectives that market participants confront. This richness of choice is due in large measure to the fact that markets have been constructed by the Traders themselves in a way that gives participants a wide range of choices. While the situations that surgeons and kayakers confront have commonly been shaped in some ways by previous actions they have taken, there is a qualitative difference between what an option Trader has probably done in creating the situation he now confronts and what a surgeon or kayaker previously contributed to the situations they confront. Below is an example of a hypothetical, comparatively simple, situation that a Trader is apt to have created and now confronts. An active Trader at any given time, it should be noted, is likely to have a half-dozen, or more, similar situations.

In this particular scenario, our Trader is long, that is, owns 2,000 SPY shares, which he purchased two months earlier at 110. SPY shares make for a good hypothetical starting point, as they reflect present-day equity markets in numerous ways. Commonly referred to as "spiders," hundreds of millions of SPY shares are traded daily. These shares represent a fund of stocks comprised of literally thousands of companies intended to mirror the Standard and Poors 500 index, which itself is intended to reflect the market values of the 500 leading large capitalization firms in the United States. SPY shares are themselves, however, comparatively new financial instruments, having only existed since July of 1997.[8] Technically they are classified as an ETF, which stands for an Exchange-Traded Fund. Each ETF share represents a share of a large, diversified stock portfolio noted above that constitutes the ETF fund. In being constituted by a diversified portfolio ETFs are similar to mutual funds. They differ in that ETF shares are exchange traded much as any other equity/stock is traded: they can be bought and sold throughout the trading hours when the exchange is open, which with US stock exchanges tends to be from 9:30 a.m. until 4:00 p.m. in New York. Mutual funds, in contrast, are bought

[8] More specifically they started trading on 1 July 1997 under the auspices of State Street Global Advisers, which is the Investment Management Arm of State Street Corporation: NYSE: STT.

and sold through various financial firms and are priced at the close of daily trading based on the prices of the instruments in the funds.

Insofar as SPY shares are exchange-traded throughout the trading day, they lend themselves to option derivatives and have, in fact, given rise to a very active option market.[9] That they reflect the equity market as a whole, can be traded second by second, can be hedged in various ways with options, and traded in large volume, giving them great liquidity, explains why they were described as a good starting point for building a market position. For illustrative purposes they are similarly useful insofar as various trading practices associated with them incorporate numerous "new" factors, such as derivatives, increased volatility, and increased trading volume, which have significantly transformed present financial markets and characterize them.

The few thousand SPY shares of our Trader noted above, serve to establish a market position, but in itself it is a very passive position. If the market as a whole goes up, the SPY shares will likely go up; if the market as a whole goes down, the SPY shares will likely go down. They are not structured to reflect sector movements within the larger market or short-term market changes or changes in market volatility. If one were to use a nautical metaphor, they are financial rafts subject to the tides and currents of the body of water in which they are. They are clearly not able to move against currents, cross eddy lines,[10] or stand still in fast-moving currents as a kayak can. On the other hand, they can be outfitted with "add-on" financial instruments that will in effect equip this SPY raft with a degree of steering and speed control. More specifically, our Trader can hedge his SPY holdings in a variety of different ways by buying and selling various option contracts.[11] Equally importantly, by adjusting his option positions, our Trader can continue to modify his overall position in response to different movements within the market as a whole.

A strong case could be made that, based on the past performance of the stock market over the past seventy years, our Trader would be better off just sticking to his SPY raft. While there have been numerous ups and downs, especially during the past few decades, the Dow Jones index rose from less

[9] It should be noted that insofar as they are traded daily the sponsors of the ETF are required to trade the stocks that constitute the ETF to keep it in line with the S&P index.

[10] Eddy lines are the lines created by two or more currents moving in different directions coming into contact with each other. A small boat, such as a kayak, needs to be repositioned as it crosses such lines or may be turned over. In financial markets, different types of instruments often move in different directions, creating their own version of crosscurrents and eddy lines. It is not uncommon that when equity ETFs, such as the SPY, are rising sharply, that a fixed income ETF, such as the TLT, may be dropping sharply. If one is trying to balance funds in a dropping ETF and a rising ETF, the cost of transferring resources from one to the other can often "flip" one over figuratively, if not literally.

[11] There are a number of other ways that the Trader could also hedge this position, but for the illustrative purposes at hand and to keep matters as simple as possible, the discussion that follows will be restricted to option strategies.

than 100 in the early 1940s to over 12,000 in 2012. There are sound reasons to believe, however, including a market doubling from approximately 750 on the S&P 500 index in April 1997 to over 1,500 in March 2000, followed by a drop back to the middle 700s in October 2002, followed by another double to over 1,500 in October 2007, followed by a collapse to below 666 in March 2009, and another doubling to 1,370 in May 2011,[12] that the steady upwards current that the market rode for the second half of the past century is not presently flowing as it did. There are reasons that go beyond the volatility of the past fifteen years that support this view, including the introduction of new financial instruments, particularly derivatives and ETFs and more recently ETNs, mentioned earlier. Whatever the eventual consensus that might emerge regarding such a market transformation, most market Traders take the transformation as real. For them the market has clearly become a more turbulent arena requiring that they respond appropriately. This has required those actually engaged in trading in the market, rather than analysts and commentators who talk about the market and those who primarily sell market instruments, to hone their acting sensibly skills.

For our Trader, this means not merely augmenting his SPY position with various derivatives, but constantly managing these derivatives in response to whatever particular objectives he has regarding his position at any given moment. As with surgeons and kayakers presented earlier, our Trader is seldom locked into a single objective. He wants to strengthen and nurture his position, but it is usually quite questionable as to whether this is best done by increasing his exposure or decreasing it. Equally, if not more important, is the question of which direction, up or down, currently presents the greatest dangers and/or the greatest opportunities. Moreover, whatever scenario might be in a given moment, it is likely to change from moment to moment. As such, the task is seldom to pick one objective, but to continually evaluate and rank a multitude of objectives. In doing this, it is not so much what one would like to choose, but what choices are possible and reasonable. The decision, especially when dealing with option contracts, isn't simply to do what one wants, either to become more aggressive or more defensive, but how one can and should do so. It is not, as when dealing with stocks, the simpler question of buying and selling, though even then one must decide what to buy and what to sell and how much of each. When one is dealing with options, the choices are much more numerous.

[12] While the mass media tends to focus on the Dow Jones Industrial Index in describing equity/stock markets, the S&P (Standard and Poors) 500 is generally considered to be a better index for doing this, which is why S&P 500 prices are used in describing the massive fluctuations occurring over the 1997 to 2001 period. These figures can be found in various places by simply searching for "S&P 500 Index Chart" online.

In the case presented, for example, our Trader is concerned about a potential short-term, modest drop in the market in response to its recent rise. He is loath to simply sell his shares, however, as they have increased in price significantly since he bought them, moving from a buying price of 110 to a present price of 125, and he would like to hold on to them if possible in order to benefit from the lower long-term capital gains tax to which he would be entitled. There is the added factor that in the rise from 110 to 125, there were two mini-corrections that held at 119, which would suggest that the 119 level is likely to be a significant support point. All of these factors favor holding on to his shares even if their price is likely to drop. On the other hand, a drop of any sort isn't to be ignored. Fortunately, there are various option strategies he might adopt to enable him to strengthen his overall position. He could elect to sell some near term out-of-the-money[13] calls to take in a few dollars per share that would partially offset the losses that a drop in the SPY would create. Or he could elect to buy some short-term puts at the present market, which would generate offsetting profits if the market went down as feared.

The puts would provide better protection if the decline became significant, but they would also cost a few points that would be lost if the drop proved momentary. In contrast, selling the calls would bring in additional funds, which would provide some protection for a modest decline. On the other hand, they could also end up costing money if our Trader has miscalculated and the market explodes up, since the cost of buying back the calls would offset profits of the SPY shares owned. Another possibility would be to put on a put spread below the present price. Rather than merely buying the twenty offsetting puts at the market as in the strategy outlines above, he could sell forty other puts at an even lower price to offset the cost of the puts he would be buying. He would probably be able to get a five-point, one-to-two ratio, spread for no cost at all.[14] This strategy would fit nicely with the 119 support point that our Trader believes has been set. Unfortunately, as explained in the last note, in a major decline this strategy could become very costly.

Whatever our Trader elects to do, it is quite likely that further adjustments will be required later. Let's assume that our Trader decided "less is more" and elected simply to sell 20 125 calls.

[13] An out-of-the-money option is a put with a strike price below the present price of the linked equity or a call with a strike price higher than the present price.

[14] Given that the two thousand SPY shares were acquired a few months ago, at the price of 110, their present market price of 125 would entail a potentially significant long-term gain. A call at the money with two plus months before expiration would likely generate approximately three points that would offset a drop to 122. A 125 put would likely cost a dollar or so more, but it will increase if the SPY drops in a manner that will probably cover half of the loss for the first five points and a greater percentage afterwards. A 1 by 2 ratio five-point put spread for two plus months could probably be done without costs. If the drop is greater than five points, however, the loss from there down will be double.

After a modest decline to 122 over the next few days, an unexpected very bullish labor report comes out and the market suddenly jumps four points, bringing it to 127. More troubling is the fact that the market looks like it is likely to continue up. Here our Trader can simply buy back his calls and absorb the modest loss, or he can try to build a call spread around his short call position to limit any significant future loses and still protect his long-term SPY position. He could do this by buying call contracts below his short position to offset them and sell other up and away call contracts to recoup some of the cost. The overall cost of doing this would be fairly modest, given the money he took in when he sold the call at the money initially, but it would expose him to a significant loss if the SPY price soared. On the other hand, it would generate an additional modest profit if the SPY price remained below the strike price of his call. Even if the price did soar, he would have his original SPY position to cover the call position, though this would eliminate his position and any hope for some long-term gains. Of course, if the market reversed itself and went down again, he would have forfeited the protection that had been acquired by selling the calls in the first place. Decisions, decisions, decisions!

Enough of this for now. The point of this exercise is simply to underscore the extent to which the management of what is actually a comparatively simple financial position requires one to continually identify and prioritize what one hopes to accomplish. There is not only no simple account or routine to follow, but no single objective to guide one's actions. For our Trader, there are additional factors that also need to be watched. In attempting to evaluate the choices available, the Trader will also need to know how each choice will fit with whatever other positions are being held at the time, particularly as to how it might impact on the account's overall margin situation. The bottom line is that in such situations our Trader is more likely to be focused on staying afloat and managing his various positions than reaching any sort of overall evaluation of his position. This requires being highly focused on the multitude of external factors that are apt to affect this position, which brings us to our second component of acting sensibly, recognizing markers.

7

Recognizing Markers

I don't know what I am looking for, but I'll recognize it when I see it!
But then there was *The dog that didn't bark!*[1]

The key difficulty with monitoring markers, as noted in Chapter 5, is that a given marker, no matter how important it might become, is not always there. When it comes to acting sensibly, markers have a tendency to come and go. They tend to exhibit other chameleon-like characteristics. They not only appear and disappear, but also intensify and weaken. Sometimes, as in the Sherlock Holmes case of the dog that didn't bark, the absence of something or of something happening can serve as an important marker. Depending upon their particular contexts, markers can suggest danger and/or opportunities, though warning markers tend to outnumber encouraging markers in most situations. Positive opportunities are desirable and no one wants to miss them if possible, but the crosscurrents and uncertainties that characterize making sense of situations are such that more attention is given to spotting warning markers.

All of these facets are linked in one way or another to the fact that in acting sensibly, markers of importance tend to be enmeshed in a flow of activities. Little is static, making it difficult to get a settled, clear picture at any given moment. The three settings presented in Chapters 5 and 6 provide a rich inventory of such markers. As in Chapter 6, the first two settings will be used to present a number of more manifest examples, followed by a more extended exploration of examples provided by financial markets.

[1] The "dog that didn't bark" is drawn from Sir Arthur Conan Doyle's short story "Silver Blaze," in which Sherlock Holmes notes that the failure of a family's dog to bark indicated that the "intruder" was known to the family and the dog. The first quote gained attention when Justice Steward Potter uttered it in the context of what constituted pornography, but it is commonly used in a great variety of different, everyday settings and has been for many years.

HERE IT COMES!

The significance of markers in kayaking has been implicitly acknowledged in the narratives of earlier chapters, particularly in regards to changing weather. The darkening of the clouds and the increase in the wind would clearly count as such markers. An increase in the number of small whitecaps in what would still have been a relatively calm ocean would probably have been an earlier marker that the weather was changing. An increase in clouds, even before they began to darken, would probably also have caught one or more of our paddlers' attention as indicating a possible change in the weather. The appearance of what might be called "pre-marker markers" addresses two related but distinct aspects of markers that have been somewhat overlooked. The first is that many markers come in various magnitudes, with different magnitudes requiring different types of responses. The second is that the ability to judge the level of any given market and its related significance requires being able to make various comparisons. Such comparisons, in turn, require that one has a model of sort in mind for comparison purposes. Such models are generally the product of two related, but quite different sources; namely, commonly accepted accounts that present varieties of virtual/hypothetical instances and personal past experiences of such markers.

Nearly all surgeries, for example, tend to generate some degree of bleeding. The magnitude varies, however, from patient to patient and from surgeon to surgeon. Whether a particular amount of bleeding will be seen as a marker requiring a response in a given operation will depend on a variety of different factors. Some will be drawn from medical treatises of varying sorts, and others will be drawn from the surgeon's personal experiences including those from internship and residency. In the end, the same amount of bleeding will be seen and treated quite differently. Magnitude counts, but variably.

For our kayakers, the situation is somewhat different. Magnitude definitely does count and needs to be gauged. There tends to be a wide range, however, as to when an action is required, which is primarily grounded in personal past experience. Most experienced kayakers know what they can handle and what they can't. Having said that, most experienced kayakers, as noted in Chapter 6 with reference to the preparation made for their crossing, will normally make use of a wide range of narratives, be they the morning weather report or survival manuals, in determining how to respond in specific situations. Kayaking requires that you navigate primarily by the "seat of your pants," but it doesn't preclude a good deal of preparation, reviewing nautical charts, tides, and scheduled traffic as well as double-checking equipment.

What distinguishes kayakers' situations most is that the crosscurrents and contingencies that they confront have little, if anything, to do with what they have done or are doing; they are not a product or even byproduct of the kayaker. They are inherently external happenings. The crosscurrents of moving water and air that a kayaker confronts are caused by forces that have nothing to do with the kayaker. While these currents are constantly changing in response to various geothermal forces in the atmosphere and ocean, the changes tend to be gradual and mutual as different currents intermingle with each other. They do change, however, and a kayaker needs to be attentive to these changes, which requires being sensitive to a range of different markers. There are times, however, when these changes are not gradual, but rather mammoth and sudden; namely, when very different geothermal atmospheric and ocean currents from previously separated weather systems come into contact with each other along the lines depicted in Chapter 2, "Stuff Happens." The result of such meetings is nearly always a serious storm of one sort or another. Not the type of weather in which one wants to be kayaking. Distinguishing between markers that indicate "rougher water ahead" and "storm coming" is not always such an easy thing to do, especially if you are predisposed to believe that the weather will be fine.

One way to handle encountering such storms would be to simply stay off the water. Unfortunately this is not a real option if one wants to kayak. A more modest choice would be to stay off the water when it is windy and choppy or there is any chance of bad weather, which many kayakers would embrace. The problem here is that weather can change very quickly as the kayak scenario presented earlier indicates. Some kayakers also want to paddle in what might be called choppy waters. Not only can it be fun, but it can also be useful for practicing one's skill in case one unexpectedly gets caught in such waters. When it comes to aggressively pursuing the unexpected and the contingent, kayakers as a group pretty much cover the range. Some try to avoid all contingencies; some are willing to milk each unusual situation for what it may be worth; and others, like the surgeon, pursue their preferred course, barring anything that strikes them as truly dangerous. Whatever their particular predilections, all of them need to be able to read the markers that they encounter if they are to be successful in meeting their own preferences.

Whitecaps and eddy lines are likely to generate different responses, but their numbers and sizes as well as changes in numbers and size require attention. Wind directions, cloud formations, time, and temperature changes also need to be repeatedly monitored, as does any other traffic that might exist. The physical condition of the equipment likewise needs to be monitored, especially when it has been subject to being manipulated in any way, such as being moved, put on, or taken off. Finally, but definitely not lastly, each kayaker needs to be aware of his or her own physical condition as well as that of the other kayakers. It could fairly be argued that these things are always important, but they carry additional weight when they might be subject to unexpected conditions and events. This is especially the case when it is likely that there will be no time or opportunity to consider them if such events or conditions materialize.

In the cases discussed above the great majority of emerging markers point to something "unexpected" or "new" that requires attention. While such attention often also entails some form of action, sometimes all that is required is simply further attention. In sea kayaking most markers tend to require serial attention before action of some sort is required.[2] These differences underscore the importance of differences in both the quantity and quality of various markers. A large rogue wave normally demands an immediate response of some sort; an increase in the number of whitecaps generally needs to be monitored for a while before any action is taken. This difference is due in large measure to how concrete a message a sighted marker is apt to convey. The message of a large rogue wave approaching is clear; an increase in the number of whitecaps is less clear. Such differences are commonly associated with the way a particular marker is framed. Sometimes, as is more often than not the case in kayaking, the marker speaks for itself or some force it reflects. In other cases, as with the increase in whitecaps, it may be unclear exactly what, if anything, is happening. While kayakers confront both of these types of markers and situations, the former are more common. For surgeons, the situation is the reverse, for reasons that will hopefully become clear.

WHERE ARE YOU?

As related in Chapter 6, parathyroid operations require surgeons to determine which and how many parathyroid glands to remove, and how extensive and prolonged the exploration for any particular gland should be. What was circumvented in this earlier discussion was the range of factors that surgeons are apt to rely upon in making their choices, and the various convoluted ways these factors emerge. To further complicate matters, the great majority of these factors may or may not be significant in any given case; in fact, many are likely to play no role at all, being absent for all practical purposes. Given the large number of possible factors, however, more than a few normally require attention. Before they can be dealt with, however, they need to be recognized, and this is not always simple as they are often easily overlooked as they are apt to be embedded in an assortment of biological parts, and/or linked to what would normally be seen as peripheral items.

A partial list of such items in a parathyroid surgery would need to include the following: the four parathyroid glands; various nerves, arteries, and veins; bleedings; and growths or scars within the surgical wound; monitors of patients'

[2] In whitewater kayaking, conditions change significantly more rapidly, which generally means that one is generally required to respond and take some action at first sightings.

vital signs; behavior, condition, and responses by attending anesthesiologist, resident, and nurses; time; room conditions including lights and temperature; and, last, but clearly not least, changes in the surgeon's own mental, physical, and emotional state. There is, of course, no way anyone could manage to actively monitor all of these factors at the same time. Even if one was capable of doing this at a given moment, pretty much all of these factors could be expected to change continually. Fortunately this is not necessary, as in most cases, most of the time, none of these factors are likely to require any special attention. What is required of the surgeon, therefore, is the ability to spot any changes in the status of any of these factors if and when they do require attention. Given the number of different possibilities that might emerge, the only way this can be done is by maintaining a highly alert, but open, lookout.

The surgeon, however, has additional resources to aid him or her in doing this that kayakers seldom have; surgeons, though equally subject to contingencies as kayakers are, operate within a significantly more structured site. Whereas kayakers primarily confront contingencies generated by external forces, the contingencies that surgeons generally encounter are generated within the relatively closed biological system with which the surgeon is dealing. As such, the markers surgeons encounter not only indicate a possible problem, they also suggest an internal source of the problem. A few concrete surgical moments can hopefully give a more grounded understanding of what this entails.

While surgery by definition entails bleeding, efforts are taken to keep it at a minimum, especially in parathyroid cases where such seepage can create other problems. This requires that surgeons remain aware of what might be considered the normal level of bleeding in any given situation. Greater than expected bleeding, like greater than expected wind gusts, quickly draws attention. For the kayaker, this attention often leads to some behavioral response. For the surgeon, there tends to be an intermediary step; namely, trying to determine where the increased bleeding is coming from and why this is happening. Analogous unexpected breathing difficulties engender a similar multistep response. The response to a "missing" gland, that is a gland that is not found where the surgeon expected it to be, is similarly shaped by the encompassing system within which the surgeon is functioning. In such a case, the surgeon is apt to try to use a recognized nerve, the recurrent laryngeal nerve (RLN) being most common, to carry out a further exploration. The surgeon is not trying to follow a pre-given map, however. He or she is, rather, responding to the particular landscape he has encountered in seeking out the missing gland, not an abstract model of it. Encountering an unexpected growth or some other type of abnormality is also likely to cause the surgeon to reconsider the situation and the action to be taken.

What is not found—Sherlock Holmes' famous "dog that did not bark"—is often as important a marker as what is discovered when working within a relatively closed system. For kayakers, absent markers are relatively uncommon, as the seascapes they encounter are continually changing. There are, of course exceptions, such as a "missing" buoy or landmass that would most likely indicate that the kayakers were not where they thought they were. On the other hand, "missing" currents might equally as well indicate significant changes in ocean conditions, as earlier Polynesian sailors/navigators were known to encounter. Within a kayak group the lack of normal chatter may signal greater fatigue, as might more "drifting" than usual. Absent "markers" in the more defined context of the organisms that surgeons encounter tend to be even more significant, giving familiarity with the terrain greater weight. This explains in part why surgeons, by and large, limit themselves to particular anatomic regions, in comparison to kayakers, who commonly seek out new venues to paddle.

Overall, however, surgeons and kayakers have more in common when it comes to monitoring markers than differences. Both, for example, need to employ all five of their senses in monitoring their markers. Both similarly need to continually balance the often conflicting inputs to which they are regularly subject while simultaneously monitoring their own emotional reactions. The multifaceted nature of these inputs not only requires them to utilize all five senses, but also to utilize what is commonly referred to as our sixth sense, the ability to transcend our basic five senses or perhaps more modestly to put all of our senses together in some form whereby the total is more than the sum of its parts. A good number of surgeons and kayakers make reference to the value of such a sixth sense. Nowhere is this more the case, however, than with market Traders, to whom having an overall sixth sense for the market is crucial.

SENSING THE MARKET

Financial markets are clearly places where "stuff happens," and as such places where acting sensibly is a valuable skill to have. In this respect, markets not only echo the two previously discussed settings, but expand upon them in combining various aspects of the two. Market Traders, like kayakers, confront external crosscurrents and contingencies, but more so insofar as they function in the middle of crosscurrents and contingencies, whereas kayakers can elect to avoid theirs.[3] There is an additional component to this in that market Traders, are dependent upon these contingencies and crosscurrents to do what

[3] We are here admittedly talking about Traders rather than merely financial investors, but even with this disclaimer, the thrust of the comment holds, as even the most conservative investor cannot avoid the contingencies and crosscurrents of the market to the degree to which most kayakers can and do.

they do. To be successful, Traders need to have access to these financial crosscurrents (Fenton-O'Creevy et al. 2005). There are some financial advisers and investors who try very hard to stay as far away as they can from such crosscurrents and contingencies, but they also are subject to them, if less so. The great majority of market professionals who are not active Traders, mirror surgeons in not seeking out the unexpected, but confronting it regularly and attempting to respond to it as best as they can.

It is one thing for a Trader to want access to financial crosscurrents and contingencies and the various markers that they generate, but quite another thing to manage to acquire such access. Kayakers need to be paddling before they can expect to encounter markers of any significance, and surgeons need to cut into patients and engage in their surgical explorations before they can hope to identify any markers of value. For a Trader, engagement in the market is less black and white. At one level, most Traders find themselves being inundated from the moment they enter their office or switch on their computers. In a split second they are likely to find themselves exposed to literally thousands of trades occurring every second, coming at them from multiple flashing screens in various colors, accompanied often by noises of varying sorts; they will, in short, find themselves enveloped by the market. For nearly all Traders, however, such a situation would not in and of itself place them in the market. They would still be only observers, much as a kayaker would be sitting on his boat looking out at the ocean, or a surgeon giving a final look at a patient's most recent scan as he or she enters the operating room. To properly experience the market and any markers it might offer, the Trader needs to be *in* the market. They need, to make use of the kayak example, to be exposed to the flows and crosscurrents of the market, which generate most markets' markers. This requires that they have various market positions.[4]

The problem is that there are considerably more flows and crosscurrents in most financial markets than those that a kayaker is likely to confront. As such, the numerous markers that continually appear and disappear are, for all practical purposes, impossible to make sense of by merely seeing them. One needs to acquire an overall sense of what is happening, much as a kayaker needs to feel the wind and the movement of the waves, but more so. The situations with surgeons, at least as they tend to report them, are somewhat different. Though a patient's unexpectedly complex situation can give rise to an overall heightened sensitivity, surgeons' commitment to maintaining control tends to dampen such responses as being counterproductive. The one major exception to this tendency is when the source of concern is linked to a junior/resident surgeon who the surgeon is mentoring. A strong feeling that things are not going well in these situations is likely to move the surgeon to

[4] The need to experience what is happening is discussed in some detail in Appendix B.

take control of what is happening. In large measure this is due to the fact that, while surgeons approach each operation with a highly detailed map of the medical situation with which they will be dealing, they don't commonly have such information about the resident with whom they are working. The maps and weather reports that kayakers rely upon tend to provide relevant information more analogous to that which the surgeon has of his resident than that of the medical condition of the patient: they generally lack specificity and are not sufficiently recent, being grounded in the past. To acquire the type of feel for the situation upon which kayakers rely, Traders also need to be within the situation, which means in the market.

To be in the market, as just noted, means to have a market position. It is only by being linked to such a position that the Trader can experience the flows and crosscurrents of the market as they impact upon his position. In this respect the Trader's situation echoes and mirrors the other two cases where fully grasping markers also requires active engagement. A brief summary of some of the most important markers utilized by Traders will hopefully elucidate this. This requires a fuller account of the specific situations in which our Trader is likely to be. A reasonable example of such a situation would be where we left our Trader in Chapter 6, holding 2,000 SPY shares bought for 110, presently trading at 127, and short 20 SPY125 call contracts sold for three points and now trading for little more than four and contemplating what to do.

In Chapter 6 we reviewed a number of the choices that our Trader might be contemplating in an effort to depict how Traders are continually forced to prioritize their current objectives. Attention was then given to some of the various possible outcomes that the various choices might produce under different conditions. In keeping with the central theme that the future cannot be predicted, the various outcomes were not specified. We rather simply hypothesized that our Trader at that moment was concerned about a short-term, modest decline in the market. While there was nothing wrong with this scenario, it was a highly oversimplified account. Not only, as noted earlier, would the situation described be merely one element in a much more complex market position, but our Trader would be wrestling with considerably more factors than those presented. To skip back, he would also be engaged in monitoring numerous rapidly changing markers related minimally to market prices of a variety of individual financial instruments, various market indexes, trading volumes, market volatility, news reports, and sentiment indexes. It should be underscored here that we are not talking about simply monitoring these parameters, but rather markers related to these parameters.

Prices, for example, are always important, but in attempting to evaluate a particular instrument, recent changes in price might be significantly more important than the actual price. Not only are such things as new highs and new lows worth noting, but price gaps, bid-ask gaps, and the size of bid and ask offers. If one is trading options, various volatility figures and their changes would also be important, as well as the comparative prices of related options. The key point here is that it would be practically impossible to keep track of all of these things, and we are talking about just one set of markers related to one parameter. What a skilled Trader needs to do is recognize changes that deserve attention, such as changes in market direction, major market moves either up or down, or significant market rotations in types of instruments in and out of favor. There exist, of course, computerized programs that are claimed to keep track of all of these things. This is an important issue to which we will return, but it is tangential to the issue under discussion since these programs are not intended to make judgments on the market but to execute transactions in response to particular factors and situations. In short, they are meant to algorithmically incorporate and thereby bypass this process. So far their performance as a whole in this particular area leaves much to be desired. When it comes to squeezing out the few extra pennies on each trade, it is another issue, but again this is tangential to the present discussion.[5]

While price, volume, and volatility have priority in the market similar to that of wind and waves in kayaking, they are not the only important factors. News and sentiment are not that far behind, or again to be more specific, changes in news and sentiment, with the latter, sentiment, normally being of more significance to Traders as it normally subsumes news. For Traders, sentiment indicators reflect how the "public" is responding to the present situation. Traders have a range of sentiment indicators, most of which are linked to the volume ratios of different types of transactions, such as short sales, up-tick versus down-tick sales, puts and calls, and changes in various types of volatility. There are literally dozens of such indicators, and Traders tend to have their favorites, which they watch more carefully than the others.

Many of these indicators have been relied upon for many decades; others, particularly those linked to option trading and market volatility, are more recent. Insofar as volatility, in one form or another, is linked to so many different markers, it is presently the overall dominant factor of the market for most active Traders. If, as noted earlier, J. P. Morgan responded to the question of what the market could be expected to do with the answer, "It will fluctuate," many would today reply that "The market is volatility." The accent and growing importance of volatility has served to underscore the importance of market markers. Most equity option Traders, for example, are normally aware of such things as the established highs and lows of the numerous individual stocks that they are following, as well their recent trading ranges. They are similarly aware of relevant news bearing on their positions. It

[5] The ability to squeeze the extra pennies out of each trade is related to our earlier discussion of the rise of what was called the croupier class of Traders. More later in Chapter 11.

is the markers that come and go, however, such as significant or unusual changes in volatility, the gap in bid and ask prices, differences between theoretical and implied volatility, differences in premiums between puts and calls, differences in trading volume levels, changes in various sentiment indicators, and overall "noise" level, which tend to be most important.

In asserting that these markers both come and go, I do not mean to imply that they actually disappear, but rather that their presence is not noted, given their low profile, reflecting the lack of any unusual activities. Much the same can be said for the ways in which the flow of news, or more accurately the way the market responds to such news is treated.[6] Even the most significant market markers over time are likely at any given moment to remain sufficiently dormant so as not to be noticed. A further complication is that some key markers take the form of the "expected not happening." These markers make their mark by continuing to remain dormant when one would expect them to materialize. The "dog that didn't bark" evidence is an example of this. The absence of any increase in the trading volume or volatility of a stock or even market sector after experiencing an unexpected earnings jump or decline would be a market example.

Equally, if not more significant than the dormant nature of many markers, is the fact that in acting sensibly it is crucial that one not over-cathect on a dormant marker. One must refrain from continually attempting to spot a particular dormant marker manifesting itself, because to do so will often serve to make one miss the emergence of some other marker. The line, "I may not know what I am looking for, but I'll recognize it when I see it," aptly describes the proper orientation when it comes to monitoring markers, and successful Traders try hard not to allow themselves or others to disrupt this studied and disciplined form of inattentive attention. In their case the line might be expanded to include, " . . . and don't try to tell me what it is."

When a marker appears, it still needs to be interpreted within the existing context. The very emergence of most markers, given that most tend to be dormant most of the time, normally indicates a change of some sort; in themselves, however, they seldom tell you the nature of the change. For a marker to be useful it not only needs to be recognized, it needs to be properly interpreted. Ideally, it should indicate something about a probable or possible near-term market change of some sort. Unfortunately, grasping what type of change it is, is often difficult. This is true even for private, personal markers, such as one's own intense emotional response, which are important "acting

[6] News, by itself, like analysts' reports and recommendations do not in and of themselves constitute "market markers" as the term is being used here. Traders cannot avoid giving such items attention, especially when hyped by the media. It is primarily the response or lack of response of the market that could act as a significant market for the Trader rather than the news itself.

sensibly" markers in all circumstances. A sudden adrenalin rush or an increase in one's irritability nearly always means something significant is happening, but it doesn't really tell you what in any particular situation. If all does become "clear" and one has a sense of the type of action that should be taken, there is still the question of exactly what, if anything, to do, which is the focus of Chapter 8.

8

Utilizing Rules of Thumb

What to do? When it comes to actually "acting" in "acting sensibly" is when "rules of thumb" comes into play. Making sense doesn't require actually doing anything beyond thinking. Routines and performances clearly do, but they don't normally require deciding "what to do" beyond initiating the relevant programmed routine or performance. Acting sensibly, in contrast, not only requires engaging in some action, but also determining what that action should be. Fortunately, the types of action required tend to be highly focused and bounded, as they are intended to respond to specific, focused, and bounded contingent happenings. As such, these actions fall under the general rubric of what are commonly referred to as "rules of thumb," which specify specific responses to specific unfolding events. Such rules and actions are generally seen to be more intuitive than most governing narratives, which are seen to be more cognitive and rational.

In recent years a good deal has been written on the differences between the "intuitive" processes governing such actions, and the more "rational and deductive" reasoning associated with making sense and explanatory accounts. Earlier references, including the works of Tversky, Kahneman, and company, have been made to these discussions. While an important and fascinating issue in itself, the cognitive differences between these different ways of processing information is tangential to the present discussion, which is concerned with the ways different contexts, particularly those entailing contingencies, shape and privilege both cognitive and behavioral responses. Comparatively little attention has been given, for example, to the different ways we experience and respond to cognitive ambiguities and sensed contingencies. These different situations differ, not only in how they privilege rational deductive reasoning versus "intuitive" reasoning, but also in how they privilege thinking per se versus action. Ambiguities solicit cognitive responses, whereas contingencies tend to call for behavioral responses that commonly, given contextual constraints, are subject to intuitive or innate judgments embodied in various rules of thumb. In focusing primarily on the different ways of thinking, it is easy to miss the extent to which we are commonly dealing with different types of problems.

"Rational" reasoning and making sense are normally cognitive responses to specified sets of inconsistent, incomplete, or contradictory indicators; rules of thumb and intuitive judgments, in contrast, are usually a part of specific behavioral responses to experienced contingencies that are still unfolding. Making sense is a cognitive effort to impose a cognitive order upon a state of affairs that are seen to be in some sort of disorder; acting sensibly, in contrast, is a cognitively informed behavioral response to cope with an unfolding event that is populated with contingencies of one sort or another. The first situation is for all practical purposes static; the second situation is dynamic and in flux. As such they are experienced quite differently. The first is perceived as a structured event; the second is experienced as a process unfolding. In the first case, we tend to focus upon the pattern of what has occurred; in the second case, our attention is drawn toward what we experience in response to the underlying causal/generative forces that are in play. Whereas the first case lends itself only to be understood, the second case lends itself to intervention; the intervention, however, needs to be immediate or its window of opportunity will disappear.

To put this matter somewhat differently, the two cases do not merely give different profiles to these two different ways of thinking: they reflect a fundamentally different stance toward the possibility of action and the level of "reality" that is prioritized. This difference lies at the core of the debate between what is commonly referred to as normative empiricism and transcendental or critical realism, which was alluded to earlier in Chapter 2 in the discussion of causal powers, open systems, and stuff happening. In the first case, "reality" is the world that we experience as given. Our task in determining how best to deal with this reality requires that we first "discover" its patterns and regularities; that is, we need to make sense of it. In the second case, we do not so much confront "what is given" but rather "what is happening," which entails the underlying causal forces that are in play, generating what is happening. From the shore, one can see the waves; in a kayak on the water one does not so much see the waves as experience them and the wind and currents that are generating them. More to the point, our response is more likely to be directed toward the wind and currents than it is to the waves per se.

Similar contrasting accounts could be given by persons engaged in what is happening and non-participative observers of a hemorrhaging surgical patient or a explosively rising stock market. From a making sense perspective we are dealing with the world of appearances; from an engaged position we are often dealing with an opaque but dynamic world of causal forces that requires some form of behavioral intervention, not to change "what is" or just "was," but what is likely "to happen." This requires confronting the underlying forces that are in play. Given the situation, such actions need to be quickly and easily implemented, which means they need to be simple and familiar. They need in short to be governed by what are commonly refer to as "rules of thumb."

While quite specific and concrete in their own right, the action-oriented rules of thumb we are focused upon are commonly quite abstract and ubiquitous in their applicability. This apparently contradictory character—specific/concrete to abstract—speaks to the multiple causal forces that shape concrete events. This admittedly sounds quite strange, if not somewhat foolish, but we actually confront and engage in such situations regularly. That we don't properly acknowledge such actions and how they operate is due in large measure to the fact that they don't comfortably fit our notions of what is sensible. As they are here being used, rules of thumb are not only action-oriented and hence about what is happening, but about what may happen; they are oriented toward the opaque forces that, while not visible, are nevertheless very real and present. Another way of describing them would be to say that they tend to be heuristic tools; if one doesn't work, it is common to switch to another. Something is generally happening, but what is often unclear, which explains in part why markers come and go and why objectives are subject to change. The changeable flow of events characteristic of these situations favors not only a plurality of objectives and markers, but also a variety of different, often opposing rules of thumb, which resonate with the contradictory maxims presented in the first chapter.

Different rules of thumb tend similarly to require different resources, as do different contexts. Time is nearly always a constraint, as are the range of options available. Accessible equipment, be it a particular surgical instrument, a towrope, a computer program, or another prop of one sort or another may be required. Supplies of one sort or another from margin credit to a special blood type may similarly be required. In many instances, backup assistance might be necessary. As implied above, the decision to apply this rule or that rule occurs within a specific context and in response to particular markers which also require continuous monitoring, including whatever feedback signals arise in response to what one has done or is doing. This often requires one to reverse or at least change gears, if not direction. It is, in fact, often the response to a particular effort that best manages to identify what is going on. Throughout all of this, it is usually also important, due to the ongoing flux of these situations, to keep one's interventions as simple and limited as possible: Don't overreact; don't oversteer; don't drop the reins; don't panic or celebrate.

Given the number of possible factors in play, a few concrete, if brief, examples drawn from the ethnographic sites introduced earlier would seem appropriate. Though examples could be drawn from a wide range of other sites, the three sites introduced above are particularly rich sources of ontological contingencies insofar as they all deal with currents and flows that transcend the cognitive terrains and streams we more commonly attempt to navigate. They cannot be thought or talked away, even when there is a collective will to do so. Our three sites differ, however, in the character of the settings in which the great majority of the contingencies of each emerge.

These different settings endow the contingencies confronted with different facets, which, in turn, tend to favor different types of behavioral responses. These different responses, in turn, generally entail the use of different, often vague if not contradictory, rules of thumb. Moreover, as is normally the case with rules of thumb, the more minimalistic the response the better, as future alternative adjustments are apt to be necessary. The proper timing of these responses demands its own range of skills. The various rules, in short, might be comparatively simple, but it is often difficult to utilize them properly as the following examples indicate.

PADDLE

The saying, "Everybody talks about the weather, but nobody does anything about it," usually attributed to Mark Twain but probably better attributed to his friend and co-author, Charles Dudley Warner, succinctly grasps the world that sea kayakers confront. They paddle on various bodies of water, but it is the weather that determines how the water will behave and the conditions that will constrain their paddling. The weather, or more specifically change in the weather, determines what they can do and need to do, but they have no ability to control or even influence it. On the other hand, if they are on the water it cannot be ignored: it demands their response.

Restated in terms of the themes introduced earlier, the stormy weather reflects and embodies the contingencies of atmospheric and ocean geothermal currents in which the kayakers find themselves. Though these currents are themselves embodied in their own atmosphere/ocean systems, they tend to be experienced by the kayakers as particular external, physical forces impacting upon them. How they fit within the particular atmospheric and ocean systems in which they find themselves embedded, is of little interest to them. In preparing for their outing, the kayakers, as noted earlier, probably spent some time checking tide charts, weather reports, and various maps, but once engaged in paddling it is what they encounter that takes priority and to which they need to respond. This is reflected in the comparatively simple types of rules of thumb that a kayaker is likely to employ in such situations.

Two of the most prominent of these would be the following: 1) In turbulent waters, or whenever your boat is being pulled along by a current, keep paddling. 2) Whenever you feel water pushing at you or your boat being pushed or falling into the water, edge/turn the bottom of your boat toward oncoming water. These actions are not intended to achieve any particular affirmative objective. The objective of both is rather to counteract the external forces that are impacting upon you. The act of paddling serves to move your boat through the water and, as such, to give it both motion and stability separate from the currents that are acting upon your boat. Edging the bottom of your boat toward the oncoming water, whether this oncoming water is coming toward you or you are being pushed toward it as occurs if you are slipping down the face of an oncoming wave, enables you to counteract your movement, as the bottom of your boat serves as a break against your movement.[1] In both of these types of situations, the responses taken are not intended to accomplish anything more than avoiding an imminent danger. There is no attempt here to try and defuse the situation, only to offset the particular threatening forces.

Most other kayak rules of thumb utilized to respond to particular unexpected happenings, such as getting a kayaker who has fallen into the water out of the water; employing a towline to a boat with a disabled paddler; "rafting-up," that is linking boats together to increase stability; cutting line that has become entangled; and various first-aid procedures are also essentially limited defensive responses to particular happenings, not solutions of any sort. They are intended to cope with a particular contingency, not eradicate it. This approach reflects the view that these contingencies, while omnipresent and pervasive, are essentially external to the kayaking activity. Sea kayakers need to be ready to deal with them, but they are not inherently part of kayaking. A strong case could be made that they are inherent to whitewater kayaking as whitewater kayakers by and large deliberately seek out what might be called contingency-pregnant kayaking venues. The difference here revolves around the internal rather than the external nature of the contingencies encountered. Such internal contingencies will be explored when we turn our attention to surgical contingencies.

The contingencies sea kayakers confront tend to be experienced as external, as they are generated by forces that originate in venues that were not expected to impact on the planned outing.[2] Put slightly differently, the kayakers experience the disorder, not as due to any sort of internal tensions, but rather as

[1] That the oncoming water when caught in a wave comes not from the wave itself, but rather from the water toward which the wave is headed is counterintuitive to most people. The physics of this is related to another fact that is caught in a familiar kayaker saying: "In moving water, this would mean streams and fast currents, water moves and waves stand still; in non-moving water, which would mean most oceans and lakes, the water stands still and the waves move." The key here is to realize that in the latter case the wave is created by the wind and is moved by the wind, not the water. It is only the height of the water that changes as the wind moves across it. In the ocean, big waves serve to lift and then drop boats, not push them in any direction. As one is lifted by an oncoming wave, the forces of gravity will pull one backwards as the wave lifts the boat up, which means that the oncoming water will be coming from the downward side not the upward side. In whitewater kayaking, the water is moving and the oncoming water comes from the moving currents. The waves generated in a rushing river are caused by the currents hitting stable rocks or other impediments and, as such, they remain in the same place.

[2] Since all systems are part of more inclusive systems, this is clearly a somewhat arbitrary distinction. The organic subsystems of a distinct organism, however, are qualitatively more related than are the distinct weather subsystems that permeate large bodies of water. The

an encounter with an external force of some sort. While sea kayakers, in preparing for an outing, attempt to inform themselves as best as they can as to the various tides, weather conditions, water traffic, and nautical maps of where they will be paddling, they do not integrate this information so as to generate a systemic picture of the venue. As such, when something unexpected happens, it needs to be responded to individually rather than as one element within a larger situation; not only is the larger situation unlikely to be clear, but the kayakers are also unlikely to have the means to deal with it in any meaningful way. This explains why each of the rules of thumb just noted entails dealing with the particular force that is impacting on them. The situation for the surgeon, as we shall see, is usually quite different, as encompassing venues play a more dominant part.

WHEN IN DOUBT, CUT IT OUT

The vague, minimalistic theme of "Do no harm!" is generally considered to be the prime rule of thumb for all physicians, including all surgeons. For surgeons, however, who are expected to cut into the flesh of their patients, there would seem to be a contradiction of some sort. This apparent inconsistency is resolved when the surgery is put into the context of an already existing "unhealthy" situation. The rule, in this context, requires the surgeon to avoid unnecessary harm in the attempt to mend the existing harmful condition, which normally consists of a failure of some sort in the normal healthy functioning of the patient's body. In these cases, the bodily system is already functioning in an aberrant manner due to internal bodily contingencies related to abnormal growths, foreign impediments, structural failures, and sundry other factors. The surgeon is not subject to contingencies in the manner in which sea kayakers might be; the surgeon is, more like whitewater kayakers, in the business of seeking them out. Like a whitewater kayaker, the surgeon generally has an advantage in doing this that sea kayakers seldom have. The contingencies that surgeons confront are grounded in a more bounded, defined venue. This relates to a significant difference in what might be called the carry-over effect of the preparations that both kayakers and surgeons make before engaging in their activities.[3]

turbulences of a whitewater river in contrast are inherent in the river and generated by the contingencies of the distinct currents fashioned by the contours of the river.

[3] The more defined and bounded world of the surgeon and others who operate in such worlds also contributes to the greater specialization that governs these practices. Sea kayakers paddle wherever they find an appropriate venue. Surgeons tend to specialize in certain more limited areas of the body, as each area entails its own specific interrelated configurations of nerves, arteries, vessels, glands, and bones.

Previously, it was noted that while both surgeons and serious kayakers prepare for their activities by informing themselves as best they can as to what they expect to find, what they actually find takes priority over any such accounts. There is an important difference, however, in the extent to which the information garnered influences surgeons and kayakers. While what is found takes precedence over what the earlier preparation indicated in both cases, for the kayaker much of the earlier account becomes extraneous, since it has been replaced with what is presently occurring. Obviously some things such as distances between points, high tide times, and other basically set factors will hold, but forecasts of the more crucial factors of weather conditions, wave heights, and currents are likely to be dismissed. For the surgeon, the location and condition of what is found will similarly take precedence over what earlier imaging and tests indicate, but the broader, more general, medical/biological accounts will continue to frame what they discover. The surgeon is not so much responding to particular causal forces as he or she is operating within a particular organic sub-system. The system may be skewed in some way and in disarray, but the basic contours of a normal system are generally in place, whereas the kayaker in the midst of turbulence of one sort or another will focus and respond directly to the primary impending force, and bracket the more encompassing turbulence of which it is a part, the surgeon is more likely to approach each particular abnormality within its encompassing system. This is clearly indicated in what might be the prime rule of thumb for surgeons dealing with cancers: "When in doubt, cut it out!"

On its face, this rule of thumb would seem somewhat inconsistent, if not contrary, to the spirit of the first rule of "doing no harm." What this response fails to appreciate is that the "doubt" in these situations refers to "something" that cannot be readily identified and hence is likely to be "out of place": it doesn't belong within the relatively closed system being explored. The surgeon deals with aberrations within recognized organic systems, not isolated oddities or contingencies. The model of the normal, while seldom if ever actually encountered, nevertheless serves as a framing within which the abnormal can be found, identified, and dealt with. Other surgical rules of thumb, particularly those related to surgical explorations are similarly grounded in the pervasive assumption that the abnormality that the surgeon is pursuing is embedded in a known structure, even if the abnormality itself is not a fully known item. Following a recurrent laryngeal nerve (RLN) in search of a potentially abnormal parathyroid gland, or using known blood vessels to lead to other known spots, similarly reflects the extent to which the "abnormal" being pursued is located in a comparatively known environment. It is in situations such as this that the surgeon integrates surgical experience with acquired medical knowledge.[4]

[4] Non-surgical physicians are also clearly focused on the physical status of their patients, but their task is to make sense out of the various "accounts" of their patients that have been generated

Other unexpected happenings, be they grounded in the patient, support staff, or the surgeon, also tend to occur within comparatively known contexts that suggest a range of possible factors that might be in play, which, in turn, suggest various rules of thumb that might be utilized to cope with the particular situation. In dealing with the patient this requires monitoring and managing the patient's various biological systems that constitute the body, each of which is in continual flow. Failures in any system be they related to oxygen, blood, temperatures, hydration, chemical balances, nerves, or anything else at least require attention, and generally some action; this can make for a challenging situation for even the most skilled and experienced surgeon. Fortunately, skilled and experienced surgeons have access to resources to assist them in these situations. They have a range of instruments to keep track of these various systems, and more importantly a very good sense of how they normally function. These resources make it possible for surgeons to better spot what is aberrant in a given case. This is possible because, while surgeons, in contrast to most non-surgical physicians, deal extensively with physical contingencies rather than narrative ambiguities, the contingencies they deal with are grounded in comparatively closed systems. Such contingencies are primarily due to internal disruptions within what would otherwise be a well-ordered comparatively closed system.

The importance of understanding these biological systems underscores the significant part that accounts play, not only in making sense, but also in acting sensibly. It is important to stress, however, that these accounts differ considerably from the great majority of accounts utilized in coping with ambiguities. These accounts are not hypothetical story accounts that revolve around assumed behavioral patterns: they revolve around various causal forces that are normally in play.

The former accounts are by and large supported by collective consensus, whereas the latter are grounded on validated empirical findings. These former accounts generally tend to predict behavioral outcomes based upon the past behavioral patterns; the latter underscore the causal forces that are likely to be operative. Though these different types of accounts often overlap, they are fundamentally different as the "Everybody talks about the weather, but nobody does anything about it" saying notes. The "everybody talks" is grounded in the first type of accounts that attempt to link past, present, and future weather conditions by various assumed hypothetical ties. The "nobody does" is a consequence of the fact that no one is able to control the various known causal forces that actually determine the weather. Based on what is known about a range of these forces, such as various recent atmospheric pressures, temperatures, jets streams, and sundry other factors, weather prognostications

by the various tests that they have been given. In preparing for a surgical procedure, surgeons also scrutinize these accounts, but in the surgical process itself, they directly encounter the patient as a physical/biological system.

can and are made, but weatherpersons, unlike surgeons, are not in the business of attempting to manage such forces. Surgeons are not alone in pursuing such goals. Plumbers, electricians, car mechanics, and others, whose jobs entail checking and fixing comparatively closed causal systems, similarly favor accounts of the latter type, not the former.

Where all of these practitioners differ from sea kayakers and weather prognosticators is that they deal with comparatively closed systems with comparatively transparent causal forces. Even their relatively closed systems, however, are subject to change and morphing, especially if the systems are organic. Such changes can be due to either internal or external impediments, as any surgeon, plumber, or electrician knows, though they tend to be called upon more to deal with internal impediments, as external impediments are normally more easily identified, as is the prognosis and likely treatment.[5] In all of these situations, descriptive knowledge of the system can be helpful, but the key is to find and cope by utilizing whatever rule of thumb seems most appropriate, given the causal powers that appear to be in play. This approach is fundamentally different from the way normatively governed behavioral systems, which are regulated by expectations and past practices, are managed when things go astray. The task then is to modify either or both the governing account or the descriptive account of what has happened in a way that makes them consistent with each other. A fairly similar approach is used when behavioral outcomes fail to conform to models generated by normative theoretical systems, such as those used in game theory. These different framings are noted because they are all used at various times in coping with markets, which makes it necessary to do some untangling in order to extricate how rules of thumb are primarily used within markets.

The first step in this untangling process is to recognize that markets entail aspects of both kayaking and surgery, as they regularly expose participants to both internal and external contingencies. To complicate things further, markets also tend to be pervaded by various types of normatively governed systems. Markets are, in short highly multifaceted, and different practitioners deal with them in different ways. Earlier a number of these different approaches were examined in our discussion of the use of narratives and accounts in Chapter 3 and routines and performances in Chapter 4.[6] In the

[5] A mechanism, be it an outdoor gas grill, an automobile, a coffee machine, a computer, or a lamp that suddenly fails to operate normally is approached quite differently from a similar mechanism that fails to operate normally after being struck by some object. In the former situation, the skill needed to effect repairs is generally required, but in the latter situation, many mechanisms are summarily discarded when the external striking object is seen to have inflicted significant damage on the mechanism whereas in the first case the problem is assumed to be due to some misalignment within the mechanism.

[6] Economic fundamentalists, insiders, cyclist–chartists, and efficient market theorists all tend to have their own "market bibles." Modern-day croupiers do not rely so much upon a narrative

present context, however, we are focused primarily upon those defined earlier as Traders, who constitute a small component of market participants as a whole. What defines nearly all of these Traders is that they see and experience the market as a dynamic, living entity constituted by the changing flows and currents of various types of financial instruments, bids and asks, buys and sells. They are aware of the narratives, superstitions, and practices that pervade the market, but it is the market that allocates and prices its various financial instruments that is their focus. Like kayakers and surgeons, they utilize a range of their own rules of thumb in their attempts to cope with these flows and currents.

CUT YOUR LOSSES AND LET YOUR WINNERS RUN

Market Traders confront a number of distinct currents analogous to the ocean currents, waves, and winds of the kayaker, and the blood, oxygen, and nerve impulses of the surgeon. The most apparent of these currents are constituted by financial instruments of various sorts which have particular monetary value. In equity markets, the main current tends to be of various equities/stocks, but there are also various derivative currents made up of options and futures. Financial markets are constituted by the flows of all of these instruments generated by the totality of transactions/allocations of these instruments. Intertwined with these allocation flows there are transactional-price currents generated by the moment-to-moment changes in the prices of these transactions. Intertwined with both of these flows, there are associated flows of ask and bid prices. In recent years, more traditional corporate instruments have been augmented by numerous equity ETFs and ETNs noted earlier. At any given moment, the numerous screens that report these transactions can be flashing literally a thousand different transactions, which in combination emit a symphony of changing rhythms and patterns. But there are other currents to contend with.

The multitude of transactional currents is accompanied by a range of different informational currents. What is commonly called the "news" constitutes the major informational flows, which are simultaneously being broadcast on numerous television and radio networks as well as in a variety of forms on the Internet. These flows contain reams of data on various companies, market

bible as they do on programmatic strategies of varying sorts. Traders, for their part, have their own favorite books, but these books do not so much tell them what to do as recommend a variety of mini strategies that need to be constructed anew in each new situation along the lines described in the text. Most market analysts, prognosticators, and salesmen, while immune from actually doing anything, tend to rely on a combination of such accounts and narratives.

actions, and national and internal news, as well as a throng of market analyses and recommendations. Interspersed with these different currents, there are innumerable more private communications as well as an unending supply of gossip. Less apparent than these informational currents, but equally, if not more important are what are commonly referred to as the sentiment currents—fear, greed, anxiety, and complacency, which reflect the shifting collective emotive tones of the multimillion number of market participants. Each of these currents, like the other major types, exhibits its own patterns and rhythms. And data derived, or at least claimed to have been derived, from these currents are publicized in a variety of ways.

At any given moment, the overall momentum of these various currents is such that it is simply impossible to keep track of everything that is happening. This limitation is offset by the fact that even if one could, it would be senseless to attempt to do so, since it would be impossible to respond to everything. There is another fact, however, that actually serves to magnify this weight of activity. The great majority of market participants are not perched safely on a hill overlooking these currents: they are somewhere in their midst. Like kayakers and surgeons, they are forced to confront the contingencies of their situation from within. What makes this somewhat more problematic is that the contingent forces of their situations tend to be an opaque mixture of the kayaker's external forces and the surgeon's internal forces. Sea kayakers by and large succeed by avoiding major contingent forces, whereas surgeons are required by and large, though not always, to engage them. Most market participants, including most professional participants, tend to follow the sea kayaker in avoiding whatever contingent forces they can. Traders, in contrast, are generally disposed to follow the surgeon, as their success lies in being able to profit from these contingencies (Fenton-O'Creevy et al. 2005). A key factor in being able to do this is to be able to untangle the multitude of currents that constitute the market and to focus on those that one feels comfortable in navigating. For most this means focusing on the flow of market transactions.

There is a powerful metaphor that nearly all of these Traders respect: "Money makes the mare run!" What this saying proclaims is that any financial market is driven by the financial resources that are inserted and withdrawn from that market. Money can flow into bonds and out of stocks or vice versa. Money can flow into different currencies and the financial markets associated with those currencies. Money can flow out of stock and bonds into stock and bond derivatives. Money can also be withdrawn from all of these markets and left in cash. Knowing a given market requires having a sense as to whether money is coming in or flowing out. At one level this is generally obvious, as money flowing in generally leads to increases in prices, and flowing out leads to decreases. Both of these moves, however, can occur in heavy or light volume. There is also the question as to where the money is coming from and to where it is going. Forty years ago, most money came from individual and institutional investors. Moreover, those professionals who had access to market specialists often had a good idea whether the orders being given were buy orders or sell orders. Today money flowing out of equity might be flowing into parallel equity derivatives. On the other hand, other money that is flowing into a particular stock may merely be hedging a much larger negative derivative bet on the same stock.

In the global markets of today, however, the flow of funds from individual investors and even institutional investors, can pale in comparison to the flow of funds from central governments and between countries. Employment rates, credit balances, saving levels, and government spending are all likely to affect the flow of funds into and out of different types of financial instruments, from bonds and stocks to mortgages, equity options, goods, and services. The numerous varied sources of funds, coupled with the currents of numerous different types of financial instruments, have fostered greater and greater specialization among market practitioners. Thirty years ago most market professionals traded primarily in listed stocks, with a mixture of over-the-counter stocks, mutual funds, and assorted corporate and government bonds. Many still stick with this menu, but most also now include a portion of options. Others, particularly among market Traders, have elected to embrace options more aggressively, often using option strategies in place of previous stock transactions. More recently, Index-based options have also generated a growing following as well as a multitude of new ETFs and ETNs, which usually have their own options. All of these instruments tend to have their own peculiarities, which further foster the increase in specialization among Traders similar to that found among surgeons. In an attempt to keep matters manageable, the concrete examples to be presented will be restricted to a few rules of thumb commonly employed in trading SPY options, which were introduced earlier.[7]

Though SPY shares are not strictly speaking equity shares but rather shares in an index ETF, the ETF is itself composed of traditional equity stocks. As such they are by and large treated much as any established equity share would be treated. This carries over to the way in which SPY options are treated.[8]

[7] I have decided to focus upon SPY instruments because, in addition to whatever other attributes they might have, they best represent today's equity markets as a whole, insofar as they are constituted by a mixture of pretty much every different type of equity being traded. They also have the greatest liquidity, and trade in the greatest volume. In some ways they are today's modern equity market.

[8] The SPY's dual identity has, however, created a few problematic situations. One of the most fascinating is how it has fostered a deadlock when it comes to classifying its options as either equity or index options. The CBOE puts out online, after the market has closed end-of-the-day put-call, ratio numbers of various types of options traded that day. During the day when the market is open, it also puts out online put-call ratios for equity options and index options. SPY options were initially grouped with equity options. Around the beginning of 2014, however, it began to run these options in its end-of-day figures as index options. So during the day they are equity options and at night index options. Throughout most of 2014 the CBOE wrestled with

Where SPY shares and SPY options differ is in the much greater than normal volume in which they trade, which tends to generate tighter than normal markets, that is, markets in which the bid–ask gap is very narrow; in the SPY case normally no more than a penny, with active options within a few pennies, which gives the SPY family of instruments superb liquidity. Insofar as the SPY is structured to mirror the S&P 500 index, it is also endowed with a high degree of market stability. While significant developments of major companies can and do impact on the SPY, it is considerably more insulated from the ups and downs of individual companies, as any given company will constitute only a small percentage of the total value of the SPY. What the SPY is meant to mirror is the market as a whole. As such it is expected to respond positively—increase in price—in response to overall positive economic and business development and news, and respond negatively to negative developments and news.

When it comes to engaging in SPY transactions, the basic rules of thumb that apply in more traditional equity transactions similarly apply, including the following: Never fall in love with your position; have established guidelines as to how you will respond to possible developments; be disciplined and patient, but act when you need to; when uncertain about taking a specific action because of conflicting factors, consider doing half of what you were contemplating; but when in serious, uncomfortable doubt, get out. What all of these rules have in common is that, like the rules of thumb of kayakers and surgeons, they offer general guidance in how to respond to possible unfolding events. There are a number of additional rules that pertain specifically to option trading; these rules pertain primarily to the hedging component commonly associated with option transactions. Options are not only derived from particular instruments, they remain linked to these instruments. They are similarly linked to other options derived from the same underlying instrument. It is specifically these ties that enable the hedging strategies for which options are known. It makes it possible to offset a given option position with another related option position by taking an offsetting position.

A corollary of this is that a large percentage of option transactions are similarly linked transactions rather than a single "buy" or "sell" transaction.[9]

how to resolve this situation for a year. During most of this time they have tried to placate those concerned with the following message run on their intra-day website: *NOTE: This webpage will be undergoing some changes in the near future, including a change in the categorization of data for options overlying exchange-traded products (such as ETFs, ETNs, and HOLDRS). Currently, depending on the particular product, data for options overlying the exchange-traded product may be included in the Index Option or Equity Option data below. Any questions about the data may be directed to the CBOE Help Desk at (866) 728–2263.* As this book goes to press the problem still exists but the note has been removed.

[9] This is not to deny that such single transaction occur regularly. Such transactions, however, are nearly always raw speculations. They entail either buying or selling a highly volatile

In trading options, consequently, the challenge is seldom to profit from a particular buy or sell transaction, but rather to extract a net profit from a group of linked options. In these situations, most applicable rules of thumb are consequently similarly directed at the group of options and related instruments in play. To note a few highly ubiquitous examples: whereas it is a fairly general rule of thumb to attempt to sell options with high volatility and buy them with low volatility, all else being constant, this is practically a prerequisite in a linked transaction. When out-of-the-money short positions, be they put positions or call positions, spreads, or simple naked positions, threaten to move into the money, rolling either down-and-away with puts or up-and-away with calls similarly tends to be "rule of thumb" semi-automatic responses. Reducing short positions when volatility increases and buying volatility when it drops are similarly subject to a form of built in response.

While these response actions and the rules of thumb that govern them are on their surface quite simple, in practice they take various, often fairly complex, forms. These particularities and intricacies, however, are not the issue here. The central point is that these rules, like the rules of thumb discussed earlier, stipulate specific action intended to offset or counteract some underlying forces, rather than an attempt to maintain or support an existing situation. Rules of thumb are not spawned by some sort of governing account or grand strategy. They are not intended to shield and preserve what was, but rather to minimize and deflect possible future damage from forces that themselves may be obscure. The value of such rules depends on whether they work or not in accomplishing these ends. If they don't, they are—with one important exception—easily and quickly abandoned in favor of other, sometimes quite contradictory, rules. The exception, which is nearly always operative in kayaking, surgery, financial markets and everywhere else when it comes to acting sensibly, is "correct mistakes"; it is the exception that proves the rule, insofar as correcting one's mistakes entails that one continues to seek out alternative ways of dealing with it until it is corrected or minimally curtailed. It is sufficiently important and pervasive to be treated as a component of acting sensibly in its own right, which we will now do in Chapter 9.

instrument that is likely to generate either a large reward or a large loss. This is not the road that most professional traders follow, at least not those who plan to be around for a while.

9

Adjusting and Correcting One's Course

In keeping with the last paragraph of Chapter 8, this chapter could have been given the title "Correcting Mistakes" rather than its present, more multifaceted and encompassing title of "Adjusting and Correcting One's Course." The present title, however, by adding the more neutral term of "adjusting" to "correcting," avoids the suggestion of an error of some sort, and the context of a "course" makes more explicit important factors that are indicated in the way the phrase "correcting mistakes" is commonly used. While the adjustments required of us are often corrections insofar as we have actively contributed to the difficulties confronted by previous actions we have taken, there are other times when we have previously done nothing wrong that requires correction: adjustments yes, corrections, no. Sometimes the need to change what one is doing is due to some force with which one had nothing to do. We didn't take a wrong turn: the path did. The "wrong turn" in the path relates to including the context of a "course" in these situations. The particular course we are on is important in other ways. While the challenge in many cases might be to avoid dangerous situations, in other cases the challenge might be to seek out rewarding opportunities. Acknowledging the importance of "the course" we are on has the added utility of sensitizing us to the constraining powers of any given situation, which commonly discourage us from making any sort of adjustment that will threaten the course selected previously. Our tendency is to continue along the path we are on.

The tendency to continue doing what we are doing relates back to the earlier discussions regarding the powers of governing narratives and routines. What we do acquires both types of influence from the moment we start by generating both a narrative and practices that become stronger moment by moment. As a consequence we often find it difficult to deviate from a particular course once we have begun to pursue it. We are more likely to 1) persevere even when there are sound reasons to believe the course is wrong—a practice commonly called "staying the course"—hoping that somehow things will improve, 2) stopping, sometimes referred to as freezing, where we are hoping for a sign as to what we should do next, or 3) turning around and returning to where we began, forsaking our original objectives. Various "mind games" commonly accompany these responses, including ignoring what we are actually encountering, and even assuming that we are not where we are, but where we would prefer to be. People—and there are many—who when lost turn to their map in an attempt to determine where they are, or more likely to place themselves where they hope they are, rather than attempting to locate themselves by seriously exploring their present location and adjusting where they are accordingly. Here we encounter a situation where a likely futile effort to make sense commonly prevails over a much more promising attempt to act sensibly. The scenarios presented earlier provide us with concrete examples of how adjusting one's course can support efforts to act sensibly. The three kayakers we left trying to decide what they should do in Chapter 6 is as good a place as any to start.

A KAYAKER'S DILEMMA: TO CONTINUE, GO BACK, OR STAY STILL

When we left our three kayakers in Chapter 6, they were faced with a serious possible oncoming storm and deciding whether to push on to the island to which they had initially intended to paddle, to head back to the mainland from which they had started, or to hold approximately their present position by rafting-up or heading for a nearby lighthouse. There were advantages and disadvantages to each of these possible choices. The simplest, and in most cases safest decision, would have been to turn around and head home. They were still closer to where they had started from than where they were going. Even if they veered off their course they would hit a landing somewhere. There was also likely to be more traffic closer in to shore and hence potential rescue assistance if that became necessary. The only serious emerging negative to this choice was that the return paddle could become difficult if the shifting wind continued to become stronger. While not sufficient to eliminate it as the course to follow, it was sufficiently troubling to examine the other choices.

Heading for the lighthouse would get them to dry land most quickly. If the storm proved to be modest or it passed, they could determine what to do next. Also, once there, they could try to contact the coastguard, though that might not be possible given the poor reception for their cell phones that far out. The major drawback of heading for the lighthouse, however, would be the possibility that with the storm picking up they might miss it, given its size and the limited visibility. They could also elect to raft-up for a while to get a better reading of the weather, but this would prove to be a mistake if the storm became worse.

The option of simply pushing on would seem to be the most reckless choice in light of what was said earlier about simply "staying the course," especially given that the island was further away than the mainland. The unexpected storm, while the source of the dangers our kayakers confronted, also presented the kayakers with an unexpected opportunity. The strong wind blowing off shore could be expected to reduce the paddling time to the island significantly. Paddling with a strong wind at your back while both fast and fun can, however, also broach a kayak and tip it over. Given that the three kayakers were experienced and skilled, this should not be a major concern for them, provided that they all felt strong and confident. This last point underscores another important factor relevant to acting sensibly, especially in relation to adjusting and correcting course. When it comes to acting sensibly, nothing is more important than determining how you as an actor feel.

In Chapter 6, I ended the presentation of the situation and choices confronted by the three kayakers, by glibly commenting, "I know what I would do." What I left out was that I would "know what I would do" only if I also knew how all of the kayakers felt. If the kayakers—all three of them—felt strong, the most sensible thing that they could do would probably be to push on to the island as quickly as they could. The island was sufficiently large not to be missed, and with the wind they were likely to get there significantly more quickly than they could get back to the mainland. They would also be running ahead of the storm rather than into it. If one or more of them felt not up to par, turning back would probably be the sensible choice, as they were likely to lose the speed advantage of heading for the island, but would have a better chance of finding assistance. The choice of the lighthouse would make sense only if there were reasons to believe that one of them would be unable to reach the mainland without assistance. Two healthy paddlers can usually manage to tow a disabled paddler to land, but in very choppy water just staying afloat can be a challenge. Whatever they elect to do, it would also be a good time to give their equipment a quick check and ensure that anything that they might need was accessible, including a few reachable flares on their decks.

There is clearly something a little paradoxical determining that the best course would be to continue toward their original destination, given that acting sensibly is generally critical of "staying the course." The results in this case, however, were clearly not a product of a "staying the course" mentality: quite the opposite. It was a product of exploring and examining the situation, the forces in play, and a range of possible future scenarios. There was not any reliance upon a previously planned route. Maps, nautical information, and past experiences were utilized, but the governing factors were those drawn from what was happening in the given moment. The route selected might have been similar to the original route, but given the different conditions, it was in fact a different route. Our other two settings provide us with similar yet also different situations.

CREATING A NEW PATH

Surgeons don't so much follow or pursue a course as create them with their surgical instruments in the surgical exploration process entailed in any operation. While surgical courses cannot be viewed in the same way that a kayaker can view various navigational courses through the surrounding seascape, surgeons can usually visualize various possible surgical courses based on their knowledge of the anatomical territory that they are about to explore. Such visualizations are usually shaped to a large extent by the various scans that have been taken of the patient. In most cases, such scans, in conjunction with what might be called normal anatomical structures, enable surgeons to stick fairly closely to the visualized courses that they initially expected to create and follow. There are times, however, when such paths lead to dead ends of varying sorts. When this occurs, the surgeon needs to amend the exploration process in an attempt to access the targeted abnormality in a manner that will enable the intended remedial changes or its removal. The parathyroid surgical scene presented earlier provides a comparatively simple example of such a situation; another somewhat different surgical example will also be presented.

Parathyroid operations, as noted earlier, usually entail the removal of one or more abnormal parathyroid glands out of the four parathyroid glands that most of us have. In many such surgical cases, the surgeon begins with one gland as the primary target, based upon the Sestambi scan that has been taken. (There are also cases in which more than one gland is suspect.) Given the normal location of these glands, two on each side with one—the superior gland—above the other—the inferior gland, such scans commonly indicate which gland(s) need to be removed. If the scan indicates that there is an enlarged gland on the lower right side of the thyroid, the surgeon is likely to begin by exploring the area in which the right inferior gland is most likely to be found. If such an exploration finds an enlarged, abnormal inferior gland in this area, the surgeon will remove it, check PTH blood level and, if the level is now within its proper range and decreased by 50 percent, call it a day. If, however, instead of finding an enlarged abnormal inferior gland, the exploration finds a small, normal inferior gland, the surgeon will need to rethink matters and, depending upon the alternative possibilities, various alternative new courses would be indicated.

The first thing that the surgeon would have to do is account for how the discovered gland appears to be normal given the pre-operative scan. Fortunately, there is a scenario with which an experienced surgeon is likely to be familiar. The enlarged, apparently abnormal gland pictured in the scan is likely to be the superior gland that has descended/migrated down the thyroid into the general vicinity of where the inferior gland is normally found. In order to determine whether this is the case, our surgeon will need to look for the superior gland. Given the hypothesis that it has descended from its normal position, the surgeon will need to explore the area where the superior gland is normally found searching not primarily for the gland itself—if the gland itself is found in this area, it would mean that the hypothesis that it was the enlarged gland and had descended would be proven false—but rather for the vessels and nerves attached to this gland. The next step would be to explore these vessels and nerves in the hope that they would lead to the now descended gland. As with the kayaker, a wide range of previously known topographical data informs the process of adjusting one's course, but the actual course followed is dependent upon what is encountered in the process, rather than upon a preset route.

In the example just given, the course adjustment is required to access a particular target much as course adjustments by kayakers are generally required to reach particular destinations. In surgical situations, reaching a particular targeted abnormality is often not sufficient, given the overriding objective of removing the targeted abnormality. Given their comparatively small size, the actual removal of parathyroid glands is seldom a problem. Removing large thyroid goiters is quite another matter, especially if they have migrated into a substernal location. When this happens, the task isn't simply finding and evaluating the abnormal organ, but finding a way to remove it with minimum collateral damage. The most direct way to do this is often to "crack open" the chest and then remove it through the opening. Skilled surgeons have also been known, however, to create a path whereby they are able to extract the goiter up through the thorax and remove it in the manner in which this is normally done. This requires creating a pathway through which the goiter can be removed, but one that under normal conditions would be difficult to imagine, let alone fashion. Here again we are dealing with behavioral responses that are clearly informed and dependent upon previously held topographic anatomical knowledge, but the particular actions are fashioned by the particular idiosyncratic and unexpected conditions encountered. Market Traders encounter situations similar to both these surgical situations and those encountered by our kayakers. They are apt, in fact, often to be even more complex than those encountered by surgeons and kayakers. The ways in which they adjust their courses also tend to be more multifaceted.

WHAT AND WHEN TO CLOSE AND WHAT AND WHEN TO OPEN?

Where a kayaker's course confronts shifting water, wind currents, nautical traffic, and other assorted moving and non-moving objects, and a surgeon's course is grounded in a variety of flows inherent in living organisms, a market

Trader's course is rooted in the flows of various financial markets, particularly in the ways in which they impact on his or her financial positions in these markets. For a Trader, managing such a course requires continually examining and evaluating these positions, both in themselves and in their relationship to the larger encompassing markets. It requires determining what to hold, sell, and buy, generally in combination with each other; it also requires examining and evaluating one's available resources. It means focusing on what is actually happening, not what might have happened, or what you would like to happen. It isn't an easy thing to do. It usually means accepting some losses that one had not expected, with little positive in return. It is primarily a process of limiting losses as best as one can and maximizing whatever profits present themselves. When it comes to "corrective" actions, less is nearly always better than more. It is important to avoid jumping out of a frying pan only to land in the fire.

Most of the actual actions taken in adjusting one's course belong to the choices described in "Juggling Rules of Thumb"; most such actions are also in response to "markers" noted in "Identifying and Monitoring Markers"; reducing one's position; building upon an existing spread or other type of strategy; buying back part of a strategy and selling an "equivalent" part "up and away" or "down and away"; "taking in" equity or buying equity to offset a position; etc. An adjustment or change in course commonly also entails reprioritizing objectives. There is, nevertheless, a distinctive tone to the ways various rules of thumb are combined when the objective is not simply to respond to some unexpected force as noted earlier, but rather to adjust one's course. This difference reflects the judgment that one is not merely confronting an unexpected force of some sort, but that this force simultaneously serves to redefine the overall context within which one is operating. It is what might be called a second level judgment. To properly appreciate this difference it is necessary to return to some points made earlier.

In earlier discussions of how Traders attempt to manage their positions in utilizing various rules of thumb, emphasis was placed on some of the ways Traders might respond to unexpected, potentially costly price movements. Insofar as these responses generally serve to alter the Trader's market positions, they also tend to adjust the Trader's overall bearish–bullish market profile. In altering this profile, they implicitly also change the bearish/bullish tone/profile of their overall market course. Their new position will be either more or less bullish or bearish. Such adjustments, however, are not necessarily deliberate in their own right. The actions are taken to deal with a specific situation, not the market as a whole. If the Trader's judgment of the market as a whole remains constant, it is quite likely that the Trader will attempt to establish the overall profile similar to its previous form.

There are times, however, when one, or more likely a series of events, will suggest to the Trader that a more fundamental market transformation is occurring that requires a broader rebalancing of the Trader's overall position.

This does not mean that our Trader has elected to adopt a broad strategy similar to those generated by market narratives and accounts discussed in Chapter 3. The situation is rather similar to those encountered by kayakers when a mix of unexpectedly large waves and wind gusts are no longer accepted to be rogue waves and rogue wind gusts, but rather signs of a brewing storm. For a Trader in such a situation, the task of managing a series of particular market actions becomes the task of restructuring an entire position. Here a more detailed description of the possible trades that this might entail for the SPY position presented earlier, in contrast to the trades contemplated earlier, might be useful.

When first encountered, our Trader was contemplating how best to respond to his concern that the market was apt to have a near term minor downwards correction. This concern, it was noted, was built on top of a more positive reading of the long-term direction of the market. Little effort was made then to explicate why our Trader felt this way, primarily because we had not yet discussed how "markers" and "rules of thumb" operate in these situations. Looking backwards, let it suffice to say that the market's previous actions had led our Trader to believe that the market as a whole, and hence his SPY holdings, were likely to continue to rise in price, but that a modest short-term correction was also likely. In light of this combination, a number of future actions were contemplated; initially we elected to have our Trader sell twenty covered calls at the present price that was 125. After the expected downward correction, however, the market rallied sharply and our Trader was contemplating buying back the calls at a modest cost. Overall, however, he had managed to protect his holding on the dip and the subsequent rise of his SPY stock more than covered his loss on the calls.

Our Trader can take some added satisfaction in the fact that if he had bought twenty at-the-money puts to offset the expected correction, he would have been no better off, since he would likely have lost the same amount of money closing the puts down when the market rallied sharply. Having said that, it is also true that if he had put on a put spread, he would not have lost anything, and he could have left it in place and possibly built something else on it later. So let's rewind our time clock and have our Trader selecting the put spread as his choice for dealing with the expected short-term correction. And then let us move the clock forward just a little bit to the point when the market moved down 3.5 point (the expected modest correction), and then a little bit more forward to when the market had come back to just under the 125 point where it had been before the correction. It is here that we want to introduce a full-bodied "adjust course" factor. This factor could take a number of different forms. What distinguishes it from the various minor adjustments presented earlier is that we want it to suggest a much more significant change of direction for the market than was previously the case.

In these situations, much like the major storm formations observed by our kayakers and the dead end encountered by our surgeon, markers are apt to signal a major transformation in the situation. Rather than indicating comparatively bounded and limited happening and forces capable of generating a modest bounded and limited down market that could be avoidable or minimally manageable, these markers indicate that there are forces in play that appear to be part of a more extensive process. In the market, such forces are normally seen to transcend the market itself. In Chapter 8, the market saying, "Money makes the mare run," was introduced. In most cases both the "mares" and the "money" being referenced are what might be called market mares and market money. There are times, however, when market markers and turbulence clearly seem to indicate turbulences beyond normal market boundaries. In these situations the objective is not merely to manage the fluctuations of the market, both large and small, but to manage major tidal changes, to keep with our nautical imagery. It requires adjusting one's course.

So what might this factor be in the situation we are focused upon and what are the Trader's available alternatives? While numerous different scenarios could be imagined, let's keep it simple and historically familiar by introducing a liquidity squeeze of a large hedge fund that gives rise to concerns that serious solvency problems might follow that shake the larger market down over a period of a few days. While this could unfold in a variety of ways, let us assume that as different rumors and reports move through the market, there is a four point drop over a two-day period, followed on the third day by a two-point rally, followed over the next two days by another three-point drop, but in lighter volume than the initial decline. At this moment, our Trader is actually not in bad shape since, with the SPY at 120, his put spread is still within the range that would generate a profit that would offset the losses his SPY shares would suffer. Equally importantly, it is still holding at the 119 level that had been a previous support level. Unfortunately, with the increase in volatility generated by this mini-crash, he can't really close his spread position because the loss generated by the 120 puts he is short have increased more sharply than the profits on the 125 puts he is long, given the two to one ration of his spread. So the question we have is the one we started with: what to do?

In attempting to evaluate what can be done in this situation, there are a number of possibilities that deserve to be considered, including some that were considered earlier. In hindsight, buying the at-the-money put clearly would have been preferable given what happened, but hindsight doesn't cut it in the market. On the other hand, one cannot discount something just because one didn't do it earlier. (Choosing to do something previously rejected can nevertheless be difficult, simply because it was previously rejected.) Selling the at-the-money call would have in hindsight also been equally if not more successful since the call would have generated a real profit and not have added the additional risk that the put spread has. Unfortunately, there is little to be gained in selling the call at the present price. All of these alternatives, however, ignore the central issue; namely, that this is not about how to manage an indicated market fluctuation, but an alert of a high probability major change in market direction. It should be stressed that this is not a prediction of such a change that a governing narrative might generate, but rather a reading of present active forces that would generate such a market collapse. The causal forces exist: it is only the outcome that has not yet occurred. It is this disparity that enables the Trader to take corrective action.

In the previous paragraph two such actions were implicitly identified. Our Trader could elect to sell calls against his SPY position as we had him do in an earlier situation, though given the situation he would probably elect to sell calls with lower strike prices since the value of the initially targeted calls will have decreased significantly. Or he could attempt to buy back the short puts in his put spread, though this would entail significant costs. He could also consider simply selling his SPY shares outright and/or a range of other option strategies. The bottom line in all of these alternatives, however, is that no strategy comes without potential costs. With this in mind, the overriding objective in this case needs to be to adjust the implicit direction of the Trader's position from being mildly bullish to being decidedly bearish, at least for the near future. Given the overall uncertainty of the situation, including the possibility that the market could for various yet unknown reasons turn around again sharply and rally, it is likely that an attempt would be made to maintain as many alternatives as possible while dealing with the immediate problem. One of the common ways this can be done is to take a number of different alternate routes simultaneously. This becomes especially attractive if it is possible to link these different strategies together in some way. With this in mind let's see what might be possible and consistent with the various stated objectives.

The first goal for our trader would be to protect his capital as best he can. This means to protect the funds invested in his 2,000 SPY position. While this position is presently protected by his 20 125 put contracts, this protection will be more than offset at 120 when the 40 120 put contracts he is short come into the money. His 2,000 shares will still be covered by the 20 125 put contracts he is long, but he would be short the 4,000 shares if he is forced to take in/buy these shares to cover his 40 short 120 put contracts. Even if he elected to act earlier and buy the 40 120 put contracts back, his losses would be significant, as the price of these contracts would have increased significantly. He could attempt to protect himself against such a situation by selling his 2,000 shares outright, which would enable him to use the 20 125 put contracts he owns to offset the 40 120 contracts he is short, but this would force him to give up the possibility of any long-term gains on his 2,000 shares. He could split the difference and sell 1,000 shares, leaving him with only 1,000 shares to protect with 10 of his 20 125 put contracts. This would also leave him with a 10 by 40 125/120 put spread. He could reduce this to a 10 by 20 spread that would be safe down to 115 if he also bought back 20 of the 40 120 put contracts he presently has. He could do this relatively cheaply or for no cost if he also elected to sell 10 125 calls against the 1,000 shares he will still own. This would not expose him to an explosive reversal of the market, though it would limit his gains. With his protective put and covered call, his 1,000 SPY shares would be locked down in a manner that should allow him to hold them peaceably for a while. He should also be able to live with his 10 by 20 put spread, given that he could still roll down and away all or part of the spread if the market continued to decline.

As complicated as the above might seem, it is actually a relatively simple adjustment as these things go. The distinguishing facet of the above, however, is not the manner in which the Trader manages to adjust to an unexpected market movement, but rather that it entailed a significant repositioning of the Trader's position. If something like this was actually occurring, the Trader would likely be involved in repositioning a half dozen to a score of such positions simultaneously. Adjusting one's course is a major undertaking in acting sensibly. Fortunately, it is something that is required only rarely as the worlds in which acting sensibly flourishes are worlds in which detailed courses are only rarely plotted out. This is particularly the case in financial markets, where things are understood to fluctuate continually. It is specifically this tendency to fluctuate continually that also makes financial markets a special arena for acting sensibly. Kayakers' and surgeons' worlds on the whole fluctuate less. Though both kayakers and surgeons consequently proceed with a clearer, if approximate, course in mind, they are also cognizant of the contingent nature of their worlds and similarly aware, as we have seen, of their need to be ready to adjust their courses. There are times, however, when even a dramatic course adjustment is not enough. There are times when it becomes necessary to close down or exit a position if one is to survive, both figuratively and actually. This brings us to the fifth component in acting sensibly, "Monitoring and Utilizing Escape Routes."

10

Monitoring and Utilizing Escape Routes

"Monitoring and Utilizing Escape Routes," though the last component of acting sensibly to be addressed, embodies what might be labeled "the prime directive" of acting sensibly. When conditions require their use, all other options, concerns, and directives are overridden. Escape routes serve as survival routes, and acting sensibly is first and foremost about survival. As such it is not surprising to realize that an implicit awareness of escape routes has been built into the four components already discussed. While generally not an explicit "objective," for example, an escape route is nearly always an implicit, fallback objective, whatever other objectives are being identified and monitored. Similarly, in monitoring markers there is often what might be called a "get out" marker. These markers indicate potentially lethal danger that may demand an escape route. Such markers take priority over all other markers. Much the same can be said for their latent powers when it comes to juggling rules of thumb with "escape" or at least "move" rules similarly taking priority when activated. Finally, "exiting" also functions as the ultimate course adjustment insofar as "fleeing" a situation entails abandoning whatever present course might have been in play.

There is a peculiar twist to all of this, however, in that despite how omnipresent and pertinent escape routes are in acting sensibly, they can become easily lost among the various objectives, markers, rules of thumb, and course adjustments that comprise acting sensibly under what might be considered normal conditions, meaning not life and death situations. Accessible emergency escape routes and exits are seldom indicated by the red lights that mark exits in theaters or the blinking lights that indicate the exit paths in commercial aircrafts. They are not designated in situations where acting sensibly is commonly required, such as kayaking, surgery, or trading options for the simple reasons that in these cases viable escape routes and exits tend to change continually as the situations change. Any attempts to pre-select an escape route is, consequently, likely to be counterproductive. In highly ordered systems where making sense is generally the coping strategy of preference, emergency exit signs can generally be usefully posted, but not in the twisting, rushing currents of situations like those often confronted in kayaking, surgery, and financial markets. As a consequence, being able to continually identify escape routes in acting sensibly situations requires ongoing attention to emerging and vanishing possibilities, rather than fixing upon a hypothetical situation or particular place.

In Chapter 9, various concrete course adjustments that a kayaker, surgeon, or market Trader respectively might employ in an attempt to circumvent danger were described. While these examples revealed a common concern for avoiding dangerous situations, the players, be they kayakers, surgeons, or market Traders, were also presented as seeking to persevere as best as they could in an effort to accomplish what they had set out to do. The objective is very different when it comes to monitoring and utilizing escape routes. An escape route is not another course adjustment; more importantly it is not concerned with what was initially planned—quite the opposite. It is an effort to disengage from the activity in which one is engaged as quickly and safely as possible. This desire to disengage is itself based on the conviction that the particular situation is no longer manageable. Moreover, this loss of control is not experienced as due to any limitation on the actor's part, but rather to conflictual breakdowns within the situation itself. The actors in these situations do not confront ambiguities but contingencies.

Given the possible perilous consequences of such situations, it would seem reasonable that anyone so exposed, whatever the activity, would be keen to maintain access to the best exits available. Unfortunately this is often not the case. One, if not the, main reason for this is that acting sensibly situations privilege actual moment-to-moment happenings, rather than the more hypothetical situations into which possible escape routes tend to fall. Within the flow of events that generally characterizes acting sensibly situations, attending to escapes routes requires an abrupt switching of gears. Weighing the various positive and negative outcomes of different actions is no longer relevant. Waiting to gather more recent information or giving matters another try are similarly not acceptable options. The only options that matter pertain to deciding the fastest and best way of exiting the present situation.

There is another factor that often makes it difficult to recognize that it is time to exit. Acting sensibly situations such as kayaking, surgery, and market trading are inherently risky and potentially dangerous situations: there is nearly always risk of significant loss of some sort involved. Danger per se, consequently, is not sufficient to signal that it is a time to exit. It is only in those situations where the danger is seen to be too damaging to be borne that exiting is required. In acting sensibly situations risk of sustainable loss is one thing; terminal loss, be it of life, money, or anything else is another thing. Grasping the difference between these two cases tends to be more difficult in acting sensibly situations than most other situations, specifically because danger and risk are inherent in most acting sensibly situations.[1] Acting sensibly situations also tend to privilege behavioral responses rather than the type of cognitive judgment that is inherent in electing to exit.

Unlike normal course adjustments discussed earlier, an escape route is not intended to put one on a safer course, but to remove one from the scene. It is in essence a surrendering. This is an important distinction that an observer can easily miss. For the actor in question, however, it is a very decisive move. A few examples from the various scenarios presented earlier might help to clarify this difference.

OFF THE WATER!

When it comes to kayaking "Off the Water!" is generally more appropriate than the more familiar nautical catastrophe command of "abandon ship." In kayaking the problem is seldom the kayak; the problem is the overall conditions in which the kayak is located. Equally relevant is the fact that in these situations the kayak is often the most efficient means for getting off the water. In Chapter 9, the course adjustment to head for the nearby lighthouse could be considered in some ways to be an exiting choice. The fact that they still needed to paddle to it and there was a possibility that they might not be able to get there, however, made it at best a semi-exit choice. A simpler and more commonly used example of "off the water" would be the decision to promptly head for land upon spotting thunderclouds or lightning. Such actions would clearly constitute an exit strategy, as they would entail not only getting off the water but also getting out of one's kayak. While such action also requires that the kayakers engage in paddling to shore, in most cases the shore isn't that far away. Even then, if a rescue boat was available, most kayakers would not hesitate to jump aboard and have their kayaks towed back to the shore if a sudden thunder and lightning storm developed. The key, of course, is determining when such a storm is likely to hit.

In the case of our three kayakers whom we left busy paddling to stay ahead of the storm at their backs, the storm had not hit and they felt that they could make it to their original island objective before it did. If they are wrong their chances of getting off the water quickly and easily are not very good.

[1] There is the added fact that many individuals in acting sensibly positions are themselves risk seekers and as such find it difficult to abandon perilous situations. Kahneman has a number of interesting things to say about risk seekers in *Thinking Fast and Slow* (2011), as well as "skills" that nicely catch many aspects of proponents of acting sensibly.

Unfortunately, their chances of doing so were not that good whatever they have decided to do. The only option they have besides getting to dry land in time would be to be rescued by a passing boat. If through fatigue or some other calamity they are unable to push on they will probably be forced to raft-up to gain stability and fire off the flares on their deck. Given the unexpected and sudden nature of the storm approaching them, the coastguard is probably on alert and the flares are equally, or more likely, to attract a rescue boat than a chance encounter. The key point here is that rafting-up and firing flares is not a course adjustment. It is an attempt to exit, with a very real possibility that the kayaks will not accompany the kayakers.

Fortunately, such exiting is not a normal ending in kayaking. What exiting does occur usually takes a much less dramatic form. It is the type of exiting that was dismissed earlier, namely exiting from one's boat. This is not a technique that is likely to improve one's position in a storm, but it is an action that might be required in coping with less threatening situations, such as having one's kayak tip over and throwing you under water. This is seldom an issue for recreational kayakers since they will normally be thrown free of their boat if it does tip over or if they simply fall out of their boat. In these situations the task at hand is normally to get back into their boat, which can normally be done, sometimes quickly and easily, especially if there are other paddlers to help, though at other times with considerable effort.

More experienced kayakers like our three paddlers, however, are seldom thrown out of their boats. To protect themselves from breaking waves that could easily swamp their cockpits, these kayakers generally wear kayak skirts that lock them into their cockpits. These skirts can be released by being pulled loose in a particular way, but without being deliberately released they will hold a paddler in the boat. When experienced kayakers go over in their boats they normally seek first to roll their boat back up rather than exiting, as this can usually be done more quickly and easily than exiting and re-entering their boats. Sometimes even quite experienced kayakers might not be successful in rolling up on their first try; fortunately most kayakers can manage a fair number of tries. Another technique when there are other paddlers nearby is to engage another paddler to assist you in what is called an Eskimo rescue. In these situations the other kayaker presents his or her boat to the kayaker who has gone over in a way that enables the upside-down kayaker to roll their boat up by holding onto the rescue boat. It is only when these attempts fail, that most experienced kayakers will elect to exit their boat. While quite different from the "off the water" exits described earlier, they are similar insofar as they entail ending the efforts to continue doing what one was doing, in recognition of the fact that it is simply too dangerous to continue. That is what all escape routes are for, though they take quite different forms in different situations as the following examples reveal.

WE'RE DONE HERE!

Surgeons do not like to "close up" or "end," a surgery before they have done what they intended to do. As noted above, good surgeons will seek out different ways to accomplish what was intended if they find it impossible to do things in the way they are normally done. There are times, however, when in keeping with the rule of "doing no avoidable harm" they will abort a surgery in process. Kayakers are also hesitant to abort a planned paddle, but doing so only entails forsaking what was intended to be an enjoyable outing. Surgeons are engaged in a very different type of activity. They are commonly seeking to alleviate a life-threatening, or at least impairing condition; failing to due this is likely to extend the patient's harmful condition. As such, the only reason for aborting a surgery is when continuing will cause greater harm than stopping, or have no further benefits. While comparatively rare, there are a number of things that can contribute to such a situation. Discovering that the growth to be removed is unresectable or otherwise inoperable, that key equipment is unavailable, or that the patient is in dire straits, would count as such a situation. At other times it might be the surgeon or another key staff person who is suddenly taken ill without a backup person available to take over. The two surgical scenarios presented earlier as settings for adjusting course lend themselves to two more idiosyncratic situations.

In the parathyroid instance introduced above, the surgeon was unable to find the abnormal parathyroid where the scan indicated it would be. In that case, the surgeon was able to find it by following a different exploratory path. Sometimes, however, missing glands remain missing. This is more apt to be the case when the initially targeted gland is found and removed, but the follow-up blood tests indicate that there is another abnormal gland to be found, or perhaps that all glands are involved. In such a situation, the missing abnormal gland or glands might be any combination of the remaining three glands and, given that none of these presented themselves in the initial scans, the task of finding and examining all three is apt to prove futile, given that any operation has a time limit of some sort. Various factors, including those mentioned above, determine when it is time to abort the operation. The responsibility for deciding when that time has arrived rests with the surgeon, though a concerned anesthesiologist is also likely to have a say in this. The key point here, as in the kayak situation presented earlier, is that once it is decided to abort, the only thing that matters is to exit as quickly and safely as possible. One more try is not an option.

The example of a thyroid operation exit/abortion to be presented is actually more similar to the earlier kayak example than the parathyroid example just presented. This is pointedly underscored by the name associated with the central causal factor in these situations: "A thyroid storm." A "thyroid storm" is the name given to a situation where the thyroid suddenly emits an excess of thyroid hormones, which cause the entire body to undergo life-threatening reactions from palpitations, fever, HTN (hypertension), etc. While such storms are not normally associated with thyroid operations, they can and do occur. When they do, whatever the specific objective of the thyroid operation in process is superseded by the need to treat the toxic conditions created by the excessive thyroid hormones released. This requires the immediate cessation of the operation in progress. Here, as in the kayak situation, the term "storm" denotes a life and death situation that trumps whatever else might have been programmed. It similarly underscores an aspect of many, if not all, acting sensibly situations that commonly deal with coping with causal forces that have life and death consequences. In other cases, such as those associated with financial markets, they often just *seem* to be life and death consequences, though at times unfortunately they actually do have life and death outcomes.

EAT IT OR IT WILL EAT YOU

From the beginning of this section, kayaking and surgery have served as introductory venues for exploring aspects of acting sensibly situations before moving on to financial markets, where matters have tended to be more complicated. When it comes to selecting and implementing survival exits we encounter a similar situation, though the bodily and life threats associated with the kayak and surgical situations are generally not factors in financial survival situations. While people have been known to jump out of windows or otherwise maim themselves in response to major financial losses, their life is seldom at risk in the same way as it is in a nautical storm or under a surgical scalpel. Financial crises, however, can and do have debilitating consequences capable of transforming lives. Such crises, moreover, commonly threaten exponentially more people than those threatened by nautical storms or surgical scalpels.

It is not just the greater number of people subject to these threats, however, that privilege these situations in the context of this book. As with the other elements that constitute acting sensibly, "monitoring and utilizing escape routes" exhibits more complications in financial market situations than in kayaking and surgical situations. The primary reason for this is that the contingencies of financial markets differ from those encountered in both kayaking and surgery as they are more hybrid in character insofar as they entail significant narrative components as well as non-narrative components. This fact has been implicitly recognized in previous sections, but not addressed. It is of particular relevance here because it underscores the difference between "adjusting a course" and "exiting," and the particular difficulty of "exiting" in financial crises. More specifically, the narrative aspects of market contingencies commonly obfuscate their inherently contingent, unpredictable, and unknowable courses. A modified presentation of the trading dilemma presented in Chapter 9 will serve to elucidate this situation.

In Chapter 9, our Trader confronted a declining market that favored a course adjustment of one sort or another. Without selecting any particular such change, a number were described. Financial markets are also subject to happenings that require more than a course adjustment. They are subject to turbulences similar to the nautical storms and thyroid storms which kayakers and surgeons encounter. It wouldn't take that much more to convert the six-point market decline over five days presented earlier into such a storm. Rather than rumors of a liquidity problem for a hedge fund, our new scenario will substitute an unexpected announcement shortly before the opening of trading in New York of a significant trading loss for a major international bank that threatens the bank's solvency. This is followed by an eight-point down gap opening of the S&P, with the SPY opening at slightly over 117 accompanied by delayed openings of numerous stocks. As in the previous situations, the central question is what actions our Trader can take.

The first thing to realize is that this situation differs significantly from the earlier situation even though the present price of the SPY is only three points lower here than in the previous situation. Even at this price, our Trader's 125/120 ratio put spread itself has a theoretical closing profit of two points. If our Trader elects to use the 20 125 put contracts to protect his 2,000 SPY shares, however, the 40 120 contracts he is short will already be three points below their closing price. Unfortunately, given the sudden drop in the market and the time left before the contracts expire, they would presently be priced significantly higher. Given that they were sold when the SPY was at 125 and the market showed no signs of declining, they were sold for approximately the same amount as the cost for the 20 125 put contracts; a reasonable price would have been three points for the 125 puts and 1.5 for the 120s. With the SPY at 117, under the conditions presented above the 120 puts would likely be trading minimally at seven and possibly a few points higher. Whereas the market drop in the earlier scenario would have made only a modest dent in the $30,000 gain that our Trader was carrying holding with his 2,000 SPY shares, the market drop in this case would probably have wiped most of this gain out. It is highly likely that the losses already taken would also require additional funds to cover the associated increase in margin debt. Given that the market collapse presented in this scenario has been a broad-based decline, it could be assumed that our Trader would simultaneously also be facing similar situations in other holdings. More importantly than what has happened, however, is what might yet happen, especially in light of the fact that all of this has happened in just a few moments.

Different things could happen. The market could suddenly reverse itself and regain its previous prices; it could even go higher than where it was. It could just as well, however, continue its sharp decline, which would transform serious losses into catastrophic losses if nothing were done. If this happened, trading could actually be stopped. While this might serve temporarily to stop the decline, it could also be followed by a gap-opening that would do even greater damage to present holdings. Whatever the consequences of such a shutdown, our Trader would not be able to take any action. In light of all of these factors, it is pretty much incumbent on our Trader to take some action. Unfortunately, nearly all of the "course adjustment" actions described earlier are unlikely to work. The market atmosphere would make it very difficult and expensive to attempt to roll his put contracts down and out as the bid/ask spreads would be extremely large, making the cost of his buybacks and the prices of his new sales undervalued. With so many other Traders selling, it would also be difficult to execute the type of multi-leg transactions that would be needed. Action is clearly required; it needs to be adequate, but also easily and promptly executed.

In the situation in which we find our Trader, the simplest exit from his present situation would be to buy back his 40 120 put contracts. The price, as noted above, is likely to be steep. Paying six dollars or more for a contract whose closing value would be three dollars hurts, especially when the difference comes to nearly $25,000 and wipes out most of a gain that has taken months to acquire. He might consider trying also to sell his 20 125 put contracts and his 2,000 SPY shares, as the 125 put contracts would probably have some additional premium in them. With the SPY trading at 117 the 125 put contracts might get nine or more, which would squeeze out an extra dollar over what he will get when he exercises his 125 put contracts. To do so, however, would eliminate the possibility of long-term gains. It would also require him to execute two additional trades when there are numerous other things to be done. Given that exiting is always a draining activity, the simpler the process the better. This is particularly true in market situations as there is another impediment in these situations; namely, a tendency to think that despite all that is happening a suitable course adjustment might yet be available, offsetting the need to exit.

The thought that there might be, or should be, a solution to the situation just presented speaks directly to a major theme of this book; namely, the difference between making sense and acting sensibly; it also speaks to the difference between ambiguities and contingencies and the difference between coping with thought-grounded narratives and accounts as opposed to physical grounded forces and currents. Markets are perhaps the best sites for exploring these differences, given their unique hybrid character.

Both the kayaking and surgical scenarios presented earlier incorporate narrative and thought-grounded components. Kayakers and surgeons function in a meaningful world filled with socially defined items and framed by numerous cognitive and normative accounts. The worlds that they confront, however, are experienced as constituted primarily by physical objects and processes governed by external, non-human, forces. Whatever cognitive and normative structures are in play, and there usually are a number as we have seen, the physical, non-cognitive, non-normative world takes precedence. Where a parathyroid gland is meant to be becomes irrelevant when it is not there. Why the wind has shifted direction and increased to 40 knots is irrelevant to the fact that it has. Situations in financial markets are more complex in this respect. Financial instruments and financial transactions are linked to human interpretations and practices in a completely different way than are wind gusts and glands; this is understandable given that they are social constructions in a way in which wind gusts and glands are not. Having said that, financial currents, resulting price changes, and reaction transactions commonly exhibit a type of independency from cognitive and normative control similar to that of waves and glands. They would not exist without humans, as wind gusts and organic life would, but they also do not remain subject to human control, as do most social constructions. This independency has increased quite dramatically over the past few decades with the introduction of computer-based trading and numerous new, often linked, financial instruments. This quite idiosyncratic situation was underscored earlier by referring to financial markets as hybrid in this respect.

The hybrid character of financial markets can have treacherous consequences for Traders as it can blur exit situations. As noted above there is always a hesitancy to abandon a situation, especially when doing so entails significant, unwanted costs. There are times, however, as in the situations presented above, when it is the only sensible thing to do; these are situations where acting sensibly trumps trying to make sense. A thyroid storm and 8-foot waves generally have the necessary power to convey this message, even to those hesitant to receive it. A market collapse such as the one just presented, unfortunately often lacks this power, as it lends itself to ongoing efforts of making sense that can seduce individuals into attempting further adjustments rather than exiting. More specifically, there is a tendency to see the collapse and transactions that constitute it as understandable, predictable, and hence manageable. Kayakers and surgeons have general understandings as to the forces behind nautical and thyroid storms, but few would claim that they have a clear understanding of the particular forces in play sufficient to enable them to manage them in a given situation. Markets as social constructions lend themselves more easily to fantasies of understanding. For Traders, their long-term survival requires that they be able to recognize when it is time to exit rather than make another adjustment. It is similarly important that they be able to do this as soon as possible since, as depicted above, exiting requires its own expertise. It is also the quintessential example of acting sensibly and rejection of making sense. It prioritizes survival over understanding, action over thought, and what is to come over what was.[2]

As essential as exiting, and all the other acting sensibly steps discussed above, acting sensibly as a coping response it clearly not always, or even usually the best path to follow, as was noted much earlier in this book. In the world in which we presently live the great majority of uncertainties encountered are primarily due to gaps and contradictions within narratives and accounts. In these situations making sense is generally a better coping process than attempting in some way or other to act sensibly. Having said that there is evidence that we are more frequently encountering uncertainties grounded in existential contingencies. This is clearly the case in financial markets where market practices, primarily in the form of trading, are playing a larger role in determining prices and allocation than governing narratives. This has wider significance, not only because of the direct impact that these fast-growing markets have had on other sectors of society, but also in the more indirect impact that they have acquired as cultural forerunners in the ways these other sectors are framed and structured. Attempts to increase "efficiency" by limiting external regulations, favoring "winner-take-all" reward structures, and "keeping score" primarily in financial terms are just a few market-generated principles that have taken hold in other social sectors. Exactly how this will play out cannot be predicted, as it is itself subject to a range of contingencies. It would, nevertheless, be wise to acknowledge such trends and strengthen the acting sensibly abilities we require to cope with them.

There is an ironic twist to this suggestion insofar as it advises that we, in effect, attempt to make better sense out of "acting sensibly," which is itself largely grounded on the principle of playing down "making sense" in coping in favor of behaving sensibly in given situations. While it is true that a major theme of this book has been the growing importance of acting sensibly, it, like any book, is primarily engaged in attempting to make sense of something. This potentially contradictory stance is mitigated somewhat by the point stressed earlier that making sense and routines, notwithstanding the growing importance of acting sensibly, retain their dominant coping status. Any book, including this one, is essentially a "making sense" instrument that is limited to making a case; that is, presenting a narrative emphasizing the importance of "acting sensibly practices" in coping with contingencies. The various vignettes

[2] Elie Ayache in his book *The Blank Swan* (2010) makes a very strong case in response to Nassim Taleb's widely acclaimed book *The Black Swam* (2007) that past probabilities, no matter how broadly presented, are a wrong-headed way to deal with financial markers. His basic claim is that markets are not controlled by the past but are focused upon the future. He goes further by arguing that it is the traders looking toward the future who actually make markets, not past transactions. This is an important book worth reading for those interested in financial markets and sufficiently skilled to follow his presentation.

and scenarios presented in the attempt to make this case are themselves merely part of this narrative. Insofar as they mirror behavioral practices, however, they provide a window into behaviorally confronting and engaging the particular contingencies presented.

Unfortunately, such story-bound encounters are able to provide neither concrete contingencies nor the experiences that they generate. All we actually have is the story. Kayakers, surgeons, and market Traders know this. They similarly know that the only way that the skills required to do what they do can be acquired is by engaging in their particular activities. While making as much sense as they can of what they do and establishing applicable behavioral practices are important prerequisites, without actually being engaged in their respective activities they cannot expect to acquire the skills required. Having said this, it is also true that kayakers, surgeons, and market Traders wrestle with a greater number of uncertainties than most people commonly confront. This raises the question of whether their particular skills are really needed by most others. From the beginning of this book an implicit case has been made that due to a pervasive increase in contingency-grounded uncertainties, they are. A related issue that has not been directly addressed is the extent to which our partiality to making sense commonly serves as a barrier to acting sensibly. Another related question so far circumvented is the extent to which these two approaches might be combined. These issues require greater attention to fully understand the challengers we are likely to confront in coping with future uncertainties. Part IV, "Teachings for Tomorrow," attempts to do this. Chapter 11, "New Teachings of the New Market," presents an overview of the transformations of the past few decades that have completely changed the market in numerous ways. In doing so this chapter offers a more detailed examination of the roots, evolution, functions, strengths, and weaknesses of both making sense accounts of the market and acting sensibly practices. Globalization and technological innovations are shown to have played a significant role in these changes. In Chapter 12, "Learning to Act Sensibly by Engaging and Doing," some strategies for dealing with these developments are suggested.

Part IV

Teachings for Tomorrow

A BRIEF OVERVIEW

This book has been engaged in exploring different types of puzzling and unexpected situations and what the market teaches us about how we might cope with them. In pursuing these objectives we have distinguished between knowledge-grounded, (epistemological), uncertainties and physically grounded (ontological) uncertainties. The first type, primarily in the form of ambiguities, have been attributed to conflicting and deficient meanings and interpretations embedded in accounts and narratives; the second type, referred to as contingencies, have been attributed to physically grounded causal crosscurrents that generate unexpected happenings. In discussing these two types of uncertainty, a recurrent theme has been that while ambiguities, both historically and presently, constitute the majority of uncertainties that we confront, contingencies are becoming more significant, due in no small way to the growth, transformation, and increased influences of modern markets, particularly financial markets. As a result of these changes we need to give greater attention to our "acting sensibly" skills to enhance our ability to better cope with these contingencies. Our pervasive partiality for making sense by relying upon governing accounts of one sort or another, however, frequently noted in earlier chapters, remains a major impediment in doing this.

In recent years the market has implicitly been wrestling with ways of merging making sense and acting sensibly to maximize the positive aspects of both while limiting their negative aspects. The process has been an offshoot of a mix of innovative attempts to master and profit from the market, which has been and remains the central objective of most market participants. These efforts have utilized a whole range of comparatively new techniques, practices, and financial instruments—many, but not all, of which have been noted in different contexts. These include derivatives, ETFs and ETNs, pricing models, algorithmic trading, high-frequency trading, and big data. All of these innovations are tied in one way or another to recent technological and digital innovations and developments, which, in turn, have been linked to the exponential global growth of financial markets. These innovations have not only dramatically transformed financial markets, but also other sectors of societies; in doing so the character of the uncertainties we confront and the ways required to cope with them have morphed in various ways. To understand these developments and the new market they have produced it is helpful to grasp their roots in both making sense and acting sensibly. The bulk of this effort will be undertaken in Chapter 11, "New Teachings of the New Market." Chapter 12, "Learning to Act Sensibly by Engaging and Doing" explores a related but qualitatively different market teaching focused not on doing per se, but rather on how we might better learn "how to do." As with much, if not most, of what the market teaches, it is not so much about having the correct answer in hand as learning how to grasp what the question is.

11

New Teachings of the New Market

This chapter examines a range of market teachings grounded in recent market developments and innovations. In doing so it revisits territory dealing with the origins and functions of both making sense and acting sensibly covered earlier. Where the primary objective earlier was to describe these two practices, our attention here will be more directed toward examining how their strengths and weaknesses have been utilized in recent years. This will be done by exploring various innovative trading strategies that seek to draw upon and combine the strengths of "acting sensibly" and "making sense" by codifying facets, usually judged experientially, of the former into data that can be used in "making sense" accounts. In pursuing this goal we will take a closer look, not only at algorithmic and high-frequency trading, derivatives and pricing models, and a range of new trading instruments noted in the preface to this chapter, but also at the croupiers introduced earlier. The feasibility of predicting the market, an issue that was skimmed over earlier, will also receive more explicit attention. Given that accounts, in the new market as in all markets, tend to play the leading role, it seems sensible to begin with them. Consistent with the last sentence of the overview to this section, we will do so by exploring more deeply why accounts exhibit the pervasive dominance they do, an issue examined in Chapter 5. We will also be doing something else. We will be highlighting many significant ways the market continues to change. So many significant ways that numerous professional market participants question whether this emerging market and the historical market they knew are the same market.

WHY ACCOUNTS REIGN

Accounts reign because, whatever their weaknesses, they are our primary means for making sense out of the "meaningful" world in which we, as minded creatures, live.[1] Without meanings and meaningful accounts human civilization would not exist. Notwithstanding the negative and harmful consequences to which they can and have contributed, they enable humans to live together collectively, cooperatively, and creatively to a degree without which human life, as we know it, would not and could not exist. Moreover, they serve to provide shared meaningful order to what we experience and encounter that serves to lessen what is commonly referred to as existential anxiety or, as it was earlier labeled, "ontological insecurity" (Giddens 1984), and generate a sense of being part of larger collectives. Though such accounts often prove to be both factually and logically inconsistent, they commonly incorporate a wide range of exempting sub-accounts that provide explicatory cover for these particular situations. The bottom line is that established accounts generally are capable of holding their own be it in the market or other situations in providing a plausible if somewhat vague explanation of the matters in question. To put the matter more concretely in the context of the market, such accounts, be they offered by brokers to clients, analysts to the public, or the majority of investors to themselves, manage to solicit general acceptance, even if the related outcomes differ substantially from what the account initially seemed to counsel.

It is one thing to understand the benefits that such accounts commonly provide and quite another to appreciate how they do this, especially when the results often prove to be factually and logically faulty. The answer was alluded to in referencing Durkheim and Mead writings on this matter in footnote 12 of Chapter 2. In brief, the ordering and legitimating power of an account is embedded in the capacity of the language of the account through its meanings to link items together. The comparatively easily grasped meaning of a statement such as "and the mother then cuddled her crying baby," for example, is dependent upon the meanings attached to "mother," "cuddled," and "crying baby." Meanings by their inherent nature serve to link designated items and happenings to a range of possible and probable expectations of other items and happenings. The particular range of other items and happenings that a given meaning is apt to call forth in a given individual, in a given situation, will be shaped by the particular mix of earlier experiences and accounts to which that individual has been exposed.

While most such situations entail a mixture of past experiences and accounts, accounts tend to dominate for the simple reason that the world most of us have personally experienced is significantly more limited than the world we have been exposed to through accounts. Accounts have an additional factor

[1] Over the centuries numerous philosophers and thinkers have attempted to explain the roots of our quite unique mental capacities that frame the world in which we live. The governing paradigm that informs the discussion that follows draws primarily upon the work of George Herbert Mead (1934).

strengthening their influence. While the meanings of both experiences and accounts are collectively grounded, the power of the collective is clearly more apparent and felt in the case of accounts than in the case of past personal experiences. Others, however, also play a central role in giving meaning to our own experiences as Mead revealed; they similarly play an important role in legitimating the meanings generated as will be shown shortly. The collective ordering and legitimating voice of accounts, nevertheless, tend to be more pervasive and apparent. The particular grounds for their powers varies depending upon the type of collective from which the account emerged, a distinction noted and commonly credited to Durkheim, and pertinent to the discussion at hand.

In referencing Durkheim earlier, his claim that shared societal meaning systems were primarily intended to foster social solidarity rather than to be accurate renditions of the world was noted. In arguing this case, Durkheim points out that the shared meaning systems of all early cultures took what we would normally describe as a religious form, which entailed being embedded within a commonly held cultural account of how the world functioned. The beliefs were shared homogenously among members and handed down from one generation to the next. The authority of these beliefs was derived from the authority of the earlier generation. This system underwent a dramatic transformation during what is commonly referred to as the Enlightenment and the rise of modernity with religious upheavals and secularization, industrialization and capitalism, the nation state, and modern science. For Durkheim these changes were due primarily to demographic changes that brought previously isolated societies into contact with each other, which served both to undermine and weaken their traditional beliefs, accounts, and practices and to expose them to other beliefs and practices. This required creating new meaningful accounts capable of fostering social solidarity within existing societies, whilst allowing for ties between members of different societies. Durkheim argued that this was done by legitimating and fostering civil and legal accounts focused upon collaborative practices and contractual obligations, the bulk of which would be grounded in the emerging division of labor. In making this switch, meaningful accounts would be built around and legitimated by shared activities, rather than the words of past generations.

Durkheim's emphasis upon the division of labor implicitly recognizes the role of markets in this transformation. In today's world, markets provide the major ties that link societies together, both internally and externally; they are structures which because of their inclusiveness bind people together more than family, politics, or religion, and thus echo the broker's comment given in the Preface to the effect that market mirrors the game of life. The only other sectors commonly seen this way are various "sports," but the market appears to have surpassed them if everyday metaphors are taken as reliable indicators. What is commonly called "the market," which can be said to represent price-setting markets as a whole, comes, as we saw earlier in Chapter 3, with its own accounts of how it works and how we should behave that function similarly to traditional religious creeds.

The fundamentalist understands the market, and commonly life as a whole, in terms of economic fundamentals that are governed by material outcomes subject to economic, behavioral, and physical laws. The insider sees the market and life primarily in terms of social and political networks, human psychology, desires, and weaknesses. Market Traders, for their part, clearly see the market and life as subject to a range of causal forces, but they tend to be more eclectic when it comes to identifying these forces than are fundamentalists and insiders. The efficient market advocate sees the market as subject to numerous different forces similar to the way the Trader does. He differs, however, from the Trader as well as the fundamentalist and the insider in believing that at any moment the market has already responded to whatever causal forces are in play. The cyclist–chartist differs from all four of these types in privileging the market itself, or more exactly the past patterns of the market, in determining its future behavior rather than external forces. All of these perspectives have their own governing narrative shared by a significant number of market participants. Moreover, all but the cyclist–chartist's narrative embrace modernity insofar as their narrative sees the market as being shaped by causal forces of one type or another.

But things are not always as they might appear. While four out of five of these perspectives frame their narrative in causal terms, only one, that of the Trader, actually attempts to ascertain what causal forces are in play in any given moment. The others are content to hypothesize how various causal forces are likely to have been, are, or will be in play. Fundamentalist and insiders might act on a surprising earning report or information about a large purchase or sales, expecting that these factors will influence the price of a given stock. For the most part, however, especially now when privileged information of all sorts is a dangerous commodity, such events are used primarily to explain why a particular price move occurred rather than to attempt to predict such a move. In this sense they act more like efficient market proponents in embracing causal forces, but refrain from predicting what the market is going to do in the near term. Reference to particular causal events tends to take the form of framing them as data that helps explain why the market did what it did. Their accounts, in short, are structured primarily to placate as described earlier rather than to predict. In contrast, cyclist–chartists, relying upon the overall patterns of the market rather than any particular non-market event, traditionally have predicted future market moves based on their theoretical narratives.

But what about croupiers? Where do they fit in? Croupiers have purposely been omitted so far because their accounts differ from all of the more traditional narratives discussed above. Like fundamentalists, insiders, Traders, and efficient market proponents, they see the market as shaped by happenings occurring in concrete reality. Where they differ from all four of these types is in their skepticism regarding people's ability to properly grasp how past happenings generate future happenings. In this respect they are in some ways similar to efficient market proponents, but in other ways different. Efficient market proponents argue that by the time one can spot a factor capable of shaping the market, the market has already responded to it. The skepticism of most croupiers revolves around the issue of whether it is possible to attribute the proper shaping forces to different happenings. They accept that what actually happens shapes the market, but are uncertain as to how and why. Put somewhat differently, they accept that facts, otherwise known as "data," shape what happens, but they are hesitant about attributing specific causal powers to these facts.

This skepticism regarding anyone's ability to properly read the causal forces inherent in particular happenings constrains them to rely upon how different happenings correlate with other happenings. Such "happenings" data, which have been subjected to detailed correlation analyses, even in massive amounts, is not capable of predicting the future, but in a relatively closed system it is normally capable of generating the probability of various outcomes. While "probability" has been an important theme in the market for some time, the croupiers and the modern market have given it a new status similar to that given to "volatility," which has replaced the more traditional "market fluctuation." The coupling of "probability" with "volatility" is not surprising as both were ushered into the market primarily by the Black-Merton-Sholes pricing model. In combination, "probability," "volatility," and "croupiers" constitute what the modern market is all about. No attempt will be made here to depict the various interdependencies of these three components as to do so is more likely to muddy the water than clarify matters. Since croupiers, or more accurately their perspective, is the issue presently under examination it is better to focus on factors that have helped frame this perspective. A number of such factors, most mentioned earlier, can be identified: The dramatic increase in the different types of new financial instruments noted earlier; the intensification of globalization that has both increased the number of market participants, and also their diversification that has generated additional modifications along the lines noted by Durkheim in governing meaning systems including legal and other types of rules;[2] an exponential growth in a variety of technological innovations, particularly in communication and computerization; and, not surprisingly given this dramatically more complex and

[2] Given all of these developments, one could argue that modern globalization is merely a continuation of the social and cultural transformations that Durkheim explored and explicated in his classic, *The Division of Labor in Society* (1933).

convoluted market, a pervasive increase of skepticism regarding both the capacity of past market practices to cope with market changes and anyone's ability to predict how the market is likely to perform. It has been this changing attitude toward predicting the market that has been the most influential factor in shaping this new market. Not the skepticism per se, which we have seen has always been present, but rather the idea that drawing upon the same changes that have made the market more complex might also provide new means for framing and mastering it.

More specifically by applying the new computer and communicative technologies and their sophisticated statistical, probabilistic, and algorithmic programs to the masses of data being generated by the exponential growth of the market in terms not only of the number of transactions, but also in terms of the numerous new financial instruments that have been introduced, the croupiers and their associates have managed, not only to identify innumerable market/pricing patterns, but also to assign them quite specific probabilities. In doing so, they clearly forsake any chance of grasping the causal forces of critical realism at work but, as already stated above, the only professionals who actually attempt to do this are a subset of Traders. Fundamentalists, insiders, and efficient market proponents talk in causal terms but their accounts are simply narratives. In forsaking even the narrative, croupiers echo traditional cyclist–chartists, but they rely upon established probabilities of a range of correlations of data, not theoretical market patterns.[3]

This lack of scientifically grounded/causal authority should come as no surprise. As we saw earlier, modern science is itself not engaged in predictions except in highly controlled, normally experimental, situations. Modern science tends, in fact, not to be that interested in behavioral patterns of everyday life be it the market, political trends, or even life styles. Social scientists admittedly do seem to get involved in these issues, but normally, at least with the best, they do so primarily post facto and in an attempt to suggest one or more underlying dynamic that appears to have played a significant role in some particular happening. A major reason for this difference is the difficulty social science confronts in managing controlled studies when dealing with issues of broad social interest. When it comes to utilizing concrete physical and behavioral processes in framing expectations of what is yet to happen, the most promising approach remains that of acting sensibly. It is not

[3] Another strategy dependent heavily upon probabilities is what has become known as "Black Swan" strategy (Taleb 2007) noted earlier. While embracing the probabilistic understanding of the market associated with derivatives and their pricing models, this perspective is critical of the probabilities assigned to market "crashes," which are seen to be significantly more likely than assumed. This highly "telescopic" framing favors buying deep out-of-the-money puts, which while likely to expire worthless, cost little and have the potential of rising explosively in a market crash. Other strategies that revolve around volatility instruments such as the VIX and VXX also rely heavily on probabilities, or more accurately, how probabilities are interpreted.

that acting sensibly allows one to do what the other approaches cannot do. Acting sensibly does not enable one to predict the future in the sense of providing an account of what will happen. Acting sensibly is limited to trying to identify the dominant causal forces in play at a given moment and consequently the more probable short-term outcomes; most importantly, it can often spot potentially dangerous outcomes. Acting sensibly is inherently negative toward the type of general account that any sort of meaningful prediction requires.

While acting sensibly cannot function as the basis for a new type of account, it does suggest particular phenomena that offer a basis for a possible alternative: actual happenings. Such actual happenings in and of themselves have limited, if any, explanatory power, but codified into "hard data," especially in large numbers, and augmented by appropriate quantitative probabilistic theory and innovative technology, they can acquire a strong voice. This is what has occurred in what I have labeled the "new market." To reiterate what has already been noted in describing the perspectives of croupiers, new technology enabled, not only the recording of multiple facets of the ever-growing flow of market transactions, but also the correlation of these facets with each other and other data in numerous different ways to create data-based, quantitative, programmable accounts. The label of "big data" noted earlier is often used in reference to these accounts.[4] While other arenas have also generated similar accounts in recent years, the market has been a leader in doing so due in large measure to the fact that market transactions are structured to lend themselves to quantitative description in both price and trading volume, the market's two most significant parameters.

In codifying the flow of these transactions, facets of them are lost; more specifically they are stripped of the "feel" and "environmental context" that market Traders have traditionally relied upon in interpreting them. Doing so, however, gives them a more universal identity that enables less "hands-on" market practitioners to utilize them. More accurately, it enables the latter to utilize this data in terms of the range of sophisticated correlational and probabilistic programmable accounts in which it is embedded. Many, if not most, of these accounts lend themselves to algorithmic programming capable of recognizing and identifying a range of market patterns, both normal and abnormal. It is unnecessary to understand why or how any particular such judgment is made, only that it is consistent with patterns identified in the assembled data. Another plus is that this can be done in a split second,

[4] An excellent overview of these accounts and their associated practices is provided in a book by Viktor Mayer-Schonberger and Kenneth Cukier entitled *Big Data: A Revolution That Will Transform How We Live, Work, and Think* (2013). It approaches this issue from a different, if overlapping, direction than the approach taken here. Another term being used to describe such accounts, primarily in medicine, is "evidence-based."

enabling what is commonly called "high frequency trading."[5] Perhaps most promising is the fact that it is possible to create a range of heuristic models and compare different models with actual performances in attempts to fine-tune them and construct new models. It helps to have sharp and advanced mathematical and programming skills to do this, which explains why mathematicians and engineers tend today to be the most sought-after hirees in the market; thirty years ago and before an Ivy League liberal arts diploma was what counted.

Given the broad and varied capabilities of these sophisticated new types of quantitative programmable accounts, it is not surprising that they presently dominate the market. They have become the "alpha" accounts, trumping fundamentalists, insiders, traditional cyclist–chartists, efficient market proponents and even traditional market action Traders. The croupiers have not been included because, as has previously been indicated, these are the types of accounts that most croupiers rely upon. This partnership speaks, however, to another facet of these new accounts that is of major importance; namely, the issue of "timing," particularly as it applies to predicting future market behavior. It is a fairly complex issue as it relates to high-frequency trading, derivatives, other types of new financial instruments including ETFs, market volatility, and increased market trading volume, but it has had a sufficiently significant impact on the market to merit some focused attention.

While the emergence of new alpha market accounts described above was dependent upon a number of different factors, as with practically all market developments the prime objective was to increase earnings. These quantitative programmable accounts clearly managed to do this by supporting a range of new financial instruments and increasing trading volume. Their ability to do this, however, was tied to the implicit claim that these new accounts, by relying upon hard data and past market action rather than assumed causal forces, traditional theoretical models, and hunches, could and would trump all other accounts when it came to predicting how the market would perform.[6] Given that their predictions would be based upon a deep grounding in a plentiful source of past behavioral patterns, in contrast to hypothetical causal models or "touchy-feely" encountered causal forces, their claim would appear to have

[5] For a sound overview of "high-frequency trading" I would re-recommend Durbin (2010) noted earlier in a slightly different context. For a fascinating follow-up to its impact on the market and a novel response, see Lewis (2014)—*Flash Boys: A Wall Street Revolt.*

[6] Links based upon simple correlations of one sort or another constitute the second major component of the perspective of "big data." Correlations have historically been treated primarily as indicators of possible "causal" links. In and by themselves, correlations tended to be seen as impostors of any sort of "true" links. In modern big data and evidence-based framings, they are commonly seen as trumping causality when it comes to predicting future outcomes (Mayer-Schonberger and Cukier 2013), which clearly deviates from the objectives of modern science, though modern science does tend to have strong reservations when it comes to the unsupported and often naïve assumptions of causality of most making sense accounts.

significant merit.[7] Having said that, documenting this superiority is not that simple. Part of the difficulty is due to the fact that the various traditional types of accounts presented earlier tend to differ considerably in what they predict. In cases where the new accounts might outperform one or more of these traditional accounts in one respect, they may not outperform some others in some other respect. The old accounts, as we saw earlier, are not ready to roll over and play dead. Unfortunately, there is a more significant problem when it comes to predictive powers discussed earlier. The predictive powers of even correctly rendered past patterns are dependent upon a high degree of closure of the system in question. The market, as with nearly all price-setting markets, is inherently an open system. This does not mean that the predictive powers of these new accounts may not be better than those of more traditional accounts, but it poses serious questions.

This problem has not been missed by the market or the proponents of these accounts. Though there exist a number of market participants who are immersed in attempts to formulate accounts and programs that will enable them to select financial instruments that will outperform the overall market, they are few and far between. The great majority of the proponents of these new accounts recognize that the open system nature of the market limits their ability to reach out into the future. What their accounts can do is guide their moment-to-moment transactions with an eye to the future. How far into the future is itself another question. Not surprisingly, in light of the fact that all else being the same the more time the higher probability of change, the "sweet spot" when it comes to future predictions is governed by the principle of "the sooner the better." This brings us back to and explains our croupiers. While these new accounts generally more than match more traditional accounts in predicting future pricing, it is their precision in predicting near-term pricing that is their basic strength. What they have been used primarily to do, consequently, is to finely tune the particular ranges of short-term volatility that different instruments are likely to generate. While this does not support taking long-term positions, since it has little to say about significant price changes over the long term, it does enable one to predict short-term trading ranges for different instruments that are sufficiently narrow to fall within normal bid/ask spreads.

This is what the great majority of high-frequency trading does. It enables one to skim a penny or half penny from a trade by buying or selling an instrument for slightly less or more than anyone else will at that moment, and

[7] While any given "causal force" encounter is by definition experienced by a given individual, the interpretation attributed to it requires a collective basis along the lines developed by Mead (1934, pp. 75–90) in explaining the way meanings emerge from interactions with others. This does not, however, fully counteract Kahneman's (2011, pp. 199–208) concern that individuals are subject to "WYSIATI" errors of "what you see is all there is" which easily translates into "what you experience is what is."

then practically simultaneously sell or buy it back for slightly more or less than anyone else will. This, of course, is exactly what the croupier does: they manage the "gambling" of others and take a commission for doing so. In these cases the croupier is taking an additional commission to the one the exchange takes. These croupiers are commonly so good at what they do that they manage to foster transactions through their middleman activities. Working with such miniscule bid/ask spreads, they often end up with no direct profit at all, but when this happens, the exchange in question commonly will reward them with a penny a share from their commission. There is a catch here insofar as the most sophisticated new types of accounts that the market has produced in an attempt to counter what the broker told me fifty years ago, "no one knows what the market will do tomorrow," have in fact confirmed this view. They have in an interesting way highlighted something else, however, that is less widely understood, namely, the central role that collectives of varying sorts play in enabling markets to function. In underscoring the collective components and aspects of markets they counter the commonly presented image of markets as sanctums for individual behavior.

In order to properly grasp how these collective facets of markets manifest themselves in market transactions, it is necessary to appreciate the various ways in which the collective legitimates and enables market transactions to occur. At perhaps the simplest level it is the collective that provides the governing narratives that produce the consensual contexts in which market transactions occur. Different participants can and do clearly hold different interpretations of what is occurring, but they do so within a basically common setting. This shared reading of what is happening enables and fosters a sense of the other and of coordinated actions. Shared meaningful accounts also support historical accounts that provide another layer of meaning bearing on what is happening. Pure data-based and data-generated accounts, no matter how sophisticated they might be, cannot provide such meaningful contexts, as they have been deliberately stripped of all such meanings.[8] These accounts are constructed to rely completely on "what was" in formulating accounts as to "what should be." One might try to speculate as to why that particular "what was" led to this particular "what should be," but such speculation would have nothing to do with the resulting "what should be" finding.

The absence of any sort of meaningful or causal attributes also serves to strip these accounts of any normative facets. There is a strong "what will be will be" tone, which has the tendency to communicate the message that whatever will be is beyond your limited ability to understand. Given the complicated form that the programs generating these accounts generally

[8] As "evidence-based" accounts were linked to "big data" accounts in footnote 6 of this chapter, it is only fair to note that they differ in this respect insofar as "evidence" in contrast to "data" seldom is presented in pure quantitative form: it normally is clothed in meanings.

take, this is probably true in most cases. This does not delegitimate the accuracy of what these accounts are apt to stipulate, but it does tend to undermine one's confidence. An example of this can be found in changes related to the way "stop" or "limit" orders are presented. These orders utilize specific "stop points" for activating a "stop–loss sell order" of a financial instrument owned if it goes below a certain point, or a "stop–buy order" to buy an instrument if it goes above a certain point.

Traditionally such "stop points" were established at previous support levels below which the stock or other instrument did not go, and at previous "tops" or resistance levels above which the stock had not gone. In both cases, the governing logic of such stop orders was that if the stock penetrated a previously established boundary it was likely to continue in that direction. Such "stop" orders are still used extensively, but the "stop points" tend not to be set by previous "lows" and "highs." They are more likely to be set by an algorithmic program that uses past prices to identify points higher and lower, which would indicate deviance from past pricing. Such points are commonly referred to as "pivot points." The particular prices generated are highly unlikely to be the same as the actual historical resistant points. Without the algorithmic program one is unlikely to be able to even judge what they would be. A trader might feel compelled to utilize such algorithmically generated "stop points," but will, in effect, be doing so based solely on blind faith.

This absence of what might be called "collective" or "human" judgment plays out in other ways. Historically most knowledgeable market participants understood the market to be governed by the actions of other market participants. As such, most sophisticated participants were continually trying to determine how people were likely to act in future situations in light of how they had acted previously. Such an orientation implicitly, if not explicitly, assumes that how people act is subject to normative constraints of one sort or another that are pervasive. Without such constraints the market is subject to more erratic action. The so-called "flash crashes" and "explosive advances" are widely attributed to the absence of such human-grounded constraints. The absence of the human touch is similarly seen as relevant in what might be called the more "ungentlemanly" manner in which trading is commonly handled.

Even the most nostalgic old-timers are willing to admit that modern algorithmically aided trading normally provides greater trading liquidity and dramatically lower commissions. Bid/ask spreads are often in pennies rather than quarters and half-dollars, and commissions in several dollars not hundreds of dollars. That doesn't eliminate the sting and irritation experienced, however, when a "market order" is executed at a price outside of what had been the trading range and what again becomes the trading range after one's own transaction has been completed. As more than one such old-timer has told me, and as I know from my own experiences, the market specialist of yore might have charged more, but most did not nickel and dime you; moreover, they were willing to take in and provide from their own inventory when possible and necessary. As another player said, "After thirty years of trading, trying to trade in this new market is like having the poker table you've frequented for years shut down and being moved to the roulette table or worse a one-arm-bandit slot machine. It just doesn't feel right."

The final words spoken by this old-timer reveals more than his distress. It indicates that it is not the absence of meaningful/causal accounts that bother him. There is something else about the new market with its high reliance upon hard data and computerized algorithmic trading that troubles him and a good number of other traditional market Traders. That he and other traditional market Traders respond differently shouldn't be that surprising as they tend also, as shown earlier, to be quite critical of traditional market accounts. What bothers them is the absence of something quite different. What he misses is more the "human touch," or more accurately the feel of what is academically frequently labeled as human agency. As a proponent of acting sensibly, he misses feeling the causal imprint of other market participants. Proponents of the new market may claim to privilege actual happenings, but they reduce such happenings to data. Such data is little more than the footprints left behind by the causal forces inherent in the happenings. Data does not interact with anything; it cannot be experienced and it lacks any sort of underlying energy. For traditional market Traders who approach the market in an acting sensibly mode, the hard data privileged by the new market is limited in another important way. In acting sensibly what is noted in the flow of events is that which catches one's attention; what we focus upon is what strikes us. The data that is used in the new accounts of the new market is preselected in terms of the categories dictated by the programs.

The new market with its new accounts present another problem for acting sensibly Traders. In acting sensibly it is not enough to experience the flow of events and the underlying forces in play. One needs to interpret them. Such interpretations, as noted earlier, are not expected to reveal what will happen. Acting sensibly is not grounded in predicting behavioral patterns. It is limited to identifying the direction and strength of various causal forces in play and to judging the general trends that are apt to result. It is sort of like what a football lineman in American football experiences when the football is snapped. He needs to feel where the various pressures are coming from as he pushes forwards or tries to hold his ground, in order to judge how he should react. The coach may have sent the quarterback a play-plan, but the lineman's objective is considerably more limited and focused.

The process of interpreting what is happening, however, on the field or in the market is not something that is done alone. The most simple of meanings, as Mead showed, are grounded in interaction. The implicit, unspoken meanings attributed to the simplest of gestures require a social grounding and social corroboration. There are times, in fact, when such meanings only exist within the particular interaction (Collins 2010).[9] Four young men throwing a ball around to each other randomly in a park, spotting an attractive young woman walking by, concurrently taking their eyes off the ball such that it goes astray, then collectively realizing what they all had done simultaneously break into smiles. The actions of each of these four young men were individual until they broke into their smiles. Finding the young lady to be attractive, focusing upon her, realizing that they had lost sight of the ball and attempting to spot it again were things that each did alone. The smiling, however, was dependent upon their collective knowledge that each of them had responded in the same way. There would have been no joint smiling if each had only recognized that the other three had responded similarly. The smile indicated that they collectively realized this. Acting sensibly in most situations, including in the market, relies on this sort of collective behavioral grounding to confirm what has occurred. It need not be present in all situations, but in a sufficient number of similar situations.[10]

What troubles many traditional market Traders concerning the high degree to which the present market relies upon big data and programmed accounts is that they are unable to get a feel for any "others" in the market. The various programs and programmatic transactions blur them from view. Most of these Traders concur with those who argue that traditional accounts failed to present the market accurately. Putting the market on various types of auto-drive, no matter how sophisticated these drives might be, is seen to have generated as many, if not more problems than it has solved. The key reason for this is that one of the prime functions of the market has been and remains to properly price financial instruments: what years ago was presented to me as "to define value." Allocating and trading value is also part of the market's business, but to many if not most of those most attached to the market, defining value is the essence of the market. And that is an inherently human

[9] Harry Collins in his fascinating book dealing with tacit and explicit knowledge argues that the only true form of "tacit" knowledge is knowledge that is embedded in collective concrete activity.

[10] The ways in which meanings and meaningful behavior are inherently social has been a continuing theme of this book as has been the acknowledgement of George Herbert Mead's contributions in making this clear. I feel constrained, however, to underscore the subtle distinctions in how the various factors that engender meanings and meaningful behavior operate in making sense and acting sensibly that this vignette reveals. The meanings embedded in meaningful accounts that enable us to make sense of matters exist and are utilized mentally. They are the thoughts of individuals though they have social origins, having been generated in interactions. The meanings, or more correctly expectations, attached to particular experiences suggest particular causal forces and, in an unspecific way, their outcomes. While not necessarily or generally explicitly validated by others, they do commonly require forms of behavioral confirmation by others, even if only a smile. Collins (2010), just noted, offers an interesting augmentation to this distinction from a different perspective in his discussion and analysis of tacit knowledge.

and collective process. As one market aficionado was heard to say regarding this issue, "They have thrown the baby out with the bathwater."

As the various aspects of the new market presented would suggest, it is generally given mixed reviews. Its greater focus on actual transactions and related happenings and its implicit critique of most market narratives have received mainly positive responses. Its capacity to manage the exponential growth in market volume has also received high marks as it has greatly enriched many market professionals. Even more peripheral market participants have tended to appreciate the greater liquidity of the market and the reduced transaction costs that they have to pay. Looking beyond its own boundaries, the market has not only been assisted and empowered by a wide range of technological innovations, it has also supported such innovations, both theoretical and material. A similar symbiotic relationship has emerged in regards to globalization, both economic and non-economic. Today's market functions as a, if not the, central player in an ever-growing global economy that has been instrumental in the global growth of all sorts of other activities. It has done so, however, at a cost. For the great majority of people, including most market professionals, the market has become more opaque. As such, it tends to generate less trust, which has simultaneously also been diminished by the regular discovery and emergence of scams, swindles, frauds, and other perceived injustices and unfairness. From the Madoff scandal to the huge incomes of hedge fund managers, from flash crashes to failed IPOs, from unintelligible derivatives and other financial instruments to insider trading, a picture and sense of a complete breakdown in any sort of responsible surveillance is projected. Taken together it seems as if the "sweet spot" generated by high-frequency trading and all that goes into it for a particular few has also generated a very strong sour aftertaste for the majority.

From a more philosophical and sociological perspective, the roots of this sour aftertaste can be traced back to the failure to properly recognize and maintain the human, collective, and interactive facets of traditional markets that echo and sustain the human condition.[11] Modern markets are clearly not

[11] There is as one might expect a vast literature on this subject. While a number of authors are referenced throughout this text, major attention has been given to Mead and Durkheim as they have most framed the perspective presented. In doing so, however, even their thoughts have only been superficially presented. To do otherwise would require pursuing a different agenda than is the objective of this book. Having said that, I feel compelled to offer a little further rendition of their thoughts, particularly as they overlap and differ from how they relate to the themes of this book. I have elected this particular spot to do so as it marks the end of the heavy use made of both of them though neither is completely ignored in the final chapter.

While Mead shared Durkheim's interests in social solidarity and the ways shared accounts fostered it, his primary objective was to explain how humans evolved the ability to interact meaningfully by taking the role of the other. Whereas Durkheim (1933, pp. 105–10, 127–9) focused on how different types of shared meaning systems link individuals together differently—what he frames as the difference between mechanistic solidarity that is supported by collective,

the only arenas in which this failure appears to be present. The market, in fact, is one of the more promising arenas in which this is occurring, given that it more clearly perceives how the opaque cloud descending upon the market might be contained if not eliminated. I refer here to the ongoing efforts of at least some participants to acquire an edge in navigating the vibrant flow of transactions that continues to be the basis of the market. The challenge would appear to be finding some way to strengthen and increase such efforts. This is the subject of Chapter 12, the final chapter.

Before doing this, however, I feel obliged, in keeping with my stated intent to acknowledge relevant differences between overlapping stances of others and those taken in this book, to address briefly some such differences pertaining to this chapter. More specifically I think it helpful to contrast some of the differences in the way Kahneman's book, *Thinking Fast and Slow* (2011), deals with various issues, including prediction, intuition, expertise, algorithms, open and closed systems, and causality, discussed in this chapter. There is clearly a great deal of similarity in the way these issues are treated and understood, but there are also a number of significant, but very subtle differences, some of which actually address the differences that Kahneman notes existed between his own understanding of how these issues are best framed and that of his colleague Gary Klein. The elusive nature of these differences is such that an earlier attempt to include Kahneman in this discussion would

shared conscience and organic solidarity that is supported by cooperative and restitutive rules—Mead (1934, pp. 289–98) explored the underlying differences between religious and economic interactions. Despite their very different ways of approaching this issue, they both end their analysis by fostering two distinct forms of social structures and associated perspectives, namely "religious" groupings and interactions based on shared values, and empathy and economic structures and interactions based on cooperation and transactions.

In contrasting "shared values" and "transactional behavior," both Durkheim and Mead implicitly recognize the differences in how "accounts and narratives" and "interactions and actions" foster social life and behavior. With his emphasis upon social solidarity, however, Durkheim gives greater weight to accounts and narratives where Mead, with his greater emphasis upon interactions, gives greater weight to "acting sensibly." Given Mead's "pragmatist" roots this is not surprising. Mead sees meanings emerging and evolving, not only in the way people process their thoughts through reflection, but also in how they experience the external world. In this respect, Mead sees the process of generating meanings as embedded in activities similar to acting sensibly. The process whereby meanings are created entails linking the universal cognitive signs embedded in language to the range of experienced responses subsumed by that sign. The word "hot," for example, is tagged to various common experiences of hot items. What holds them together and links them to the sign is the fact that the various experiences/response call forth the same sign. This is a socially embedded process since it is only when this is a commonly shared experience that the linkage/tagging can be established. Connecting a set of appropriate experiences to a given sign is what gives that sign meaning. The bottom line here for both Durkheim and Mead is that while economic/market interactions and transaction generate and foster a qualitatively different type of meaning than do religiously grounded collectivities, a strong collective component runs through both. Without this collective component, meaning as we know it is impossible, which means so is human activity. This condition holds for markets whatever form they might take.

more likely than not have generated more confusion than clarification. At this point, however, addressing these differences should be helpful in clarifying the case being made.

Before focusing upon the differences, a brief review of the many similarities and overlaps is in order. Perhaps the most visible shared claim is the pervasive failure of predictions, especially in situations designated as open systems in this text and what Kahneman describes as insufficiently regular situations. Both texts acknowledge that causal narratives generally have a stronger explanatory hold on us, even when they prove to be factually and often logically inaccurate. Both express a similar appreciation for expertise in dealing with unexpected, threatening situations, as well as a strong feeling that true expertise can only be acquired by means of significant, long-term exposure to similar situations. Insofar as "intuition" plays a role in such expertise, both texts see such "intuition" itself to be dependent upon extensive previous exposure to similar situations. Finally, both texts judge algorithmic narratives, especially in relatively closed systems or stable situations, to be have greater predictive powers than other types of narratives.

Despite these various agreements, there are a number of fundamental differences in how and why these various stances are attained. Kahneman views these issues as a cognitive psychologist, that in effect means in terms of how we make sense of our world. In doing so he identifies, describes, and analyzes the numerous limitations built into our efforts to make sense of our world. Many of these same limitations are presented in the discussion of making sense in this book. The substantive nature of "intuitions" for his colleague Gary Klein, with whom he differs, is due to Klein's implicit acceptance of such intuitions as responses to causal forces of the sort claimed by critical realism rather than merely responses to past behaviors. For Kahneman these causal forces simply do not exist. There are causal narratives and items cognitively identified as causes, but not causal forces that can be directly experienced independently of their cognitive representations. What is more accurately called the "empirical" rather than the "real" world when cognitively framed is accepted as "reality": there are no layers of reality to be directly experienced. In ignoring the existence, or even the possibility of such an existence, it is extremely difficult to identify the script component attached to objects and even "causes" that are presented in cognitive/narrative form.

Much of *Thinking, Fast and Slow* focuses upon what Kahneman sees to be a misguided reliance upon causal explanations. Unfortunately, he never actually addresses, let alone embraces, causal forces. All he deals with are causal narratives that fail because the so-called causal forces are never actually affirmed in any meaningful way. The narratives might just as well be based on mythical stories or findings in the stomachs of pigeons. It is the power of the familiar, explanatory narrative that seduces people, not any grounded causal account. Interestingly, when Kahneman presents what he considers to be statistical, formula and algorithmic accounts on which to base decisions, as he discusses what he calls "intuitions versus formulas," the limited items upon which his formulas are based are exactly the types of items that one would assume had inherently true causal powers.

This is even more the case with the types of experiences that his colleague Gary Klein relies upon in explaining what he sees to be the acquired "intuition" of the experts he has studied. Kahneman attributes the "intuition" of Klein's subjects to the memories they have from the many experiences that have had over the years. What Kahneman misses here is that the types of experiences related to the unexpected, threatening situations that Klein focused upon tend to be quite idiosyncratic. Kahneman speaks of the recognitions obtained from these experiences that are stored in memory. He is, I believe, correct in attributing such "intuitions" to aspects of previous experiences, but these previous experiences are not stored in memory as recognized behavioral patterns as he suggests. It is the lived experiences of the various causal forces that are stored, and they are not stored in memory as commonly understood. They are stored in one's body and the types of situations encountered. Obviously, one's memory is engaged in this recall process, but one's whole body is commonly in action at the same time.[12]

This critique in no way is meant to reject Kahneman's central critique of the false dependency that we commonly give to governing narratives of one sort or another. It is directed only at his dismissal of both our ability, admittedly our very limited ability, to experience the world we live in at a different level and the impact that this level has on the world in which we live. I refer here to the pervasive ontological contingencies that subject us to "stuff happening." In dismissing this aspect of reality, Kahneman exposes himself to another serious error. In supporting and adopting algorithmic and probability accounts over what I would agree are false causal narratives, he fails to recognize the inherently dangerous nature of these accounts. Probabilistic accounts work only in closed systems. As Ayache (2010) has argued even Taleb's (2007) "black swans" cannot be relied upon. Any narrative based upon the past cannot predict the future in a world subject to contingencies. Algorithmic accounts in which not only are both the formula and the particular items/

[12] A case could be made that ethical constraints commonly function in a similar "total body embeddedness." Such constraints have not been dealt with in this text and are not dealt with by Kahneman, but they certainly do play a role in the market. The best I can offer this late into our discussion is that ethical constraints commonly do function as causal forces in shaping behavior. Where they reside is a difficult question to answer, but in most cases they seem to be embedded not only in mind, but also throughout one's body, and often in given situations. What is fairly clear, however, is that not only do they often trump what might be called normal cognitive decision-making, but they are also expected to be able to do so. A person free of such constraints and who insists on acting purely in terms of his or her stated values can be quite frightening, as the phrase "Never trust a person of principles" is intended to convey.

values utilized subject to their own self-governing algorithmic monitors, but are also opaque to humans, would seem to be as scary as most ungrounded causal narratives of which Kahneman is so critical. None of this is meant to negate the power and value of these account or narratives in most situations. It is meant, however, to underscore the importance of enhancing our abilities to act sensibly, which is the topic of Chapter 12.

12

Learning to Act Sensibly by Engaging and Doing

It ain't what you don't know that gets you into trouble. It's what you know for sure that just ain't so.

(Mark Twain they say, but who knows)

From the ground covered, particularly in Chapter 11, it would appear that accounts, be they traditional narrative accounts or sophisticated quantitative programmable accounts, will not enable us to cope with all the many and varied uncertainties we can expect to confront in the future. It is not the weaknesses of these accounts, which are actually quite good in doing what they were made for, be it calming us in confronting the uncertainties we regularly confront or linking them to a massive amount of data derived from past behavior patterns. The problem is that accounts were never meant to assist in managing contingencies: they are meant to assist us in tolerating them. Unfortunately, contingencies appear to be rapidly growing in conjunction with the growth of crosscultural and cross-societal currents linked to continuing globalization. Modern technologies and the exponential growth of financial markets have played and are likely to continue to play major roles in this process. Together, by boosting the flow of events and new crosscurrents, they have muddied the waters of pretty much everything thought to be known as populations confront other populations that think and act differently. To survive in such waters, let alone thrive, one needs to get one's hands dirty. One cannot simply think about what is happening: one needs to become behaviorally engaged in what is happening. This generally entails adopting a highly pragmatic perspective and orientation in judging and determining what to do. There is also a need to tolerate "muddling through," which requires an interesting mix of self-confidence and humility.

"Muddling through" is another colloquial phrase similar to "stuff happens" that often seems to be a non-descript utterance of little meaning. In actuality, like "stuff happens." it conveys a very multifaceted and insightful message. While "muddling" is commonly understood to mean mixing things up in a disordered manner, its Dutch roots link it to "muddying." As such, the expression "muddling through" implicitly acknowledges the muddy context in which one is operating; another way of framing this is that in situations of "muddling through," things are normally already mixed up, lacking any recognizable order. In these situations, one cannot hope to plan and follow a course to a desired destination, because one cannot properly assess the territory one intends to traverse. All one can do is move from one situation to what appears to be the most promising next situation as they appear. From a philosophical perspective such an approach embraces a pragmatic orientation in which the reality we experience is privileged over a conjectural version of what we expect to encounter. Checking things out as they are encountered is an approach that is commonly referred to as "trial and error." One cannot expect to find things in muddy water by imagining where they might be or by simply looking into the water: one needs to reach down and search out what is there by hand. If nothing is found where you stand, it generally makes sense to move to a different spot and initiate another hand-search. That is what muddling entails. The idea of "muddling *through*" augments the process by recommending that one persevere until one succeeds in one's objective or ceases to be interested in obtaining it. The latter situation is normally due to finding that one has in some way or other emerged from the muddy waters or no longer needs what one was looking for.

In privileging the world as experienced, muddling through is an approach that implicitly mimics acting sensibly. It differs from the acting sensibly examples presented earlier in applying to more everyday, mundane situations rather than the more exotic situations dealt with earlier. It also reflects the drudging and more menial character that acting sensibly commonly entails, especially when it is applied to everyday, mundane situations. This menial tone is also due to the dismissive ways in which the "doing" character of acting sensibly is commonly treated in comparison to the more cognitive character of making sense. In comparison to making sense, acting sensibly is commonly seen to be low-bred. This is perhaps understandable given that it generally requires getting one's hands dirty. If, as suggested above, globalization and technological innovations are subjecting the world to more and more contingencies, more people will have to get accustomed to getting their hands dirty more often. Acting sensibly, dirty hands and all, will need to become a mainstream ability, not the comparatively fringe skill it has become in most circles. We will need to enhance our skills to recognize and correct mistakes rather than investing our energies in attempting to think out ways to preclude them. If the uncertainties and volatility of financial markets has taught us anything, it has taught us that mistakes will be made. For those less familiar with these markets, the same lessons are being offered by increases of uncertainty and volatility related to the weather, sectarian conflicts, medical epidemics, and various other arenas.

The skills and attitudes required to cope with these situations are unlikely to emerge of their own accord, at least not in the quantity or quality required. We need to dramatically rethink and reshape the way we educate ourselves. A scary thing here is the extent to which education itself presently suffers from its own obsessions with "making sense" and abandonment of "acting sensibly." The ironic twist to this is that skill-based, hands-on, acting sensibly education has an illustrious history, both within different educational systems and beyond. From science labs to athletic fields, including music and art classes, apprenticeships, shop courses, home economics, entrepreneurial activities, and numerous other forums, students have been engaged in different types of learning practices. Pretty much all of these sorts of activities, which primarily utilize acting sensibly skills have been reduced due to financial restraints and efforts to give more time to "academic" fields which emphasize texts and "making sense" skills.

Though different in numerous ways, educational experiences that embrace "acting sensibly" tend to include learning methods usually absent from the more "making sense" formats. Ten such components are particularly common:

1. The great majority entail bodily involvement in one way or another in the learning process, not just cogitation. This is the case not only in gym classes and sports, but laboratory experiences, and most art and music classes.
2. Such experiences tend also to be grounded and linked to physical objects of one sort or another, be they particular instruments or equipment or particular physical objects.
3. Acting sensibly learning experiences tend to be more interactive, be they with particular people or within a group setting. Framing and decision making in these situations also tends to be more consensual, both explicitly and implicitly, with the latter process commonly requiring being able to "read" other participants.[1]
4. The interactive nature of most of these situations also generates a teaching–learning mix in which students are required to teach as well as to learn. These activities commonly unfold simultaneously.
5. The interactive dynamics of these educational experiences generate highly multifaceted happenings as different aspects of what is occurring are noted by different participants.

[1] The practice and need to read "others" being noted here echoes the fuller discussion in the Chapter 11 that drew upon Mead (1934) and Collins (2010).

6. The practices associated with these educational experiences tend to be repetitive, as they require a considerable amount of doing that itself cannot be done in a single try. This is true as much in doing a chemistry laboratory assignment as in playing a piece of music or doing a somersault dive. Different settings and different partners also often require repeating activities (Gladwell 2010).
7. Acting sensibly educational experiences tend to be more emotive than making sense experiences insofar as they engage one's body more and are more experiential, including the ups and downs associated with success and failure.
8. A significant number of acting sensibly learning experiences also entail stronger aesthetic sensitivities as a direct result of the aesthetic aspect of the activity.
9. Many acting sensibly learning situations exist in uncharted territories that favor experimental and innovative efforts. Often there does not exist a specific correct action.
10. The complexity and uncertainty of the situations within which these educational experiences occur tend to generate multiple feedbacks that need to be acknowledged and addressed in their own right.

All ten of these factors have been noted and addressed in one way or another earlier in exploring acting sensibly. The purpose of locating them in a range of traditional educational situations is to underscore the fact that acting sensibly has historically been an integral factor in education. (Others could be added, but these ten should be sufficient for the purposes at hand.) While the dramatic cutback of these types of educational experiences over the past few years has tended to be explained in terms of cutbacks in educational funds, it has clearly also been due to a widespread disparagement of these forms of education in comparison to making sense education. A very similar reprioritizing of forms of education has occurred in a general cutback of apprenticeship types of training versus increased classroom instruction and classroom testing, in which knowing how certain things should be done has taken the place of learning how actually to do it. Teacher/coaches who repeatedly illustrate a practice, then watch those they mentor perform, and then offer suggestions have to a large extend been replaced by structured accounts to which students are expected to respond with structured answers. It is commonly described as "teaching to the test," which has value if the objective is to implant a specific account. If critical reasoning is the goal, teaching to the test is commonly counterproductive.

To be fair, apprenticeships of varying sorts are still employed in numerous situations. Interestingly, however, these are not the various skill-focused educational situations that have traditionally been looked upon as requiring little intellectual ability, such as plumbing, electrical work, carpentry, cooking, automobile repair, tailoring, and so on. Where "apprenticeships" continue to flourish are in various high-end professions such as litigation, consultancy, corporate management, and, as indicated in the various vignettes presented in this text, surgery, and engagement with economic markets. The term "apprenticeship" is seldom used in these contexts, however, as it is commonly seen to apply to simpler types of work. Academic laboratory instruction, athletic and musical training, and various high-end mentoring positions, though clearly forms of apprenticeship, are similarly seldom designated as such. In all of these situations, the need to be actively engaged in a particular practice is understood to be linked, not only to the need to master various physical activities, but also to experience the range of contingencies that one is likely to encounter in these activities. It is not enough to "know" what is happening since there will be many occasions when one will not be able to "know." Moreover, in these situations it will not be sufficient to grasp what is happening: one will also have to be able to respond properly to it.

No one wants to be operated upon by a physician, no matter how medically knowledgeable, who has not previously done a similar operation numerous times. This can and does generate a good deal of tension in deciding what a resident-in-training can and should do in particular surgical situations. The situation is usually quite different when it comes to getting the right person to do the more mundane repairs and jobs. More often than not there isn't even an option for a repair in our present world. If something is broken it usually needs to be replaced. The reasons are multifold. Comparatively simple utensil and machine parts commonly entail micro-circuitry of some sort and are stamped out as single closed units. Even if one were able to get inside such units, identifying the internal failure would be difficult, and finding proper replacement parts all but impossible. This does not mean that there are not numerous situations where hands-on experiences are a critical asset in both determining what needs to be done and providing guidance in how things should be done. Whereas the great majority of first responders to such situations in earlier times were often able to deal with such situations, presently it is commonly the case that first responders are restricted to reporting back to more senior colleagues who are then required to determine if the situation merits the attention of a more skilled practitioner. Karl Weick, whose work was referred to earlier, emphasizes the importance of expertise and deferring to those with past experiences when dealing with unexpected crises. To be able to do so, however, requires having someone so skilled present.

The widespread decline in the ability to deal creatively and responsively to accidents and unexpected happenings has been linked to more than an increase in the number of stamped replacement parts. There has also been an increase in the pressure and expectation to do things by "the book," which is the antithesis of acting sensibly.[2] Acting sensibly requires one to fashion responses to the particular situation, which generally means each unique situation produces a relatively unique response. Going by the book requires sticking to a particular path. Lack of adequate training makes it difficult to respond in a creatively useful way; going by the book makes responding in a creative way inappropriate, no matter how successful it might prove to be. Moreover, it makes it difficult for observers to even recognize, let along appreciate, the strengths of creative and unique actions that are not stipulated in the approved book. I remember two such events that left their marks on me. One was market related and the other more political.

The market-based incident occurred in the mid 1990s. At the time I was exploring some of the changes that were occurring in the way universities were managing their endowments (Smith 2000). What I was particularly focused upon was the attempt by various institutions to be more aggressive in how they invested their funds by selecting a number of different hedge funds in which to invest parts of their endowment. How the total endowment was allocated was subject to annual evaluations that were used to maintain, increase, or decrease the amount allocated to each fund. The guidelines and criteria used by each university tended to become more and more complicated year by year. While the gains and losses played an important role, equal if not more attention was given to the different degrees of risk that the different funds were seen to be generating. How this risk was determined varied from one institution to another, but for all practical purposes every institution relied to some extent upon a mixture of quantitative programmable guidelines in determining what risk was entailed by each fund.

There was one particular fund that caught my attention for a number of different reasons. I had better than normal access to one of the firm's principals; the firm had been allotted a significant share of the endowment of an institution with which I had good contacts; and they had established a very impressive record over the past few years. There was another factor that caught my attention; namely, that its approach to the market was more traditional than most hot hedge funds at the time. They did little with derivatives and made little to no use of quantitative programs and accounts to guide their investments and trading. The firm's guiding philosophy was a mix of old-fashioned economic fundamentals and sentiment indicators. The number of Traders were few and they focused on relatively few stocks that they tended to hold for the long term, but which they were also willing to buy

[2] There is clearly a minor conundrum here as Weick has written a few "books" (such as 2007) on dealing with unexpected crises. From the perspective of this book, Weick gets a good deal right by presenting a number of guiding principles that fit with acting sensibly. Where he goes astray is in formally describing how to respond to the various situations when acting sensibly would suggest that this can only be done in the given situation.

and sell in volume. They were extremely astute investors and traders and did very well over the two-year period I followed them.

What gives this story its punch is that after putting together a three-year record that not only outpaced the other firms to whom funds had been given, but also most major stock market indexes, they received word that the funds that they had been allocated to invest were to be reduced by 20 percent in the following year. The simple reason given was that the significantly higher than normal gains they had generated were evidence that their investments entailed higher than normal risk. What made the whole business a bad dream was that at that time risk was being measured primarily in terms of deviation from normal return on capital. In short, at that time superior returns on capital would generate higher risk regardless of how the money had been invested. Risk management is presently more sophisticated than it was then, but volatility still plays a dominant role in both risk indicators and abnormal returns on capital. To put the matter somewhat differently, volatility and quantitative programmable accounts had not only become the foundations for managing financial portfolios, but had also co-opted the means and instruments for judging the trustworthiness of different investment/trading practices. Risk management has evolved since then, but this thread still runs through most such programs. Were they right in reducing their funds to this firm? I really don't think so but the "alpha" program they relied upon said they were.

The second event related to the risks entailed in deviating from doing things "according to the book" regardless of how successful an innovative approach might be occurred in a very different type of setting than the event just described. It happened in the late 1960s on the college campus where I was teaching at the time, in the midst of a student anti-war takeover of one of the college's major buildings. The students had been occupying this particular building for a number of days. Throughout each day and night various issues covering a wide range of possible future actions were discussed and debated. During these discussions and debates arguments in favor of occupying other buildings were regularly made, as were arguments for leaving the building presently being occupied. In both cases, the impact that one action or the other might have on the administration, particularly the administration's willingness to call in the police, which they had refrained from doing so far, was central. While some students wanted to force the administration to call in the police, the great majority were not in favor of this. For days the collective of students and numerous faculty members who had joined them in various degrees discussed and debated these issues while issuing various other statements. What was most impressive throughout these activities was the degree of order in which the discussions were managed. A major factor in this order was what was, and still is, a very innovative way of governing who could speak at different times.

With literally hundreds of people in the auditorium, representing numerous different positions on numerous different issues, pretty much all with something to say and wanting to be heard, keeping a degree of order was not something to be taken for granted. The mike was assigned to a number of informally appointed leaders who regularly passed it to each other. These leaders were allowed and expected to keep everyone informed as to what might be going on outside, to pass particular messages on and otherwise maintain a level of order. Their primary job, however, was to give the mike to different speakers. When functioning in this leadership position, they were prohibited from expressing their own views on pretty much everything.

The way in which it was decided to allocate the mike to different speakers proved to be quite innovative. The system had a number of familiar aspects. At any given moment there was an attempt to restrict comments to a particular issue. Individual speakers were requested/limited to several minutes. An effort was made by the person in control of the mike to rotate it between people with different positions on the issue being discussed at that moment. When it appeared as if a limited number of shared positions had been presented, there was commonly an attempt to articulate the two, three, or more positions presented and get a general response as to whether the major positions had in fact been identified. After this was done, an attempt was also made to get a straw vote as to how the body as a whole, that is the entire group, felt. It is at this point that a more innovative practice was adopted. When a particular position obtained a dominant position, speakers in favor of that position were for all practical purposes denied the right to speak. The mike was given instead to those supporting minority positions. After those in opposition to the dominant position had spoken, another straw vote would be taken. If the speakers in favor of these minority positions managed to win a sufficient number of supporters, speakers in favor of other positions were given the opportunity to rejoin the debate. If the support for the dominant position remained or increased, those in opposition would likely be offered another attempt to change people's opinion.

In practice, the number of people supporting such minority positions commonly became fewer as they spoke without gaining more support. Without rebutting what was said, the majority position actually acquired strength. At a certain point, usually after the major points of the minority view had been repeated a number of times without changing anyone's mind, the group as a whole, including the minority, tended to embrace the majority position as the position of the body. This process became so instilled in this particular group that if anyone came back into the room after a break and heard a half dozen speakers push for a particular action with no counter arguments being offered, they would know that the position being supported was a minority position that had little to no future. Unfortunately, why unfortunately will become clear shortly, most people unfamiliar with this practice, entering such a room and hearing a half dozen speakers argue for a particular position without any counter arguments being offered would conclude that this was the majority position. They would conclude this, not only because all the speakers took this position, but because in most such situations the majority not only tend to dominate based on their size, but they also tend to squash contrary views from being expressed. Such a conclusion would be "going by the book": it would be consistent with what we would expect.

A scene very similar to the one just described occurred shortly before the spring break, when the number of people present had already shrunken a good deal. The issue under discussion was whether to attempt to take over the central administration building, where some administrators were in residence. The dominant position in the group was not to since spring break was near and it would probably force the president to authorize the police to come onto campus and arrest the students occupying the building they presently were in. The small minority that was in favor of the takeover had been the only speakers for a considerable period of time. During this time two senior faculty members close to the administration elected to observe what was going on in the occupied building. (All college students and faculty had free access to the room; others needed permission of the entire body to enter.) After listening to the minority speak for approximately a half hour, they hurried back to the president and the other college administrators and officials. With full confidence in what they had heard they informed the group that the students had decided to take over the administration building and from the tone of what they heard it would be happening very soon. Within a brief period of time the president, to the surprise of practically everyone since the protest was ending on its own, requested the police to enter the campus. The results were messy and unnecessary. Here again we have a case where an assumed understanding as to how things are ordered failed to recognize a sound acting sensibly practice.[3]

The two cases just presented demonstrate not only that accounts, which are assumed to be able to interpret and understand particular situations—to make sense out of what is happening—cannot only badly read what is actually occurring, but also foster counterproductive actions. These situations are sufficiently widespread to cause one to wonder how and why such accounts are so often proposed. There are a number of reasons for such actions, some of which were noted earlier. Familiar, apparently sound accounts are highly reassuring insofar as they present an ordered, sensible reading of what might otherwise be a complex, anxiety-provoking situation. The familiar and orderly character of these accounts also serves to create a sense of

[3] Other explanations have been offered as to why the president acted as he did, including a need to avoid future protests, but having observed what happened, I'll stick with the account given in the text.

community that offers additional calming powers. This is what making sense accounts do. There is often an additional, more self-serving factor in play in reaching out to these accounts. They can normally be used as a form of protection when and if things go wrong. Those who embrace such an account can usually point to it and claim that what they did was obviously reasonable, given the account. Even when such an account actually contributes to things going wrong, it can be used to take the blame for what happened. This endows these accounts, whether right or wrong, with a great deal of value. When it comes to protecting oneself from after-the-fact criticisms, one might say that using "making sense" accounts is a prime instance of acting sensibly. The only difference is that acting sensibly in these cases is a step removed from what the original matter requiring action was. It could even be considered a special example of the familiar saying, "A good offense is the best defense."

The two cases presented above speak to another interesting contrast between making sense and acting sensibly; namely, the way in which meanings are related and dependent upon collectives and interactions. The symbiotic relationship of shared making sense accounts and collectives has been noted repeatedly throughout this text. Though sociologists tend to credit Durkheim and other early sociologists with establishing and ascertaining the collective character of meaningful accounts and their primary social function, the mutuality of the two has been noted by thinkers for millenniums. While recognition is normally given to the constructive role each partner of this relationship plays in the flourishing of the other, the role that shared narratives play in maintaining collectives tends to overshadow their inherently collective character. George Herbert Mead's vision as to how mind and meanings evolved is somewhat an exception to this more common weighting of the relationship. For Mead, human mind and meanings would never have emerged without the idiosyncratic nature of human behavioral interactions. More importantly, Mead gives great weight to the behavioral responses inherent in these interactions in which these meaning are structured; to a large extent such meanings are seen to mirror these responses.

While true in large measure, it is also true that meanings tend to remain dependent upon human interactions. While the great majority of meanings in any given moment exist in accessible definitive form, other meanings are likely to be embedded in behaviors in less definitive forms. The closing price of a particular stock shortly after the market has closed can usually be assigned a definitive value.[4] The price of that same stock while trading is ongoing, however, is clearly not definitive in any normal sense of the word definitive. It is not just that trades are occurring at different prices, but different bids and

[4] Aftermarket trading has actually changed this situation in many cases, though for most stocks for most people, closing prices are accepted as the definitive price until trading begins again.

asks figures are simultaneously appearing and disappearing. While no specific price is likely to emerge from these transactions, various price parameters may. The actions and reactions of traders serve to shape their future actions. While the price in any given moment is likely to change, a high price and a low price boundary of sorts may emerge for a period of time and be recognized and acknowledged by most market professionals.

Under these conditions, Traders actively engaged in trading are likely to operate—buy and sell—within these boundaries. As the boundaries change, so the active territory will change. The key here is that while the Traders' actions would be shaped by these boundaries, the boundaries themselves would be shaped by their actions. At any given moment the Traders who were engaged would by and large agree on where the boundaries were, but their agreement would not be dependent upon their individual or collective thoughts alone. Rather, their individual and collective thoughts would be interlinked to their individual and collective interactions. I stress interactions rather than actions as the proceedings that are of importance are trades that are inherently interactions. While a strong case can be made that making sense relies upon a richer set of meanings than acting sensibly, when it comes to generating meanings, acting sensibly trumps making sense.

This is evidenced pretty much everywhere, be it in scientific laboratories, in sporting activities, in art studios, playing musical instruments, or any other sort of creative activity. It is in the encounters with uncertain responsive environments that are simultaneously mirrored by others in person or hypothetically that new connections and meanings emerge. Kayaks are meant to stay upright, but they are used in situations that are apt to cause them to roll over. Skilled kayakers cannot only roll a kayak that has turned over into an upright position, but the really skilled, drawing upon technique that Inuit kayakers perfected many years ago, are able to roll their kayaks up in many different situations where particular rolls are required. Surgeons have similarly fashioned new ways to access tumors and remove organs by being forced to improvise in specific cases. In sporting events, different athletes have repeatedly discovered new ways to hurl objects and jump higher and further in confronting unexpected obstacles. In most of these situations, a given individual commonly played a pivotal role in the emergence of the new way to do the act in question, but recognition and suggestions from others played a crucial role as well. Entrepreneurs emerge in much the same way.

What makes this process significant in the context of coping with uncertainties is that it underscores the broader importance of acting sensibly in dealing with contingencies. The skills and ability to act sensibly are required, not only to cope with particular instances of unexpected happenings, such as a sudden thunderstorm, a thyroid storm, or a financial market flash crash, but also for fostering new skills and abilities. In acting sensibly, particular skills commonly generate new skills. A skill and orientation that emerges unexpectedly in a momentary situation can become a common skill useful in dealing with reappearing situations and events. Another way of framing this is that most practices are generated in response to or connected to other practices, not in response to mental cogitations of one sort or another. Ideas tend to generate other ideas. This does not mean that inconsistencies and conflicts identified within a given account cannot foster changes in the account, but only that encountering such problems in the midst of some activity tends better to highlight their existence and to require a solution of some sort. Making adjustments to accounts, while an option, nearly always produces other stresses and contradictions, making it easier to ignore the original problem. The overall soundness of the account commonly trumps the soundness of any particular situation, provided one is not engaged in that situation. This explains in large measure the power and resilience of most fundamentalist accounts, be they economic, political, or religious, even when there exist numerous examples that contradict them.

In the highly turbulent world in which we presently live, we confront a myriad of challenging, changeable, and uncertain situations. Global warming, pollution, energy use and resources, volcanic eruptions, tsunamis, and other types of natural disasters by themselves are enough to overwhelm us, but they constitute only part of what we confront. Globalization and chemical and genetic research have dramatically increased the possibilities of pandemics and other health-related crises. Political upheavals and the spread of related armed conflicts of varying sorts have contributed their own share of unexpected events. Technological innovations, particularly in the area of communication, have served to redefine, not only the ways in which divergent populations communicate among themselves and with others, but how education is being restructured. At the same time work and employment at all levels has been subject to ongoing changes that shape and reshape what, how, and where things are produced, allocated, and priced. These changes have, in turn, dramatically altered the economic and political structures within and between different societies and nation states. These developments in combination have also served to reshape demographic profiles, including birth rates, life expectancies, and various lifestyles. Health practices and medical care, including proper treatments, accessibility, and funding, have been drawn into these overlapping developments. Accounts and plans, which argue for this and that solution in all of these different areas, abound. While various more grounded explorations have also been undertaken, they are comparatively few in number. This is unfortunate since analyzing different hypothetical situations, while often useful, cannot generate the type of rich findings that concrete experimental trials can. We are capable of learning a great deal from accounts and reasoning, but when it comes to multifaceted situations, direct experience is qualitatively superior. What makes it superior is that experiences expose one, not only to the particular actual flow of events, but also to the causal forces in play. This additional asset of experience is commonly overlooked. The popular advice to "learn from experience" is often incorrectly interpreted to mean that you should remember and learn from what happens, but that is not the essence of the advice. What happened is not what was experienced. What was experienced was the process whereby what happened came into being. A somewhat similar misreading is generally applied to another related saying: Santayana's "Those who cannot remember the past, are condemned to repeat it." Santayana was in most ways a pragmatist. He understood that history did not actually repeat itself in a concrete way. Rather, he is clear that we need to learn *from* history rather than simply the *what* of history. What we are meant to learn are the causal dynamics of the past, which are repeated in different future settings. He was not recommending that we use past events to generate rubber stamps of the behavioral pattern of that event.

There is another facet to grasping these underlying causal dynamics, which has been alluded to, but not sufficiently recognized; namely, the part they play in coping with contingencies. Experiences enable us to grasp inherent causal dynamics insofar as they are able to convey types of liminal knowledge that accounts are not able to convey. Accounts are limited to conveying explicit information. Such information can normally be interpreted in different ways, but as information it is precisely given. The information conveyed by the flow of events that constitutes experiences is more multilayered. It needs to be read from various different angles. This is where the presence of others is so valuable. Different people sharing a given experience not only experience it from different angles, but also serve to mirror what they are experiencing to the others present. The information exchanged in these encounters is commonly described as liminal knowledge as it exists at the boundaries of what is explicitly present and what is subliminal, not seen.[5] The future path of a vehicle suddenly swerving in the midst of a number of different people located in different places is anticipated by each individual, not only in terms of its own immediate path, but also the distinctive responses of the other people present. It all tends to happen simultaneously. Another way of saying this is that the future is not best read in the behavioral patterns of the past, but in the interrelated actions and reactions of those engaged in the pertinent flow of events. Ayache (2010) expresses this nicely, and underscores the relevancy of the market to our understanding of this process, when he claims the future markets are created by market Traders, not the past patterns/probabilities of markets.

Even the most sophisticated modern computers cannot function in this manner. While they can actually communicate and exchange information

[5] See H. Collins (2010).

with each other many times faster than people can, they cannot grasp liminal information embedded in the flow of events. Neither can humans, for that matter, except when they are jointly engaged in the flow of events. There is more involved here than the distinction between thinking fast and slow as described by Kahneman (2011), which in some respects overlaps reasoning in terms of accounts and reasoning in the flow of events. The difference does not revolve around different ways of processing our thoughts as much as it does around thinking and doing. Thinking, by its very reflexive character, seeks to filter out what it identifies as external input. Doing, in contrast, depends upon the flow of non-cognitive input to grasp what is happening. Such input includes the full array of sensual inputs that we receive, as well as the emotive inputs to which we are often hard wired. While we generally process all of these inputs individually, there is a sense in which some of them are commonly experienced collectively.

There is another important difference in the way we confront the world when we are primarily engaged in doing versus when we are engaged in thinking. When we approach the world in a primarily thinking mode, we are normally interested in answers. Our thinking mode is normally energized and sustained by questions not answers. A good lecture or play is one that manages to present us with various questions that pull us in and hold us as the lecture or play presents us with possible answers to accept, reject, or at least wrestle with. The basic assumption in what might be called making sense situations is that there are proper answers as there is a governing order of some sort. When people are actively engaged in an activity, be it kayaking, surgery, or trading, they tend to be more involved in monitoring and privileging possible questions than answers. The assumption in these situations is that the flow of events they confront is pregnant with contingencies of varying sorts. The primary task is to recognize those contingencies that are most likely to require one's attention.

The last paragraph echoes the central theme that runs through this text; namely, that greater acknowledgement and attention needs to be given to the contingent nature of the world in which we live and the coping strategies of acting sensibly that such contingencies require. Here, as before, the central role of making sense and accounts is not being rejected or denied. The argument being made is simply that contingencies and acting sensibly need greater attention than they appear to be receiving. The related contention of this chapter is that there is a critical need to increase and expand acting sensibly forms of education throughout our educational system, rather than cut back on them as has recently been the trend. Learning by doing should become an educational objective. We similarly need to recognize the limitations of assuming we live in a world of closed systems where order prevails and there are sound answers to all issues. Teaching to the test is wrongheaded to its core. Few arenas manage to validate these principles better than concrete financial markets, despite massive attempts to impose on them market models that are often embodiments of the purest, most sophisticated forms of making sense accounts. This is not an instance of one or the other, but to echo the quote with which this chapter began, recognizing and acknowledging what we don't know and what is not to be known. The future falls into this category. While we cannot know the future, we had better prepare ourselves for dealing with it.

There is an old saying that you don't want to put a fox in charge of the chicken coop. The warning signals not only the predatory relationship between fox and chicken, but also the fact that the fox is a particularly skilled predator when it comes to chickens. There is an ironic twist to these warnings, however, in that we actually do train and use close cousins of these predators, namely dogs, to protect these animals. It is the same inbred canine skills that foxes utilize to catch chickens that dogs utilize to protect these animals. Wolves and dogs exhibit even stronger complementary skills in attacking and in protecting sheep. As another old saying goes, "It takes a thief to catch a thief." Success in all of these instances is clearly not based on similar intentionality. It is based on skills that are grounded in particular activities. Our ability to cope with the unending number of contingencies that we are destined to confront, given that we live in an inherently unpredictable world, depends upon our acting sensibly skills. Such skills cannot be expected to replace our more cognitively grounded reasoning abilities, which are essential for coping with ambiguities and other uncertainties grounded in the narratives and accounts we rely upon to make sense out of our world. We clearly need both types of coping techniques. Unfortunately, at a time when acting sensibly skills have become more important, they have been abandoned and discarded, often in favor of new types of accounts. Modern financial markets have evidenced the dangers that such actions can create. Acting sensibly cannot be restricted to small groups of kayakers, surgeons, and Traders.

There are a number of added benefits in expanding the number of opportunities we provide for engaging in acting sensibly situations both formally and informally, both as part of our educational system and beyond. Three deserve special notice. In doing so we will unavoidably be increasing the number and range of concrete experimentally grounded findings to augment the hypothetical findings of various mind games and untested theories that presently dominate most discussions and issues. Most such experiments and their findings are likely to be flawed in one way or another, but so are the findings of most mind games and theories. Actually they are not flawed in the sense of being wrong, but rather limited to the particular conditions of the experiment that did not conform to the conditions assumed and specified. Whatever the findings are, they will be findings. A good number, however, are likely to be sufficiently promising to foster further experimentation. In education, healthcare, climate control, organizational structures, parole practices, disciplinary issues, and on and on, actually trying out different practices under different conditions would provide a treasure chest of valuable findings. Even conflicting findings are likely to be useful, as they would likely result in the need to give closer examination to previously taken-for-granted conditions. Whatever the results, the learning experiences will be worthwhile.

A second benefit of fostering a multitude of experimentally grounded findings is less obvious, but perhaps even more important. The very range of unexpected findings that experiments are likely to generate serves as a powerful antidote to simplistic, fundamentalist, and doctrinaire thinking. This is not meant to dismiss doctrinary thought in all situations. There are times when it works as it is meant to work, but there are also times when it hinders our ability to cope with dangerous situations. This adversarial relationship is, of course, a rerun of the adversarial relationship between making sense and accounts on the one hand and acting sensibly and practices on the other that has run through this text. As the roughest representatives of their respective camps it somehow seems appropriate to pit them against each other, if only figuratively. My hunch is that if actually tested, a generation whose education entailed a broad range of experimental experiences would be less prone to simplistic thinking than one educated in a "teaching to the test" modality.

The third benefit of privileging teaching by doing, which is another way of framing the extensive use of experimental experiences, is that doing is nearly always more fun. The sense of agency in successfully accomplishing a difficult task is nearly always enjoyable, but the more behaviorally engaging the task the more enjoyable it usually is. Surgeons enjoy a successful operation, especially one that is demanding and utilizes their skills considerably more than pre- and postoperative duties. Kayakers take great pleasure in the beauty and magnificence that they encounter, but the rewards of controlling and managing their kayaks successfully, especially in challenging waters, are normally sweeter; there is something quite special about performing a successful roll when conditions require. For their part, the pleasure Traders take in executing a successful transaction entails much more than the pleasure of making a profit.

In all of these cases, successfully coping with challenging, often unexpected situations serves to confirm and celebrate one's very being. Purely cognitive successes can and commonly are also rewarding, but they generally lack the existential timbre of completing an activity, even when the results, as is always the case, might have been better. Surgery is clearly off limits for most people, and the market and kayaking, while open pretty much to all, are likely to strike many as somewhat threatening, which in their own ways they are. This is not surprising given that "learning by doing" is often a gentler way of saying "learning by one's mistakes." Neither the "doing" or the "mistakes" are likely to generate much learning in themselves. Reflection, which entails others in some way, is also required. This is clearly not a new message in any way as the numerous references in footnotes throughout this text would indicate. Unfortunately, it is a message that seems to have been smothered by a range of more cognitively sophisticated methods that are more fixated on identifying and mastering the hidden orders of the world in which we live than with coping with the contingencies of this world.

In today's world the market stands somewhat alone in making the case for acting sensibly. The central thesis of this book is that we would do better trying to grasp the teachings of the market than attempting to master it. If the market teaches us anything it is that what works in one situation is unlikely to work in another and vice versa. Having said that, the market also suggests that accounts and attempts to make sense out of things, especially in trying to predict the future, are more likely to err than judgments grounded in a range of past experiences. Put more simply, teachings grounded in "doing" tend to trump teachings grounded in "explanatory accounts"; acting sensibly bests making sense. And when all else fails, the market is committed to keeping us humble. A final teaching.

Postscript

Given that the numerous multifaceted teachings of the market presented above have often been intertwined and even implicit, a brief summing up seems in order. Though different cases can be made for the relative importance of different teachings, when it comes to the scope of relevancy few, if any, arenas demonstrate and illustrate the pervasive reliance and use of descriptive and "explanatory" accounts and narratives more than the markets. Without such accounts markets could not function. The market makes it very clear, however, that it is not that these accounts are inherently factually or logically correct, but rather that they enable the cooperative and interactive practices required by markets. Markets are clearly not unique in this regard, but given the multitude of different accounts that pervades them, the market reveals that its primary function is not to get things "right," but merely to enable transactions to happen. The more general lesson here is that in the great majority of open systems within which we commonly function, accounts capable of retaining their devotees are more likely to be those that can adjust to changing situations, rather than those determined to be factually and logically correct. The fickleness of much knowledge has its pluses as well as its minuses. Accepted accounts, whatever their factual or logical weaknesses, also often have the ability to impose order, generate consensus, and lessen anxiety.

The market provides us with quite similar teachings regarding the strength and weaknesses of routines. As with accounts, the reasons, both factual and logical, given for embracing a particular routine are commonly false, but the routines nevertheless often have positive consequences. The worth of routines, however, rests not so much with their ability to maintain collective ties, though they often also do, but rather in their ability to pull us through turbulent currents. It is here that the market teaches us that not all threats require intellectual solutions. Some are inherent in the world we confront and they require that we at least keep moving. In underscoring this reality, the market makes it very clear that we not only need to recognize that we confront an external reality, but that this reality is constantly changing. It is in this recognition of an external world pervaded by crosscurrents of varying sorts, that the market's teachings transcend that of most other arenas, including it might be added most sporting arenas. It is also within this context that the market teaches us about acting sensibly.

The acting sensibly practices do not lend themselves to being judged as factual or logical as in the case of accounts or even routines for the simple reason that though they are intended to function as coping mechanisms, much as accounts and routines do, they are not intended to provide answers. Their objective is rather to aid us in avoiding perils of one sort or another. The market teachings, however, seldom if ever come in the form of answers though they commonly critique answers. In acting sensibly situations, the market's teachings tend to be focused upon identifying the various steps and actions that go into acting sensibly. Acting sensibly as such is clearly not mindless: it is embedded in minded behavior. Teachings in such contexts tend to take more of a coaching form than the more familiar didactic teaching form. They are clearly teachings nevertheless.

In privileging minded behavior over what might be called pure reasoning, acting sensibly and the markets in which acting sensibly has flourished, particularly with Traders, exhibit both their pragmatic and existential heritages. Given that it could be argued that these two philosophic movements were the two most powerful philosophic movements of the past century, this would seem to be quite appropriate, given the growth of the market and markets in general during this period. The irony here, of course, is that most academic, particularly economic, accounts have sought to frame markets as paradigms of rational behavior. And to a large extent they have been quite successful in doing this with the exception, of course, of "the market" itself. This is not to deny that most markets, including financial markets, tend to function in an orderly manner most of the time, but much like their cousin, the weather, they are capable of suddenly generating great disruptions. And like the weather, markets are forever changing. In the end markets teach us that they, like life itself, can neither be mastered nor ignored.[1] They teach that

[1] Throughout this book it has been asserted that there is a major divide between the world that most academic economists inhabit and the world that most market professionals inhabit. There are, of course, individuals who try, and sometimes succeed, in keeping a foot in both worlds, such as the market professional who seeks to keep up with academic developments and might even teach part time and the academic who engages regularly in market transactions. While the performances of these individuals tends to be modest at best, there have been some who have excelled in both worlds. Among the winners, few if any seem to have matched John Maynard Keynes (1936), who excelled in both arenas. His success, I would suggest, rested on his grasp of the central themes of this book. In his words: 1) "Markets are moved by animal spirits, and not by reason"; and 2) "The market can stay irrational longer than you can stay solvent." The first quote speaks to the causal forces operative in the market and their erratic nature; the second to the inability of governing accounts to predict future markets. Two basic themes of this book. There are a number of other market savvy economists, many of whom are cited in various places in this book, whose market advice strikes me as generally sound though I cannot vouch for their market success. Two, who regularly write for *The Financial Times*, are Martin Wolf (2014) and John Kay (2011).

there is a need for fewer ungrounded answers and explanations, and more grounded explorations: Less bravado and certainty, and more humility. Not bad, for an institution that in the big picture of human history, civilization, and culture is still a growing adolescent.

Appendices

APPENDIX A

Understanding Markets from a Sociological Perspective

Though markets, especially financial markets, are considered by most people to fall within the province of economics, they have solicited from their early beginnings many centuries ago the interest of a wide range of non-economists. Among academics these non-economists have come from numerous different fields, including anthropology, various subgroups within psychology, political science, history, philosophy, and sociology. They have also been scrutinized in various ways in numerous fictional writings. A far as sociology is concerned a strong case could be made that the emergence and growth of sociology was symbiotically entwined with the emergence of markets and other economic structures as reflected in the writings of Durkheim, Simmel, and Weber, to say nothing of Marx. Numerous early American sociologists exhibited a similar interest in economic practices and structures. George Herbert Mead (1934), for example, who is commonly considered to be the father of the school of symbolic interactionism, not commonly seen as tied tightly to economic and market practices, deals with these practices in great detail.

It was only in the mid-twentieth century that sociologists and numerous other social scientists elected to cede the realm of economic behavior to economics. The primary factor in this development was the ascent of "neoclassical economics," which embraced an economic model that framed economic behavior in terms of individuals rationally maximizing their own utility, which in turn governed such things as supply and demand, pricing, output, and distribution. In adopting this definition of economics, the discipline in effect relinquished the more social and philosophic features of economic behaviors, which played important roles in the writings of earlier classical economists such as Adam Smith, generally considered to be the father of modern/classical economics. In ceding economic behavior to the economists, the other social sciences, particularly sociology, acquired greater control over all other interactive social/cultural arenas. While this arrangement continues to hold throughout most of academia, it has been subject to continuing erosion from both sides from its very beginning.

A subset of economists, for example, have both introduced and reintroduced parameters dealing with various psychological and sociological factors that are seen to minimally augment if not conflict with the dominant neo-classical model. Oliver Williamson (1975, 1985) received a Nobel Prize for his work dealing with such areas as "transactional costs" and other things that revealed the impact of organizational structures upon economic behavior. Williamson's work is often seen to have been influenced by that of Herbert Simon (1957, 1972), the author of the phrase "bounded rationality." The sub-discipline of behavioral economics, noted on numerous occasions in the text, also questions the dominant neo-classical model insofar as it fails to incorporate adequately various psychological factors. Kahneman, Tversky, and Thaler, noted in the text have shaped and contributed to this sub-discipline. Other major economists who have been critical of the manner in which the neo-classical model has been used include Hayek (1989), Albert Hirschman (1985), Schumpeter (1950), Amartya Sen (1977), and Lester Thurow (1983). The list could go on, but these names should suffice to support two central themes of this book: 1) There are serious weaknesses in the way markets are generally framed and depicted; and 2) Despite the weaknesses of these accounts, given their authoritative, established, consensual status, they are highly immune from such critiques.

Subsets of sociologists and other social scientists have also emerged that have elected to refocus upon economic behaviors and structures. This re-emergence has been greatly influenced by the work of Karl Polanyi (1944, 1957), an economic historian, various aspects of whose work are presented in this book. Another scholar whose work influenced this reemergence, especially studies that relied in large measure upon ethnographic data, was the anthropologist Clifford Geertz (1973). In both of these cases, rethinking the ways in which markets actually function, specifically in how prices are determined and how items are allocated, revealed numerous factors that transcended the "rational choice" and "utility" paradigms assumed in the neo-classical economic model. Each also underscored the importance of structural and cultural factors. It has been specifically these structural and cultural factors that have been the focus of concern of those associated with the comparatively recently emergent sub-discipline of sociology commonly referred to as "economic sociology." Over the past few decades scholars associated with this sub-discipline have contributed a wide range of publications focused on the various ways different social and cultural factors interplay with economic behavior.

The classic article by Mark Granovetter (1985) dealing with "embeddedness" that shows the ways in which markets are embedded in encompassing social structures is commonly cited as one of the earlier works that gave rise to this sub-discipline. Numerous other authors including an A to Z list of Mitchel Abolafia, Wayne Baker, Jens Beckert, Michel Callon, Bruce Carruthers, Paul DiMaggio, Amitai Etzioni, Niel Fligstein, Karin Knorr Cetina, Greta Krippner, Donald MacKenzie, David Stark, Richard Swedberg, Harrison White, and Viviana Zelizer have made additional cases relying upon different sorts of data, utilizing different methodologies and theoretical framings. These scholars in recent years have been joined by numerous younger scholars who have both deepened and widened the issues and arguments of their mentors. All of these authors make very strong, if different, cases to the effect that the neo-classical economic model not only ignores numerous important factors in the way it approaches and explains large segments of economic life, but also fails to adequately appreciate broader aspects of economic behavior and life.

The concerns of this book clearly address only a small part of the subject area that presently engrosses economic sociology. Financial markets are only one type of market, and markets constitute only one segment of economic structures and behaviors. Focusing primarily upon the various ways participants seek to cope with ambiguities and contingencies in these markets as this book does, establishes significantly tighter boundaries. This highly focused approach has the offsetting advantage, however, of freeing and decoupling the various meta-practices of making sense and acting sensibly from the market-grounded behavior in which they are found. In this way, a sociological framing not only enables us to have a richer understanding of these markets, but they provide us with a deeper understanding of a broad range of social practices. This exchange has broader implications that transcend academic disciplines.

As noted often in the text, the past few decades have seen an exponential global growth of financial markets, whose influence has been magnified by their impact on other sectors of society. As a consequence, the numerous emerging issues generated by these markets have spread to these other sectors. The decline in normative orders and the increase in contingencies characteristic of global financial markets has similarly spread to these other sectors. As a consequence, the range of coping skills that modern financial markets require, is likely to be required in these other sectors. "What the Market Teaches Us," in short, is clearly relevant to a wide range of happenings, issues, and activities beyond the market.

The wide-ranging utility of these "Teachings" has even framed this book in ways that were not immediately recognized. I refer here to the way in which the market served to amend the methodology that was relied upon to explore it. This is a subject that, while closely linked to what might be considered to be a "sociological perspective," deserves to be discussed in its own right. This is the objective of Appendix B, "The Interplay of Ethnography and Markets."

APPENDIX B

The Interplay of Ethnography and Markets

While markets have received a good deal of attention throughout this book, the methodologies used in obtaining the data for this book have been given comparatively little attention beyond a few autobiographical inserts. Whether the various methodologies, primarily ethnography, used in gathering and evaluating this data deserve to be relied upon for getting things "right" was not addressed. This is not uncommon in ethnographic narratives such as this, as methodological asides tend to interrupt the flow of the text. The different methodologies used are normally understood in general terms and either accepted as appropriate or not, the exception being instances where detailed quantitative data is included and analyzed. Each method tends to be known for both its strengths and its weaknesses, and where it is most likely to be appropriate and where not. The objective, regardless of the specific methods used, is to gather useful "facts" and to get them "right."

It is in the various claims of getting things "right" that strong differences of opinion arise regarding the value of different methodologies. Getting things right generally means getting things as they actually are, not as they might be seen to be. This normally requires that different observers should "get it" fundamentally the same. Simple variables such as place and time and physical parameters lend themselves to consensual judgments. Written texts and quantitative data that are accessible also lend themselves to consensual judgments. When reported data is not easily accessible and when the intentions and values of observers are likely to play significant roles in properly classifying actions, reported facts and data are quite likely to be questioned. Ethnographic findings are commonly subject to such questioning as it generally entails all of these qualities. The problem in most such situations is not so much the ethnographic methodology in use as the highly subjective character of the findings being gathered. Such findings tend to be interpretations and responses of both individuals and collectives associated with ongoing concrete, everyday interactive behaviors of multiple participants.

Strictly speaking, one can never hope to get such behavioral findings "right" if they are presented only in terms of particular actions, since particular acts that appear to be basically the same are often very different in their intent. Scores of different buyers might buy a particular stock at approximately the same price at approximately the same time, but their actions are likely to entail a wide range of differences that if ignored prohibit getting these behaviors "right." The most that can normally be hoped for is an account that grasps the core character of such actions, which requires somehow grasping the opaque forces and constraints operative in the behaviors observed. This, in turn, commonly requires focusing, not only upon what is happening, as well as when and where, but also how and why it is happening. This requires acknowledging the motivations and thoughts of the actors engaged in what is occurring. Getting such motivations and thoughts "right" unfortunately is difficult, as behaviors are subject to projections and misrepresentations, deliberate and unintentional, from both observers and participants. These factors have led some ethnographic researchers to adopt a positivistic stance to their research that in effect requires limiting their data to observable actions, leaving their interpretation to rest upon the behavior itself. The great majority of ethnographic researchers rely not only on observed behavior, but also on accounts and reports offered by those engaged in these behaviors. Yet others, who often label their methodology as auto-ethnography (Ellis, Adams, and Bochner 2011), have adopted a very different path. Rather than attempting to filter out their own responses to what they observe and experience, they seek to build on them. Their argument is that their own responses are more reliable in understanding and getting to the core of what is happening than that commonly suggested by the offered positivistic accounts. Over the years the most respected ethnographic or "participant-observation" findings have tended to rely on all three types of information/data as evidenced in the appendix of William Foote Whyte's classic *Street Corner Society* (1943/1955).[1]

The methodology pursued in this book, which has evolved over many decades, seeks to follow this middle road. It does this by utilizing three overlapping yet distinct "ethno-methodological" practices. What makes these practices of special interest in the context of this book is that they have taken form primarily in the context of exploring markets, and in many ways mirror the practices of markets. The label I have given this form of ethnography is "collaborative transactional ethnography." It is itself, as just noted, a product of the "What the Market Teaches Us" insofar as it mirrors key exploration practices and actions taken to get things "right" inherent in the markets. It is constituted by three distinct practices: 1) Selecting and scrutinizing data pertinent to the market; that is, what is grasped by the term "observation" in the concept of "participant observation" and that mirrors in some ways the more positivistic ethnographic camp; 2) Personally engaging in the various market practices; that is, what is covered by the term "participant" in the same phrase and favors to some extent the autoethnographic camp; and 3) Soliciting and exchanging information, opinions, and perspectives with a range of market insiders as a market insider. All three of these practices are ongoing and require continual updates. As there are wrinkles to all three, each merits further discussion.

Practice 1) "Selecting and Scrutinizing Data," mirroring "positivistic" ethnography as it does, entails what many consider to be the prime objective of any methodology; namely, collecting relevant data. A good deal of such data can be found in earlier research and other publications. The special contribution of ethnography is that it is capable of generating behavioral data drawn directly from ongoing, everyday behavior. Such data often serves as the "bread and butter" of a given study as it often seems to provide a new, grounded portrait of what is under investigation. The limitation of such portraits is that, as with any portrait, what we see is what the person responsible for creating the portrait claims to have seen, not necessarily what others might have seen. There is also the problem of misinterpreting what was observed, as well as the problem of being subject to deliberate misrepresentations of those being observed. Despite these very real shortcomings, as ethnographic data goes, this type of data is probably the

[1] While all of the factors noted in this paragraph continue to be evaluated and debated, the question of how much weight should be given to what people say versus what they do probably continues to be the issue of major concern. For a recent discussion of this issue, see Jerolmack and Khan's (2014) article "Talk is Cheap," and the critiques from Maynard (2014), Cerulo (2014), DiMaggio (2014), and Vaisey (2014), and Jerolmack and Khan's response.

closest there is to what is commonly referred to as hard data. In depicting the various settings presented in this book, I relied upon masses of such data dealing with historical pricing of financial instruments, trading volume, different types of financial instruments, and other structural factors. Personally I prefer to think of this data as cold data rather than hard data, as it is inherently dormant.

Practice 2) "Engaging in the activities being observed" entails a very different set of behaviors from those of Practice 1. The goal is clearly not to gather hard or cold data: it is to experience directly what is happening in order to get a living "feel" for it. This is the primary objective of most auto-ethnographers (Ellis, Adams, and Bochner 2011). While most self-defined auto-ethnographers focus primarily upon their own experiences and attempt to use these experiences to understand the culture and collective they are studying, other researchers, who generally don't define themselves as auto-ethnographers, are more concerned with using their own experiences to better grasp the experiences of those they are studying and as a way to understand and define what they are doing. The key distinction in the context of this study is that this approach, which emphasizes fully "experiencing" the situation with all of its emotional attributes, is directed more toward the underlying causal forces in play and less toward the behavioral patterns generated than is the first approach. My own research has clearly used this approach to grasp both my own experiences and, through them, the experiences of others engaged in the activities that concerned me. Trying to access the experiences of others based on one's own experiences, alas, is at best a tricky business. In an attempt to support this process I found myself utilizing the third practice noted above of directly soliciting and exchanging information and experiences with other participants. This third practice, which is generally seen to be peripheral if not alien to ethnography, evolved in a manner that made it central to my own ethnographic methodology.[2] In hindsight, it has become clear that this fit rested upon the inherent transactional character of both the markets I was studying and the research process I was utilizing.

In order to appreciate the importance of the interactions between researcher and those associated with the practices being explored, it is necessary to recognize that their primary objectives differ. Those engaged in the practices being explored are first and foremost interested in successfully obtaining their own objectives and goals related to the various practices. The researcher is primarily interested in understanding the practices themselves and various facets of the participants. These different objectives favor different presentations of self; they are also apt to generate various degrees of suspicion, especially from those who see themselves as being scrutinized. There is nothing surprising about this. Such suspicions and lack of trust is often given in validating and rationalizing the two types of ethnography first presented. In the first instance, this is used to support the practice of limiting interpersonal filters and framings and focusing upon hard/cold data. In the second instance, priority is given to obtaining first-hand experiences on the part of the researcher, and avoiding depending upon the questionable reports of others. Each of these approaches unfortunately ignores the richest veins of data held by those engaged in the practices being explored; namely, their own understandings and perspectives. There is, of course, a dilemma here, as a researcher soliciting this sort of data without validating filters of one sort or another is very likely to mine only "fools' gold."

[2] The process of formally soliciting information is normally considered to be in the realm of interviewing.

The two primary sources of this dilemma, as noted, are the pervasive mistrust that those being queried commonly have in these situations, and the different objectives that they and researchers commonly have. Given this situation, why should they share their professional and personal concerns and ideas with an outsider? Why should they even waste their time in doing so? It is here that markets present us with an interesting model and answer. People participate in markets when the markets offer them something that they want. Researchers who rely heavily upon questionnaires and interviews and experimental studies have sought to deal with this situation by paying subjects for their time. Ethnography doesn't normally lend itself to this technique, though the process of "buying" attention and information is not unknown. Personal introductions can also help when past ties and favors are part of the package. When the participants being solicited are individuals of substance who are financially comfortable and professionally established, modest monetary rewards are apt to backfire. Close friends and family members may open doors, but then even a large network of family members and friends will not have access to all doors.

So what does that leave us with? Interestingly, there is one commodity that researchers and most participants, particularly those in professional practices, value highly; namely, information. This is clearly true of most market participants. Equally important, they normally prefer to pay for such information with information of their own. It is relatively cheap. In nearly all settings, there are admittedly boundaries regarding what types of information can be exchanged. In financial markets, for example, there are laws against insider trading; in most other settings there are commonly rules, if not laws, against revealing various private or personal items and issues. There are usually, nevertheless, vast amounts of information available for legitimate exchange. In order to engage in such exchanges, however, one needs to have sufficient informational capital of one's own, For ethnographic researchers this means that they need to acquire sufficient knowledge of what they are studying before attempting to engage in any sort of serious discussion with participants. This is what the label "collaborative transactional ethnography" is intended to reflect. It is a joint exploration of an arena that both researcher and participants embrace not only individually, but collectively.

This collective, collaborative, interactional facet of markets and other research sites is often instrumental in fostering ethnographic research in other ways. Gaining initial access to many research sites, as noted above, commonly requires a range of introductions from insiders or individuals with strong relationships with insiders. A classic example of such a mentor who continued to function as a prime informer is described by Whyte in the appendix of his 1943/1955 classic referred to earlier. I have myself relied on a number of such introducers, some of whom also became in differing degrees prime informers as was the case with Whyte. In order to explore situations on one's own, however, one needs to be able to engage in informational exchanges by oneself. Such exchanges can and do take a variety of forms, from simply exchanging one bit of information for another to using information to question a dubious response given. While the latter situations constitute a crucial tool in avoiding being fed false information, it is necessary almost always to avoid entering into a combative relationship. The most common and best way to avoid doing so is to establish oneself as personally invested, knowledgeable, and on the whole respectful of the practices being explored. Over the years I had a number of interactions with various market participants that evidenced these dynamics. One that speaks to pretty much all of the various components just noted, however, stands out. I commonly refer to it as my "Bobby, Bobby!" interaction.

This particular interaction occurred in the early 1980s when I was studying various types of auctions. I was in Kentucky attending the fall thoroughbred horse yearling auctions with the expectation and hope of not only observing the auction but also of speaking with a number of major players including a key auction manager. I had not only already gone through the process of being introduced by name to this auction manager through a network of friends, but had also talked to him on the phone, been invited down graciously, and promised some face-to-face time. When I arrived, however, I quickly saw that upon meeting me, he was hesitant to engage in any sort of serious dialogue with me. He kindly arranged matters so I could attend the auctions and meet other people, which was not something I could have done on my own. Every time I approached him to engage him in a serious conversation, he brushed me off with an excuse of some sort. On the third day in desperation, seeing him walking from the auction tent to his office, I managed to get his attention by yelling out to him a simple question: "Do you always use the same signal to indicate a no-sale?"

The practice of camouflaging a no sale auction outcome, which occurs when no one is willing to pay the minimum/reserve price, is accepted practice in thoroughbred auction, though illegal in most other types of high-end auctions. The reason for this is that announcing a "failed sale" can undermine numerous other sales scheduled for that day involving the same sire. To offset this camouflaging practice, such "no sales" are reported after that day's auction has ended. These reports also carry the name of the under-bidder in each sale which is not done in any other auctions I know and serves as an added guarantee that things were done honestly. In any case, in response to my question, the manager stopped, turned to me and quizzically asked, "What do you mean? What signal?" I yelled back "Bobby, Bobby!"

To understand what was happening here, a little more information is necessary. In these auctions, once a sale is made, the buyer is required to sign various documents immediately, at which time the buyer takes possession of the horse. If the horse dies walking out of the tent it is the buyer who is the loser. This is why all buyers need to establish a line of credit before being empowered to bid. Getting the buyer's signature is the responsibility of the spotter who has relayed the buyer's bid to the auctioneer. Here again these auctions differ from the more familiar fine art and antique auctions often presented on television and in movies where the auctioneer takes bids directly. In these high-end horse auctions numerous spotters tend to be in constant communication with a subset of buyers, some of whom seek to camouflage their own actions. In support of these buyers' desire to maintain a low profile, the auctioneer identifies the present bid in terms of the spotter who has taken the bid. It is important that the auctioneer does this because at times the actions of a spotter may be misinterpreted by the auctioneer, and he may attribute a bid to a spotter that the spotter never intended to give. The problem in the "no sale" situation is that the auctioneer not only needs to inform all of his spotters that the bidding is over, but he also need to get one of the spotters to behave as if he is getting the signature from the assumed winner bidder. The signal that I recognized was being used was to double call the name of the spotter when such a "no sale" happened. A single name call would not be sufficient because, even if the spotter knew he had not made the final bid, some action of his could easily have been interpreted by the auctioneer as if he had.

The bottom line of all of this was that as soon as I had yelled out "Bobby, Bobby" the auction manager hurried over to me to ask me how I had figured out what the double naming meant. My brief answer was something along the lines that this is what I did. I not only studied auctions of varying sorts but was fascinated and intrigued by them. Without missing a beat, he grabbed my arm, turned toward his office and said, "Let's talk!" That is what we did for the next hour and a half, exchanging auction experiences and probing each other on a range of different related points. He wanted to know about how other types of auctions functioned; I wanted to know how his auction functioned. To top things off, he not only offered to continue our conversation the next day but to introduce me to a number of key people who could and did share with me their own understandings of these horse auctions. In all of these interactions, I was clearly seen as a thoroughbred horse auction outsider, but I was also seen as a very keen insider when it came to the wider world of auction, to which most of the people I talked to were outsiders. This was commonly the situation in my interactions with participants in a wide range of commodity auctions from fish to tobacco. The situation in financial markets was somewhat different. Here I was pretty much an insider having been in the market for decades. I was able to function as a sounding board based on my forty plus years exploring these markets for what traders and others were experiencing as changes in the market.[3]

Acquiring the experience required to engage in the types of collaborative transactional practices described above takes time and patience. Any research site worth exploring is highly unlikely to be a quick study. There is a hidden benefit to this, however. Most situations worthy of study tend not to be static. They are subject to change, and such change can only be grasped over time. Change, of course, tends to undermine given accounts. It also, however, tends to shed light upon the various causal forces in play. Collaborative transactional practices are also better at raising interesting questions about what can be expected in the future than in presenting final answers. As an ethnographically oriented sociologist, I find all of these lessons valuable not only in doing good ethnography, but also in trying to both make sense of and act sensibly in the world in which we live. As someone who has embraced price-setting markets, particularly financial markets, both professionally and personally for nearly fifty years, I can attest that few if any sources have provided us with a richer set of teachings for doing this than what we generally call "the market."

[3] Each of my earlier publications focused upon financial markets and auctions (1981, 1989, 2001) contains a methodological appendix that spells out in detail the various parameters of the ethnography utilized in gathering data for these publications. This book clearly depends heavily on these earlier explorations. They have been augmented, however, by literally thousands of additional hours engaged in following various markets, trading in these markets, and maintaining ongoing dialogues with scores of other participants, as well as time spent in scrutinizing the continual flow of both academic and trade publications focused on these markets, some of which are cited in the Selected Bibliography. The data upon which the kayak and surgery discussions rest also had ethnographic sources, but of a somewhat different nature. As noted in footnote 8, in the case of kayaking my personal experience of literally thousands of hours on the water in a variety of different locations, of paddling many thousands of miles, of many hours of instruction, and of interaction with hundreds of different kayakers have provided the bulk of the data utilized; this data has also been augmented by a variety of "how to books" that stress various survival procedures. As I am not a surgeon, the surgery data presented is not based on personal experience. The bulk of the data utilized was provided, rather, as noted in Chapter 1, note 9 and Chapter 6, note 2, by a prime informer. This data was also augmented by the literature cited and the fact that I grew up in a very dense medical context with both parents physicians: a slight ethnographic component.

Selected Bibliography

Abolafia, M. Y. (1996a). *Making Markets: Opportunism and Restraint on Wall Street.* Cambridge, MA: Harvard University Press.

Abolafia, M. Y. (1996b). "Hyper-Rational Gaming." *Journal of Contemporary Ethnography*, 25/2: 226–50.

Ayache, E. (2010). *The Blank Swan: The End of Probability.* Sussex, UK: John Wiley and Sons, Ltd.

Baker, W. E. (1984). "The Social Structure of a National Securities Market." *American Journal of Sociology*, 89: 775–811.

Bang, P. F. (2008). *The Roman Bazaar: A Comparative Study of Trade and Markets in a Tributary Empire.* Cambridge: Cambridge University Press.

Beck, U. (1992). *The Risk Society: Towards a New Modernity.* London: Sage.

Beckert, Jens (2013). "Imagined Futures: Fictional Expectations in the Economy." *Theory and Society*, 42: 219–40.

Beckert, Jens and Aspers, Patrik (eds.) (2011). *The Worth of Goods.* Oxford, UK: Oxford University Press.

Bernstein, Peter L. (1998). *Against the Gods: The Remarkable Story of Risk.* New York: John Wiley & Sons.

Beunza, D., and Stark, D. (2003). "Tools of the Trade: The Socio-Technology of Arbitrage in a Wall Street Trading Room." *Industrial and Corporate Change*, 13/2: 369–400.

Bhaskar, R. (1975). *A Realist Theory of Science.* 2nd edn. 1978. Atlantic Highlands, NJ: Humanities Press.

Bhaskar, R. (1979). *The Possibility of Naturalism.* Brighton: Harvester Press.

Bourdieu, P. (1984). *Distinction: A Social Critique of the Judgment of Taste.* Cambridge, MA: Harvard University Press.

Bourdieu, P. (2005). *The Social Structure of the Economy.* Cambridge, UK: Polity Press.

Callon, M. (1998). *The Laws of the Market.* Oxford: Basil Blackwell Publishers.

Callon, Michel and Fabian Muniesa (2005). "Economic Markets as Calculative Collective Devices." *Organization Studies*, 26/8: 1229–50.

Carruthers, Bruce G. and Sarah L. Babb (2000). *Economy/Society: Markets, Meanings, and Social Structure.* Thousand Oaks CA: Pine Forge Press.

Carruthers, Bruce G. and Arthur L. Stinchcombe (1999). "The Social Structure of Liquidity: Flexibility in Markets and States." *Theory and Society*, 28/3: 353–82.

Cassady, R. Jr. (1967). *Auctions and Auctioneering.* Berkeley and Los Angeles: University of California Press.

Cassell, J. (1991). *Expected Miracles: Surgeons at Work.* Philadelphia, PA: Temple University Press.

CBOE (Chicago Board Options Exchange) (2010). *Annual Market Statistics*, <http://www.cboe.com/data/AnnualMarketStatistics.aspx> (accessed 27 January 2015).

Cerulo, K. A. (2014). "Reassessing the Problem: Response to Jerolmack and Khan." *Sociological Methods & Research*, 43: 219–26.

Chancellor, E. (1999). *Devil Take the Hindmost: A History of Financial Speculation.* New York, NY: Farrar, Straus & Giroux.

Collins, H. (2010). *Tacit and Explicit Knowledge.* Chicago and London: The University of Chicago Press.

Collins, R. (2004). *Interaction Ritual Chains.* Princeton, NJ: Princeton University Press.

Collins, R. (2008). *Violence: A Micro-Sociological Theory.* Princeton, NJ: Princeton University Press.

Dewey, J. (1925/1929). *Experience and Nature.* Chicago, Ill.: Open Court Publishing Co.

Dewey, J. (1939). *Theory of Valuation.* Chicago, Ill.: University of Chicago Press.

DiMaggio, P. (1997). "Culture and Cognition: An Interdisciplinary Review." *Annual Review of Sociology*, 23: 301–20.

DiMaggio, P. (2014). "Comment on Jerolmack and Khan, 'Talk Is Cheap': Ethnography and the Attitudinal Fallacy." *Sociological Methods & Research*, 43: 232–5.

DiMaggio, P. (1994). "Culture and Economy." In *The Handbook of Economic Sociology*, edited by N. J. Smelser and R. Swedberg. New Jersey: Princeton University Press: 27–58.

DiMaggio, P. and Powell, W. W. (1983). "The Iron Cage Revisited: Institutional Isomorphism and Collective Rationality in Organizational Fields." *American Sociological Review*, 48/2: 147–60.

Durbin, Michael (2010). *All About High-Frequency Trading.* New York: McGraw Hill.

Durkheim, E. (1933). *The Division of Labor in Society*, G. Simpson (trans.). New York, NY: Free Press.

Elliott, Ralph Nelson (1938/2012). *The Wave Principle.* New York: Snowbook Publishing.

Elliott, Ralph Nelson (1946/2011). *Nature's Law: The Secret of the Universe.* New York: Snowbook Publishing.

Ellis, C., T. E. Adams, and A. Bochner (2010/2011). "Autoethnography: An Overview." *Forum: Qualitative Social Research.* Vol. 12/ Historical Social Research Vol. 32: 273–90.

Espeland, W. and M. Stevens (1998). "Commensuration as a Social Process." *Annual Review of Sociology*, 24: 313–43.

Etzioni, A. (1988). *The Moral Dimension: Toward a New Economics.* New York: The Free Press.

Fenton-O'Creevy, M., N. Nicholson, E. Soane, and P. Willman (2005). *Traders: Risk, Decisions, and Management in Financial Markets.* Oxford: Oxford University Press.

Festinger, Leon, Henry W. Riecken, and Stanley Schacter (1956). *When Prophesy Fails.* Minneapolis: University of Minnesota Press.

Fligstein, N. (2001). *The Architecture of Markets.* Princeton, NJ and Oxford: Princeton University Press.

Gawande, Atul (2002). *Complications: A Surgeon's Notes on an Imperfect Science.* New York: Henry Holt & Company.

Geertz, C. (1973). *The Interpretation of Culture.* New York: Basic Books.

Gibson, James J. (1979). *The Ecological Approach to Visual Perception.* Boston: Houghton Mifflin Harcourt.

Giddens, A. (1984). *The Constitution of Society: Outline of the Theory of Structuration.* Berkeley, CA: University of California Press.

Gillespie, Alex (2005). "G.H. Mead: Theorist of the Social Act." *The Journal for the Theory of Social Behaviour*, 35/1 (March): 19–39.

Gladwell, M. (2010). *Outliers: the Story of Success.* New York: Back Bay Books.

Goffman, Erving (1959). *Presentation of Self in Everyday Life.* Garden City: Anchor Books.

Graham, Benjamin and David Dodd (1934). *Security Analysis.* New York: McGraw Hill Book Company.

Granovetter, Mark S. (1985). "Economic Action and Social Structure: The Problem of Embeddedness." *American Journal of Sociology*, 91: 481–510.

Granovetter, Mark S. and Richard Swedberg (1992). *The Sociology of Economic Life.* Boulder, CO: Westview Press.

Guseva, Alya and Akos Rona-Tas (2001). "Uncertainty, Risk and Trust: Russian and American Credit Card Markets Compared." *American Sociological Review*, 66/5: 623–46.

Harré, R. (1981). *Social Being.* Totowa: Rowman and Littlefield.

Harré, R. (2009). "Saving Critical Realism." *Journal for the Theory of Social Behaviour*, 39/2: 129–43.

Harré, R. and E. H. Madden (1975). *Causal Powers.* Oxford: Basil Blackwell.

Harré, R. and P. Secord (1973). *The Explanation of Social Behaviour.* Oxford: Basil Blackwell.

Harvey, D. L. and M. Reed (1996). "Social Sciences as the Study of Complex Systems." In *Chaos Theory in the Social Sciences: Foundation and Applications*, edited by L. D. Kiel and E. Elliott. Ann Arbor, Michigan: University of Michigan Press: 295–321.

Hayek, F. A. (1989). *The Fatal Conceit: The Errors of Socialism.* Chicago: University of Chicago

Heft, H. (2001). *Ecological Psychology in Context: James Gibson, Roger Baker, and the Legacy of William James's Radical Empiricism.* Lawrence Erlbaum Associates, Publishers.

Hirschman, Albert O. (1985). "Against Parsimony." *Economics and Philosophy*, 1/1: 7–21.

Jerolmack, C. and S. Khan (2014). "Talk Is Cheap: Ethnography and the Attitudinal Fallacy." *Sociological Methods & Research*, 43: 178–209.

Jerolmack, C. and S. Khan (2014). "Toward an Understanding of the Relationship Between Accounts and Action." *Sociological Methods & Research*, 43: 236–47.

Kahneman, Daniel (2003). "Maps of Bounded Rationality: Psychology for Behavioral Economics." *The American Economic Review*, 93/5: 1449–75.

Kahneman, Daniel (2011). *Thinking Fast and Slow.* New York: Farrar, Strauss and Giroux.

Kahneman, Daniel, Paul Slovic, and Amos Tversky (eds.) (1982). *Judgment under Uncertainty: Heuristics and Biases.* New York: Cambridge University Press.

Kahneman, Daniel and Amos Tversky (1979). "Prospect Theory: An Analysis of Decision under Risk." *Econometrica*, 47/2: 263–91.

Kahneman, Daniel and Amos Tversky (1982). "The Psychology of Preferences." *Scientific American*, 246: 160–73.

Kahneman, Daniel and Amos Tversky (2000). *Choices, Values and Frames*. New York: Cambridge University Press and the Russell Sage Foundation.

Kay, J. (2011). *Obliquity: Why Our Goals Are Best Achieved Indirectly*. New York: Penguin Press.

Keynes, J. M. (1936). *The General Theory of Interest, Employment and Money*. London: Macmillan.

Knight, F. H. (1921). *Risk, Uncertainty, and Profit*. Boston, MA: Hart, Schaffner & Marx; Houghton Mifflin Company.

Knorr Cetina, K. (1999). *Epistemic Cultures: How the Sciences Make Knowledge*. Cambridge: Harvard University Press.

Knorr Cetina, K. (2003). "From Pipes to Scopes: The Flow Architecture of Financial Markets." *Distinktion*, 7: 7–23.

Knorr Cetina, K. (2009). "The Synthetic Situation: Interactionism for a Global World." *Symbolic Interaction*, 32/1: 61–87.

Knorr Cetina, K. and U. Bruegger (2000). "The Market as an Object of Attachment: Exploring Postsocial Relations in Financial Markets." *Canadian Journal of Sociology*, 25/2: 141–68.

Knorr Cetina, K. and U. Bruegger (2002). "Global Microstructures: The Virtual Societies of Financial Markets." *American Journal of Sociology*, 107/4: 905–50.

Knorr Cetina, K. and A. Preda (eds.) (2012). *The Oxford Handbook of The Sociology of Finance*. Oxford: Oxford University Press.

Krippner, Greta R. (2001). "The Elusive Market: Embeddedness and the Paradigm of Economic Sociology." *Theory and Society*, 30: 775–810.

Krippner, G. R. (2005). "The Financialization of the American Economy." *Socio-Economic Review*, 3: 173–208.

Lewis, Michael (2014). *Flash Boys: A Wall Street Revolt*. New York: W.W. Norton & Company.

Loeb, Gerald M. (1957). *The Battle for Investment Survival*. New York: Simon and Schuster.

Lorenz, Konrad (1963). *On Aggression*. New York: Harcourt Brace & World, Inc.

Lyng, S. (1990). "Edgework: A Social Psychological Analysis of Voluntary Risk Taking." *American Journal of Sociology*, 95: 851–86.

Lyng, S. (1993). "Dysfunctional Risk Taking: Criminal Behavior as Edgework." In *Adolescent Risk Taking*, edited by N. J. Bell and R. W. Bell. Newbury Park, CA: Sage: 107–30.

Lyng, S. (1998). "Dangerous Methods: Risk Taking and the Research Process." In *Ethnography at the Edge*, edited by J. Ferrell and M. S. Hamm. Boston, MA: Northeastern University Press: 221–51.

Lyng, S., and Snow, D. (1986). "Vocabularies of Motive and High-Risk Behavior: The Case of Skydiving." In *Advances in Group Process*, Volume 3, edited by E. J. Lawler. Greenwich, CT: JAI Press: 157–79.

McDermott, J. (1973/1981). *The Philosophy of John Dewey*. Chicago, Ill.: University of Chicago Press.

MacKenzie, D. (2006). *An Engine, Not a Camera: How Financial Models Shape Markets*. Cambridge, MA: MIT Press.

MacKenzie, D. and Y. Millo (2003). "Constructing a Market, Performing Theory: The Historical Sociology of a Financial Derivatives Exchange." *American Journal of Sociology*, 109/1: 107–45.

MacKenzie, D., F. Muniesa, and L. Siu (2007). *Do Economists Make Markets? On the Performativity of Economics*. Princeton, NJ: Princeton University Press.

McMillan, L. (2002). *Options as Strategic Investments*, 4th ed. Paramus, NJ: Prentice-Hall.

McMillan, L. (2004). *McMillan on Options*. Hoboken, NJ: John Wiley & Sons.

Malkiel, Burton (1973). *A Random Walk Down Wall Street*. New York: Norton.

Manicas, P. T. (1987). *A History and Philosophy of the Social Sciences*. Oxford: Basil Blackwell.

Manicas, P. T. (2006). *A Realist Philosophy of Social Science: Explanation and Understanding*. Cambridge: Cambridge University Press.

Marx, Karl (1959). *Capital: A Critique of Political Economy*, Volume III. Moscow: Foreign Language Publishing House.

Mayer-Schonberger, Viktor and Kenneth Cukier (2013). *Big Data: A Revolution That Will Transform How We Live, Work, and Think*. New York: Houghton Mifflin Harcourt.

Maynard, D. W. (2014). "News From *Somewhere*, News From *Nowhere*: On the Study of Interaction in Ethnographic Inquiry." *Sociological Methods & Research*, 43: 210–18.

Mead, G. H. (1934). *Mind, Self and Society*. Chicago, IL: University of Chicago Press.

Merton, Robert K. (1987). "Three Fragments From a Sociologist's Notebooks: Establishing the Phenomenon, Specified Ignorance, and Strategic Research Materials." *Annual Review of Sociology*, 13: 1–28.

Natenberg, S. (1994). *Option Volatility and Pricing: Advanced Trading Strategies and Techniques*. New York, NY: McGraw-Hill.

Nazaretyan, Akop P. (2003). "Power and Wisdom: Toward a History of Social Behavior." *Journal for the Theory of Social Behaviour*, 33/4: 403–26.

Nazaretyan, Akop P. (2005). "Fear of the Dead as a Factor in Social Self-Organization." *Journal for the Theory of Social Behaviour*, 35/2: 155–70.

Polanyi, K. (1944, 1957). *The Great Transformation: The Political and Economic Origins of Our Time*. Boston: Beacon Press.

Polanyi, K. (1957/2001). "The Economy as Instituted Process." In *Trade and Market in the Early Empires*, edited by Karl Polanyi et al. Glencoe, IL: Free Press. Republished in *The Sociology of Economic Life* edited by Mark Granovetter and Richard Swedberg. Boulder, CO: Westview Press: 31–50.

Porpora, Douglas (2007). "Sociology's Causal Confusion." In *Revitalizing Causality: Realism About Causality in Philosophy and Social Science*, edited by Ruth Groff. New York: Routledge: 195–204.

Preda, A. (2009). *Framing Finance: The Boundaries of Markets and Modern Capitalism*. Chicago: University of Chicago Press.

Reith, Gerda (1999). *The Age of Chance: Gambling in Western Culture*. London: Routledge.

Schumpeter, Joseph A. (1950). *Capitalism, Socialism, and Democracy*. 3rd edition. New York: Harper and Row.

Sen, Amartya K. (1977). "Rational Fools: A Critique of the Behavioral Foundations of Economic Theory." *Philosophy and Public Affairs*, 6/4:317–44.

Simmel, G. (1990 [1907]). *The Philosophy of Money*. London and New York, NY: Routledge.

Simon, H. A. (1957). *Models of Man*. New York: John Wiley.

Simon, H. A. (1972). *Human Problem Solving*. Englewood Cliffs, N.J.: Prentice Hall.

Smelser, Neil and Richard Swedberg (1994, 2005). *The Handbook of Economic Sociology*. Princeton & Russell Sage Publications.

Smith, C. W. (1981). *The Mind of the Market: A Study of Stock Market Philosophies, Their Uses and Implications*. Totowa, NJ: Rowman and Littlefield.

Smith, C. W. (1989). *Auctions: The Social Construction of Values*. New York, NY: Free Press.

Smith, C. W. (1993). "Auctions: From Walrus to the Real World." In *Explorations in Economic Sociology*, edited by R. Swedberg. New York, NY: Russell Sage Foundation: 176–92.

Smith, C. W. (1999). *Success and Survival on Wall Street: Understanding the Mind of the Market*. Lanham, MD: Rowman and Littlefield.

Smith, C. W. (2000). *Market Values in American Higher Education: The Pitfalls and Promises*. Lanham: Rowman and Littlefield.

Smith, C. W. (2005). "Financial Edgework: Trading in Market Currents." In S. Lyng *Edgework: The Sociology of Risk-Taking*, edited by S. Lyng. London: Routledge: 187–200.

Smith, C. W. (2007). "Markets as Definitional Practices." *Canadian Journal of Sociology*, 32/1: 1–39.

Smith, C. W. (2011). "Coping with Contingencies in Equity Option Markets: The "Rationality" of Pricing." In *The Worth of Goods*, edited by Jens Beckert and Patrik Aspers. Oxford: Oxford University Press: 272–94.

Smith, C. W. (2012). "Auctions and Finance." In *The Oxford Handbook of the Sociology of Finance*, edited by Karin Knorr Cetina and Alex Preda. Oxford: Oxford University Press: 134–51.

Smith, Vernon (2000). *Bargaining and Market Behavior: Essays in Experimental Economics*. New York: Cambridge University Press.

Stark, D. (2009). *The Sense of Dissonance: Accounts of Worth in Economic Life*. Princeton, NJ: Princeton University Press.

Stark, D. (2011). "What's Valuable?" In *The Worth of Goods*, edited by J. Beckert and P. Aspere. Oxford, UK: Oxford University Press: 319–39.

Swedberg, Richard (1993). *Exploration in Economic Sociology*. Russell Sage Publication.

Swedberg, Richard (1998). "Max Weber's Vision of Economic Sociology," *Journal of Socio-Economics*, 27/4: 535–55.

Swedberg, Richard (2005a). *The Max Weber Dictionary*. Stanford: Stanford University Press.

Swedberg, Richard (2005b). "Interpretive Economic Sociology: On the Relationship between Max Weber's Basic Sociological Terms and his Economic Sociology." CSES Working Paper Series: #29.

Taleb, N. N. (2007). *The Black Swan: The Impact of the Highly Improbable*. New York: Random House.

Thaler, Richard (1991a). *Quasi-Rational Economics*. Russell Sage Foundation.
Thaler, Richard (1991b). *The Winner's Curse: Paradoxes and Anomalies of Economic Life*. Free Press. (Princeton University Press paperback, 1993).
Thurow, Lester C. (1983). *Dangerous Currents*. New York: Random House.
Tversky, Amos and Daniel Kahneman (1986). "Rational Choice and the Framing of Decisions." *Journal of Business*, 59: S251–S278.
Tversky, Amos and Daniel Kahneman (1991). "Loss Aversion in Riskless Choice: A Reference-Dependent Model." *Quarterly Journal of Economics* (November): 1039–61.
Vaisey, S. (2014). "The 'Attitudinal Fallacy:' Is a Fallacy: Why We Need Many Methods to Study Culture?" *Sociological Methods & Research*, 43: 227–31.
Weber, Max (1947). *The Theory of Social and Economic Organization*. New York: Free Press of Glencoe.
Weber, Max (1949). *The Methodology of the Social Sciences*. New York: The Free Press.
Weick, K. E. (1979). *The Social Psychology of Organizing*. 2nd ed. New York: McGraw Hill.
Weick, K. E. (1993). "The Collapse of Sensemaking in Organizations: The Mann Gulch Disaster." In *Administrative Science Quarterly*, 38: 628–52.
Weick, K. E. (1995). *Sensemaking in Organizations*: Thousand Oaks, CA: Sage Publications.
Weick, K. E. and L. E. Sandelands (1990). "Social Behavior in Organizational Studies." *Journal for the Theory of Social Behaviour*, 20: 323–46.
Weick, K. E. and K. M. Sutcliffe (2007). *Managing the Unexpected*. San Francisco: Jossey-Bass.
Williamson, Oliver E. (1975). *Markets and Hierarchies: Analysis and Antitrust Implications*. New York: Free Press.
Williamson, Oliver E. (1985). *The Economic Institutions of Capitalism*. New York: Free Press.
White, H. C. (1992). *Identity and Control*. Princeton and Oxford: Princeton University Press.
White, H. C. (2002). *Markets From Networks*. Princeton, NJ and Oxford: Princeton University Press.
Whyte, W. F. (1943/1955). *Street Corner Society*. Chicago, Ill.: University of Chicago Press.
Wittgenstein, L. (1953). *Philosophical Investigations*. New York, NY: Macmillan.
Wolf, M. (2014). *The Shifts and the Shocks: What We've Learned—and Have Still to Learn—from the Financial Crisis*. New York: Penguin Press.
Zaloom, C. (2006). *Out of the Pits: Traders and Technology from Chicago to London*. Chicago, IL: University of Chicago Press.
Zelizer, Viviana (1979). *Morals and Markets: The Development of Life Insurance in the United States*. New 1983. Brunswick, NJ: Transaction Books.
Zelizer, Viviana (1987). *Pricing the Priceless Child: The Changing Social Value of Children*. New York: Columbia University Press.
Zelizer, Viviana (1997). *The Social Meaning of Money*. New York: Basic Books.

Index